Corporations Are People Too

Corporations Are People Too

(And They Should Act Like It)

Kent Greenfield

Yale UNIVERSITY PRESS

New Haven & London

Published with assistance from the Mary Cady Tew Memorial Fund.

Yale University Press books may be purchased in quantity for educational, business, or promotional use. For information, please e-mail sales.press@yale.edu (U.S. office) or sales@yaleup.co.uk (U.K. office).

Set in Janson Roman type by Integrated Publishing Solutions, Grand Rapids, Michigan.
Printed in the United States of America.

Library of Congress Control Number: 2018937838

ISBN 978-0-300-21147-4 (hardcover : alk. paper)

A catalogue record for this book is available from the British Library.

This paper meets the requirements of ANSI/NISO Z39.48-1992 (Permanence of Paper).

10 9 8 7 6 5 4 3 2 1

Introduction

Americans have an odd relationship with corporations. We love our Apple iPads, Sony big-screen televisions, and Ford F150s. We obsess about where to get the best deals on Black Friday and eagerly await the commercials during halftime at the Super Bowl. We attend baseball games at AT&T Park and football games at MetLife Stadium. We lionize successful business people such as Douglas Branson who captivate us with their extravagant lifestyles and idiosyncratic personalities. We wear our favorite brands on our sleeves—not to mention our caps, shirts, purses, and jeans—as if to borrow the branded image of our favorite corporations as our own. In effect, we pay corporations to advertise for them; clothing with a corporate logo emblazoned on it is often more expensive than a plain version. My local hipster coffee shop has a huge Mobil sign adorning an inside wall, intended as art.

But in our popular imagination corporations and their leaders are also among our most ubiquitous villains. Rapacious businessman Henry Potter bedevils sweet George Bailey in *It's a Wonderful*

Life. The corporate drive for profit motivates the extraterrestrial recklessness of *Alien*, the environmental genocide of *Avatar*, and the android slavery of *Blade Runner*. George Clooney heroically fights against corporate mendacity in *Michael Clayton*. Gordon Gekko has become a Hollywood franchise, a synonym for corporate villainy. After the global financial crisis of 2008, Hollywood portrayed Wall Street investors as cocaine-fueled children in *The Wolf of Wall Street*.

In the very real world of politics, a skepticism of corporate power has fueled populist movements through much of our nation's history. More than a century ago, politics centered around Republican Teddy Roosevelt's trust-busting and Democrat William Jennings Bryan's populist railings against big banks. Franklin Roosevelt warned against the concentration of business, saying that "liberty of a democracy is not safe if the people tolerate the growth of private power to a point where it becomes stronger than their democratic state itself."[1] Dwight Eisenhower's farewell message from the Oval Office focused on the risks of the military-industrial complex.[2] More recently, we had Tea Party activists fulminating against Wall Street excesses and anti-corporation activists energizing Bernie Sanders's insurgent candidacy for president. Especially when corporations roam outside of the world of commerce and into the realm of politics and public governance, Americans distrust the corporations' distorting influence on legislation, regulation, and public debate.

None of this has prevented corporations and their executives from exercising immense influence in the public sphere. Twenty years ago, Bill Clinton offered overnight stays in the Lincoln Bedroom to rich business people as an enticement to contribute to his various political funds.[3] Later, Vice President Dick Cheney convened an "energy task force" at the White House that reportedly included executives of Enron, Exxon, and other energy company representatives.[4] In his two presidential campaigns, Barack Obama raised more money than any candidate in history, much of it from Silicon Valley, Hollywood, and Wall Street. During the global financial crisis, the U.S. government bailed out auto manufacturers to the tune of nearly $80 billion and committed several trillion dollars to save the financial industry.[5] And in 2016, we elected to the presidency a self-proclaimed billionaire who owns a gilded penthouse on Fifth Avenue.

Our conflicting views about corporations exist in the law as well. Some landmark constitutional decisions have featured the assertion of constitutional rights by corporations. For example, the 1971 Pentagon Papers case, *New York Times v. the United States*, protected the right of the newspaper to publish classified information about the Vietnam War leaked by Daniel Ellsberg, who, before Edward Snowden, was the most famous whistleblower in U.S. history.[6] No one doubted that the *Times* could claim free speech rights despite its for-profit, corporate status. A few years later in 1976, the ideologically progressive group Public Citizen, co-founded by Ralph Nader, won a case at the Supreme Court recognizing the First Amendment right of businesses to advertise. The case, known as *Virginia Pharmacy*, was about whether pharmacies could be prevented from advertising the prices they charged for drugs, but the constitutional question was a broader one about whether companies had a constitutional right to commercial speech. In that case the rights of businesses were championed by the left; the lead dissent in the case was written by Justice (later Chief Justice) William Rehnquist, one of the most conservative jurists of the modern era.[7] Speech rights, even those of businesses, were a progressive cause.

Fast forward to 2010. When the Supreme Court decided in *Citizens United v. Federal Election Commission* that corporations have a First Amendment right to spend unlimited amounts to influence elections, the decision quickly joined the rogues' gallery of despised

Supreme Court rulings.[8] As many as 80 percent of Americans believed the decision was wrong,[9] and President Obama scolded the justices to their stony faces during a subsequent State of the Union address. Constitutional amendments to overturn the decision, and indeed take away all constitutional rights of all corporations, gathered steam. Public Citizen said that "rights protected by the Constitution were intended for natural people"—a view that would upend its work from thirty-five years earlier.[10]

Constitutional law has been in conflict about corporations since our very beginnings. In the early nineteenth century, the state of New Hampshire sought to change Dartmouth College's corporate charter to make it a public rather than a private institution. The college sued, saying its constitutional rights would be violated by the change. When the case made it to the Supreme Court, the great chief justice John Marshall wrote that corporations are "creatures of law."[11] He went on to recognize that the college, even though an artificial, state-created entity, had constitutional rights. His statement explaining the holding contained a straightforward assertion of the artificial nature of corporations: "Being the mere creature of law, [the corporation] possesses only those properties which the charter of its creation confers upon it. . . ." Then he finished the sentence with a seeming contradiction, saying a corporation would receive not only those rights given "expressly," but also those "incidental to its very existence." *Trustees of Dartmouth College v. Woodward* remains our foundational constitutional case on corporations, and it contains an illogical notion: the corporation is a creature of the state and receives whatever rights the state bestows—except for the rights that the state *must* bestow and cannot rescind.

It is not surprising that constitutional law is conflicted and unsettled about corporations since the underlying foundational doctrines and theories of corporate law are themselves conflicted and unsettled. The law of corporations governs the obligations of managers, the structure of corporate decision-making bodies, and the rights of shareholders and other stakeholders. In deriving and evaluating these obligations, structures, and rights, courts and scholars struggle to get a handle on such amorphous and complex entities. Agreement or consistency on exactly how best to conceptualize a corporation is nonexistent. Some scholars and courts say corporations are property. Some see them merely as a collection of contractual relationships. Still others assume they are best seen as teams; for some they are instead creatures of the state.

Consider this fundamental and foundational question: To whom do managers owe obligations? To the company itself? To shareholders alone? To other stakeholders such as employees? To society in general? We simply cannot answer those questions without deciding what a corporation *is*. If it is a piece of property owned by shareholders, the answer is that obligations run exclusively to shareholders. If it is a contract, the answer depends on the explicit or implicit deal among the parties. If it is a grant from the state, the answer would be whatever the state requires. If it is a team, then the obligations should run to everyone on the team. And so on.

One might have thought that corporate scholars would have reached consensus on how best to explain what corporations should do and how we should think of them. For a while in the late twentieth century, we did come close in that the corporation was seen as a "nexus of contracts" with the powers, obligations, and rights that its various parties negotiated. This view of the corporation was part of a broader dedication in the legal world to the principles of "law and economics," which was, in turn, an application of a libertarian mindset with a respect for personal choice and a skepticism of government intervention into the free market.

But this consensus has collapsed. Corporate law is experiencing a level of intellectual churning that has not been seen in generations. Scholars applying psychological and sociological insights to economics revealed profound limitations on the assumptions of human rationality and choice built into the conventional, libertarian economics framework. And the global financial crisis brought us all face-to-face with the real-world dangers of trusting an under-regulated "free" market. Basic questions about the nature, purpose, and limitations of corporations became topics of scholarly and political conversation.

It is not an exaggeration to say that we are experiencing a pivotal intellectual moment in the history of business. Both corporate law and constitutional law are in flux and conflict over fundamental and foundational questions relating to the obligations and rights of corporations and their place in society. Should corporations be seen as citizens? Should they be able to claim rights of free speech, religious conscience, or due process? Should they owe obligations to society? If so, what are those obligations?

These questions could hardly be more important or touch on a more diverse range of interests and topics. And they cannot be answered in isolation. The questions of constitutional rights depend on assumptions of corporate law. Questions of corporate law depend on constitutional law. Constitutional problems and dilemmas might be addressed by adjusting corporate governance. The appropriate mechanisms of corporate governance might depend on what we see as the appropriate role of corporations in the public and constitutional space.

Unfortunately, in the U.S. legal academy and in legal scholarship worldwide, constitutional law and corporate law are seen as distinct intellectual silos. Constitutional law is considered public law; corporate law is considered private law. Constitutional law is a matter of federal law; corporate law in the United States is primarily derived from state law. While both areas are characterized by significant debate, it is certainly fair to say that most leading constitutional law scholars are ideologically liberal, while in corporate law, the leading scholars are ideologically conservative. Few scholars work in both areas.

This book bridges the divide, offering a way to think about corporations that is consistent in both the constitutional and corporate fields and helps bring about a resolution to the unsettled aspects of doctrine and policy in both areas. In effect, I will set out a unified theory of the corporation. My claim is not that I will solve all the difficult cases or persuasively answer all the troubling questions. Rather, my claim is that the analysis in both areas of law will be clearer and more consistent than at present. Both corporate law and constitutional law will be better for it.

ONE

In Defense of Corporate Persons

Are corporations people?

This is an easy question. Of course corporations are not people. Corporations are businesses that make stuff or provide services in exchange for money. They do not have brains or hearts or consciences. They do not feel love, fear, desire, hunger, pride, or spite. They do not suffer from indigestion or take pills for their cholesterol or have bags under their eyes when their kids lie awake coughing all night. They do not worry about their aging parents. They do not feel awkward at holiday parties. They do not share secrets or moments of pride with friends.

The truth of corporate inhumanity borders on the obvious. Over two hundred years ago, the Lord Chancellor of England pointed out that a corporation "has no soul to be damned, and no body to be kicked."[1] In modern times, Wall Street protesters shout, "Corporations Are Not People!" When 2012 Republican presidential candidate Mitt Romney declared that "corporations are people, my friend," it helped doom his campaign.[2] Despite political and social polarization on everything from abortion to climate change, the truism that corporations are not people is something almost all Americans can hold to.

The problem with the clear, obvious, and apparent notion that "corporations are not people" is this: it is wrong.

It is wrong in three ways. First, corporations have been, are, and should be legal persons. They are separate entities with a set of individual capacities, limitations, rights, and obligations that are distinct from those who work for them or invest in them. Corporations are independent legal personalities and can sue, be sued, enter into contracts, own property, buy stuff, and sell stuff—all in their own name and legal capacity. If a company manufactures a dangerous car, the people who are injured by that car sue the company—a legal person—and not the company's shareholders or employees. This legal personhood of corporations is not an ancillary characteristic. Legal separateness is perhaps the most pivotal legal quality of corporations, helping to make the corporation the most powerful creator of wealth the world has ever seen.

Second, corporations are people in the sense that they are made up of people. Corporations are collective bodies in which humans come together as employees, investors, managers, or suppliers to create goods and services to sell for a profit. Some corporations do exist only on paper, often to shield real people somewhere else in the legal chain. But most of the businesses we think of when we think of "corporations" are comprised of a mix of people, each doing their part to make a go with the business. Some people are the investors, holding either stock or debt in the company. Some are employees, offering their sweat or expertise or charm to the betterment of the whole. Some are the managers, in charge of making the decisions of what to do, with what resource, when, and where. Some of the managers are legal agents of the corporation, authorized to act on its behalf.

Sometimes when people come together as a corporation, the collective efforts are aimed only at creating wealth—that is, of course, the *sine qua non* of corporations. The social and institutional purpose of the corporation—as opposed to that of the church, the family, the university, the government, and the charitable sector— is to make money over time. But many corporations have other reasons to exist as well. The *New York Times* exists to make money, but it also has the purpose of producing the principal newspaper of record in the United States. The people who make up the *New York Times* corporation have organized themselves around an idea that is more than just making money.

These first two ways corporations are people—that they have separate legal status and are made up of people working collectively— do not raise much controversy. But the third way that corporations are people is that they are holders of constitutional rights. And this is the area of most controversy.

Corporations have been able to assert constitutional rights for most of the nation's history, stretching back to the earliest years of the nineteenth century.[3] And even though corporations have claimed an increasing number of rights over time, the question of when and where they could assert constitutional rights was mostly in the background, not arousing much sustained attention from activists or even legal scholars. This all changed, however, in 2010, when the Supreme Court issued its ruling in *Citizens United v. Federal Election Commission*, striking down limits on corporate expenditures in federal elections.[4]

The case arose when a politically conservative group called Citizens United wanted to use "video-on-demand" services on cable television to distribute the film *Hillary*, a harsh documentary about Hillary Clinton. The film—no matter how mean-spirited—would normally be considered political speech, lying at the core of First Amendment protections. Such pejorative critiques are part of the rough and tumble of American politics. But the problem was that Citizens United was organized as a nonprofit corporation, and federal law imposed limits on corporate money in elections. Specifically, the Bipartisan Campaign Reform Act of 2002 prohibited "corporations and unions from using general treasury funds to make direct contributions to candidates or independent expenditures that expressly advocate the election or defeat of a candidate, through any form of media."[5] Because the film was considered express advocacy and was financed by a corporate entity, it violated the statute. The question was whether the statute was unconstitutional under the First Amendment.

The 2002 law was of recent vintage, but it was akin to laws on the books for decades limiting corporate spending in politics. And it had long been assumed that such laws were constitutional. The laws were based on the fear that corporations would use their considerable financial resources to skew electoral results in their favor. And even though the Supreme Court had (in the 1970s) struck down limits on political spending by individuals,[6] the limits on political spending by corporations were analyzed with more deference. Corporate involvement in politics was not seen as the same as the involvement in politics by human beings. The Supreme Court had, in fact, upheld restrictions on corporate political spending in a case handed down in 1990.[7] In that case, *Austin v. Michigan Chamber of Commerce*, the Court recognized that corporations receive "state-created advantages" that "not only allow corporations to play a dominant role in the nation's economy, but also permit them to use 'resources amassed in the economic marketplace' to obtain 'an unfair advantage in the political marketplace.'"[8] The Court ruled that the corporations' free speech interests were outweighed by the compelling interests in limiting "the corrosive and distorting effects of immense aggregations of wealth that are accumulated with the help of the corporate form."[9]

4

When *Citizens United* was argued, *Austin* was still on the books, and the Court recognized that the group's constitutional claims could not be decided without squarely considering whether *Austin* should be overturned. In a rare move, the Court set the case for a second argument—during the summer, no less, when the Court is not usually in session—and asked the parties explicitly to answer whether the Court should overrule *Austin*. The *Citizens United* case immediately became a Big Deal.

In the end, the Court ruled in favor of Citizens United. It could have limited its judgment in any number of ways that would have made its decision less pivotal. It could have said the statute was not intended to cover films like *Hillary*. It could have limited its free speech protections to nonprofit groups like Citizens United itself. But the Court issued a ruling that proclaimed broad and muscular protections for corporate speech—and corporate money—in politics. And it overruled *Austin*.

The Court said that corporate voices were important in the "marketplace of ideas" and that fears about corporate money giving those voices an "unfair advantage" were not an appropriate basis for regulation under the First Amendment. The limits on spending were violations of the corporations' rights of free speech, whether the corporation was nonprofit or for-profit, small or large. The Court gave its stamp of approval to corporations' full participation in civic debate as holders of free speech rights like any (human) American. The Court did not say explicitly that corporations were people. (It referred to corporations as "associations of citizens.") But it did say that corporations could claim the same free speech right as individuals to spend money in electoral politics to support a candidate or cause.

The ruling in *Citizens United* was extraordinarily controversial. An army of opponents rose up to resist it with their *cri de guerre* as "corporations are not people." And opponents of the ruling expanded their fight to all assertions of constitutional rights by corporations, not just speech rights. They use the phrase "corporations are not people" not to mean that corporations lack brains and hearts (which is obvious) or even that corporations should not have separate legal status (which is uncontroversial). The phrase instead means that "corporations should not be holders of constitutional rights."

There is much to criticize in the Court's free speech jurisprudence generally and its *Citizens United* ruling in particular. But the Court was correct in assuming corporations are rightful holders of constitutional rights. That does not mean that the Court was correct in striking down limits on corporate political spending. Free speech doctrine could be nuanced enough to recognize the dangers posed by unlimited spending in elections, whether from individuals, unions, or corporations. But to answer the mistakes of *Citizens United* by opposing all corporate rights, or even all corporate speech rights, is like dealing with a termite infestation by burning down the house.

The question of corporate personhood does get tricky. Corporations do, and should, receive constitutional protections. But they do not, and should not, receive all the protections and rights as human beings. The breadth and scope of the rights corporations can claim will turn on both the nature of corporations and the purpose of the right. In other words, when it comes to the Constitution, corporations are people some of the time. And sometimes they are not.

I. The Opposition to Corporate Personhood

After *Citizens United*, a broad and energetic movement has sprung up to overturn it by way of constitutional amendments of various stripes. They range from relatively limited and contained grants of congressional authority to regulate campaign finance to broad attacks on corporate constitutional personhood.[10]

While the opposition to *Citizens United* in particular and corporate personhood in general enjoys bipartisan support, these ideas are particularly energizing and unifying for progressives. President Obama criticized the decision in his 2010 State of the Union address, when the ruling was only days old, and continued the critique during his 2012 reelection campaign. After Mitt Romney asserted on the stump that "corporations are people, my friend," Obama responded by declaring, "I don't care how many times you try to explain it, corporations aren't people. People are people."[11] During the 2014 midterm elections, Senator Elizabeth Warren kept the issue fresh as she barnstormed the country to rally the faithful. According to the *Washington Post*, her most dependable applause line in her stump speech was "Corporations are not people!"[12] In the 2016 election, presidential candidate Hillary Clinton promised to nominate justices to the Supreme Court who would overturn *Citizens United*.[13] Her opponent for the Democratic nomination, Bernie Sanders, railed against the case and pointed to his sponsorship of a constitutional amendment taking constitutional rights away from corporations.[14] And even though the political pendulum swung on other matters in 2016, the opposition to *Citizens United* and corporate rights remained broad and robust. Voters in four states passed anti–*Citizens United* referenda by landslide margins.[15] At this writing, seventeen states, more than seven hundred localities, and more than two hundred members of Congress have endorsed a constitutional amendment of some kind.[16] In addition, a petition to the Securities and Exchange Commission to require public corporations to disclose political spending to shareholders received over half a million comments, most of which were in favor of such a rule.[17]

A number of advocacy groups have emerged to fight corporate personhood or have rebranded themselves by newly taking aim at it. Most of these groups oppose the right of corporations to assert any First Amendment speech rights, and some have gone further, calling for disabusing all corporations or businesses of any constitutional rights. Common Cause, for example, uses former secretary of labor Robert Reich to tout its support for "a constitutional amendment declaring that 'Only People are People' and that only people should have free speech rights protected by the Constitution."[18] Public Citizen, the liberal litigation group founded by Ralph Nader, argues that "rights protected by the Constitution were intended for natural people."[19] Free Speech for People, one of the groups most influential in the anti-personhood movement, is pushing a "People's Rights Amendment" to the Constitution.[20] The version introduced in the U.S. Senate by Jon Tester of Montana and in the House by Jim McGovern of Massachusetts would declare that "the rights protected by this Constitution [are] the rights of natural persons." The proposed amendment goes on to provide that "People, person, or persons as used in this Constitution does not include corporations, limited liability companies or other corporate entities . . . and such corporate entities are subject to such regulations as the people . . . deem reasonable." These efforts are part and parcel of a larger attack on corporate involvement not only in politics, but also in society broadly.[21] The skepticism about corporations is so profound that the ban on corporate rights in the People's Rights Amendment would extend even to nonprofit corporations. The organizations fighting corporate personhood—Common Cause, Public Citizen, Free Speech for People—would lose the right to speak about the amendment they have championed.

This movement against corporate personhood has benefited from the intellectual heft offered by a number of prominent legal scholars.[22] In a moment when the progressive left seems otherwise to be fighting rearguard actions, the movement against corporate personhood has genuine energy.

But taking a sledgehammer to corporate personhood is a mistake. Corporate personhood deserves a more nuanced analysis than we have seen from opponents of *Citizens United*. In fact, corporate personhood can be marshaled in arguments *against* corporations being able to assert constitutional rights. Moreover, the concerns motivating the movement against corporate personhood can be ameliorated with adjustments in corporate governance rather than constitutional law. And in corporate law, what we need are changes in corporate governance to make corporations *more* like persons, not less.

II. The Importance of Separateness

Before we begin the discussion of corporate constitutional rights, it is worthwhile to note how important corporate separateness is. In 2014, the Supreme Court heard arguments in *Burwell v. Hobby Lobby Stores, Inc.*, a case contesting the "contraceptive mandate" in the Affordable Care Act (ACA) that required companies over a certain size to provide its employees with health insurance that included contraceptive care.[23] Hobby Lobby—an arts and crafts retailer—sued under the Religious Freedom Restoration Act (RFRA),[24] which provides that the government "shall not substantially burden a person's exercise of religion" unless that burden is the least restrictive means to further a compelling governmental purpose.[25] Hobby Lobby argued that under traditional canons of statutory construction and under the Dictionary Act, it should be considered a "person" under RFRA.[26]

Hobby Lobby is a big company, with over twenty thousand employees and more than six hundred stores. But it's a "closely held" corporation—meaning its stock is not publicly traded. The stock is owned by members of one family—the Greens of Oklahoma City, who are devout Christians. The Greens believe that four of the methods covered by the contraceptive mandate of the ACA are "abortifacients," and they argued that the mandate would cause them to violate their belief that human life begins at conception.

Though the Greens' claims appeared at first glance to depend on corporate personhood, they ironically depended on a *rejection* of corporate personhood. A group of law professors with expertise in corporate law argued in a brief to the Court that a dedication to corporate personhood should lead the Court to reject Hobby Lobby's religious claims.[27] The brief explained that corporate personhood expresses the idea that "for-profit corporations are entities that possess legal interests and a legal identity of their own—one separate and distinct from their shareholders."

The brief emphasized that the distinction between the company and the shareholders is not ancillary but the very purpose of the corporation as a legal form. This separateness means, among other things, that shareholders are not held liable for the debts of the corporation. That makes it possible for people who do not wish to oversee the day-to-day activities of companies in which they invest —and do not wish to risk every penny they own if the corporation goes bankrupt—to invest in corporate stock. In other words, corporate personhood is what makes capital markets possible, and capital markets are essential for the development of a vibrant national economy. Beyond that, corporations can exist long after the life of any individual who invests in or works for them. This means, as legal scholar Lynn Stout has pointed out, that corporations provide a mechanism for society to make long-term, intergenerational investments that are not linked to government or a specific family.[28] In this light, it is not an overstatement to say that corporate separateness has been one of the most important legal innovations in the development of national wealth.

The corporate law brief argued that this separateness meant the Greens should not be able to attach their own religious beliefs to the corporation. The Greens chose to form a corporation in order to operate the business without running the risk of losing their personal assets if the corporation went belly up. They *wanted* separateness. But when it came to religion, they argued the corporation and its religious shareholders were one and the same. Hobby Lobby was not a religious corporation, but the Greens wanted to claim it was because of the beliefs of its shareholders. Corporate law professors argued they should not be able to have it both ways.

The Supreme Court disagreed. It held, 5–4, that the Greens could project their religious beliefs onto the corporation and refuse to provide their employees the required contraceptive-care benefits. The Court considered the shareholders and the company to be identical for purposes of RFRA. Though Justice Samuel Alito's opinion for the Court reached the conservative outcome, its sin was not an embrace of corporate personhood but a rejection of it. If the Court had taken corporate personhood seriously, it would have ruled against Hobby Lobby.[29]

Hobby Lobby is not the only example of when corporate personhood has implications that should be applauded by progressives.

One aspect of corporate personhood—of corporate separateness—is to create a mechanism in law to hold corporations accountable. Consider the Deepwater Horizon oil spill disaster. For three months in 2010, Americans woke to the news of another fifty thousand barrels of crude oil spewing into the Gulf of Mexico.[30] Americans were justifiably outraged. In a legal system without corporate personhood, the channel for that outrage would have been limited to lawsuits and criminal inquiries against individual human beings responsible—managers, workers, and contractors. In any legal jurisdiction worth its salt, the search for culpable individuals has to be part of the settling-up of any man-made disaster. But few human beings would have enough money to compensate those harmed by a massive disaster like Deepwater Horizon. Because a corporate entity is also on the hook, there's a chance for something approaching real compensation or real responsibility. This same rationale applies for any number of thousands of corporate misdeeds and mistakes, from negligently produced pharmaceuticals to fraudulently marketed securities. Corporate personhood is thus not only a mechanism for the creation of wealth by encouraging investment or for distinguishing the interests of shareholders from those of companies. It is also a mechanism for enforcing accountability by providing a deep pocket to sue.

III. Corporate Constitutional Rights: A Null Set?

The concept of corporate separateness—of corporate personhood —in corporate law is not particularly controversial, even if misunderstood by the Court in *Hobby Lobby*. Not surprisingly, the leaders of the movement against "corporate personhood" do not spend much time talking about its corporate law aspects. Even though their arguments in regard to constitutional standing are inconsistent with these long-standing corporate notions in some ways, they do not appear to advocate for an eradication of corporate personhood in the sense of a corporation's having a capacity to sue and be sued, to hold property, or to borrow money and issue stock in its own name. Instead, the assertion "corporations are not people" is meant as a placeholder for the assertion that corporations should not be able to claim the constitutional rights that human beings can.

While the question of which rights corporations should be able to claim does not have straightforward answers, one piece of analysis is easy. The argument that corporations should not have standing to assert *any* constitutional right is quite weak. The opposite of a constitutional right is a governmental power. If corporations have no rights, then governmental power in connection with corporations is at its maximum. That power can be abused, and corporate personhood is a necessary bulwark. For example, in 1971, the government sought to stop the *New York Times*, a for-profit, publicly traded media company, and the *Washington Post*, which had gone public as a corporation only a few weeks previously, from publishing the leaked Pentagon Papers. The Supreme Court correctly decided that the newspapers had a First Amendment right to publish.[31] That was one of the most important free speech decisions of the twentieth century. At the time, no one suggested that the *Times* and the *Post*, as corporations, had no standing to bring a constitutional claim. In 1992, Planned Parenthood won a hard-fought battle to have the Supreme Court reaffirm *Roe v. Wade*, which recognized abortion as a fundamental right protected by the Fourteenth Amendment to the Constitution.[32] Planned Parenthood is organized as a corporation, but no one suggested it had no standing to object to limits on its ability to provide abortions. Today, Google and other media companies are fighting government demands to disgorge the contents of their servers.[33] No one suggests that the government's power should be unchecked because the media companies, as corporations, have no Fourth Amendment rights to be free of unreasonable searches and seizures. If corporations were not able to claim the Fifth Amendment rights to be free of government takings, their assets and resources would always be at risk of expropriation. No one would invest in corporations, undermining the reason we have them in the first place.

Some of the leading opponents of corporate personhood have begun to concede the weakness of the argument that corporations should never be able to assert any constitutional rights. An update of the Free Speech for People website, for example, seeks to reassure supporters that its advocacy of the People's Rights Amendment (PRA)—the proposed amendment ending constitutional rights for corporations—would not affect the freedom of the press. The site argues that press freedoms would still be held by the individual human beings engaging in press activities, even when those individuals operate in a corporate form. According to this update,

"The freedom of press applies to press/media functions regardless of whether a corporation owns and operates those functions."[34]

This interpretation of the People's Rights Amendment by its own authors embodies what appears to be a striking concession that the corporate form is immaterial if speech or press freedoms are in play. What counts is the *function* at issue, not the status of the claimant. Corporate personhood is immaterial. If a government law infringes on the function of the press, then it will be subject to constitutional scrutiny, "regardless of whether a corporation owns and operates those functions."

This is an important concession, inconsistent with the language of the proposed amendment that "corporate entities are subject to such regulations as the people, through their elected state and federal representatives, deem reasonable."[35] The language of the amendment would seem to allow a reasonable regulation of corporate-owned newspapers; the explanation of how it would operate would seem to say the opposite. Perhaps the amendment is not meant to apply limits on corporate rights when they are used to the benefit of natural persons or require the actions of humans to put them into operation? If so, when is that *not* the case? In *Citizens United*, the corporate claimant was asserting a First Amendment right to speak on behalf of, and to, natural persons. If the PRA includes an implicit exception when a corporation is acting through, on behalf of, or for the benefit of natural persons, then it would not change the outcome in the very case that motivated it.

The PRA does include a provision saying, "Nothing contained herein shall be construed to limit the people's rights of freedom of speech, freedom of the press, free exercise of religion, and such other rights of the people, which rights are inalienable." But that provision focuses on the rights of *people*. If it operates as a savings clause for *corporate* rights of speech, press, and religion, then the amendment is toothless indeed.

Another part of the PRA's explanatory website purports to answer the criticism that it would subject corporations to uncompensated takings. Such takings are unconstitutional under the Fifth Amendment, which provides that no "private property be taken for public use, without just compensation." If the PRA means what it says, then corporations would not be able to use the Fifth Amendment to defend against a government expropriation of their property. The Trump administration could order the seizure of printing presses owned by the *New York Times;* Georgia could order Coca-Cola to hand over its secret formula; the National Security Agency could take control of Google's servers. If corporations lack all constitutional standing and are subject to whatever regulation government officials wish to put into place, then the Constitution would pose no obstacle to such actions.

But the PRA's website explains that "While corporations are not among 'we the people' by and for whom the Constitution exists, corporations and other property are nonetheless secure from unconstitutional conduct by government."[36] This could mean one of two things. It could mean that those who own corporations—which appears to mean shareholders (a contested claim)—can assert a constitutional claim any time a corporation's property is taken. Let me call that "property standing." Or it could mean that the corporation can derivatively assert the interests of its shareholders. Let me call that "derivative standing."

The website suggests that the People's Rights Amendment would allow both "property standing" and "derivative standing." As for property standing, it asserts that "human beings who have had their property taken . . . (including the shares held by people in the corporation) may invoke remedies under the 5th or 14th Amendment." As for derivative standing, it says, "The corporation may also have standing to bring those arguments on behalf of their shareholders."

It is unclear how these arguments are consistent with the text of the proposed amendment and the overall goal of refusing constitutional protections to corporations. As for "property standing," are courts to consider corporate property as really belonging to shareholders? If so, any time the government takes or burdens the property of a corporate entity, a shareholder would need to be the plaintiff in a court challenge. Not only would this be extraordinarily messy (who decides which shareholder or group of shareholders speaks for the company?), but it is also inconsistent with the very notion of corporate separateness. The purpose of the corporate form is to separate the interests—and the property rights—of the corporate entity from the shareholders and other investors.

Perhaps instead we are to understand that *corporations* cannot raise constitutional claims but *shareholders* can any time their shares decrease in value because of some government act. That would turbocharge shareholder rights like never before and transform any regulation of corporations decreasing shareholder value into an unconstitutional takings claim. What's more, there would be no conceptual difference between a taking of corporate property that decreases shareholder value and a limit on corporate speech that decreases shareholder value. The "property standing" of shareholders would thus be the exception that swallowed the rule of no constitutional rights for corporations. Corporate speech rights claims under the First Amendment would simply arise as shareholder property rights claims under the Fifth Amendment. Surely that is not what anti-corporate personhood activists would prefer.

Another oddity created by the supposed work-around of "property standing" is that many corporate entities do not have shareholders. My home institution, Boston College, is organized as a corporation; it would not be able to claim any constitutional rights under the proposed amendment and would be subject to "such regulations as the people . . . deem reasonable." If the Commonwealth of Massachusetts wanted to seize a swath of land from the university for a new road, "the "property standing" of shareholders could not come to the rescue because Boston College has no shareholders. This is true of all nonprofits—whether they are hospitals, charitable organizations, or political advocacy groups like Free Speech for People itself. Boston College is a legal person under Massachusetts law, but under the PRA it would have no constitutional rights and could be subject to uncompensated takings of its land, property, or other assets. Without shareholders, there would be no human beings who could claim "property standing" to protect the corporation from governmental overreach. The irony of the "property standing" exception to the amendment's ban on corporate rights would be that for-profit corporations would be protected because they have shareholders, but nonprofit corporations would not. Any constitutional amendment protecting Exxon and General Electric more than Boston College and Planned Parenthood is fundamentally flawed.

The notion of "derivative standing" is similarly problematic. This is the same kind of exception to the "corporations have no rights" rule that was claimed to save the freedom of the press. The corporation itself has no standing to bring constitutional claims, but the "corporation may . . . have standing to bring those arguments on behalf of [its] shareholders."[37] There are multiple problems with this work-around, however. First, as mentioned above, many nonprofit corporate entities do not have shareholders. Second, the authors of the amendment wrongly assume that most shareholders are human beings. In today's economy, most shares in most companies are owned by institutional investors such as insurance companies or mutual funds. And companies routinely organize themselves in several layers of corporate subsidiaries, which means that many corporations have only other corporations as shareholders. Under the proposed amendment, those corporations presumably would not "have standing to bring [constitutional claims] on behalf of their shareholders" if those shareholders are also corporations. The resulting patchwork—corporations with human shareholders could claim constitutional rights but corporations with no shareholders or with only institutional shareholders could not—would be awkward at best.

Worse, the "derivative standing" argument would undermine corporate separateness where it is most important. In effect, Hobby Lobby asserted "derivative standing" to bring its shareholders' religious claims. If such derivative standing became the norm, it would result in a drastic *increase* in corporate constitutional claims seeking exemption from regulations conflicting with shareholders' freedoms of speech or religion, whether those regulations pertained to contraceptive mandates or anti-discrimination laws.[38] We see those very cases arising around the country. One case concerning a bakery refusing to sell a wedding cake to a gay couple on the basis of the religious beliefs of its dominant shareholder made it to the Supreme Court in the fall of 2017.[39] Increasing corporate claims like that one is not what the anti-corporate personhood activists are looking for. But their arguments allowing corporations to assert the rights of their shareholders will have that very effect.

The argument that corporations have no constitutional rights is simply unsustainable. Even the most adamant opponents of corporate constitutional rights cannot hold the line, offering up exceptions that recognize and even expand corporate rights. They, too, find themselves trying to determine which rights corporations may claim and which they cannot. Their answers are problematic and inconsistent, but they recognize the necessity of the task.

IV. Corporate Constitutional Rights: Some But Not All

The question of which constitutional rights corporations can claim has bedeviled the Supreme Court and commentators for two cen-

turies. It is obvious that corporations are not genuine human beings and should not automatically receive all the constitutional rights
that human beings claim. At the same time, it is similarly obvious that
corporations should be able to claim *some* constitutional rights. So:
which ones, and when?

The answer to that question turns on both the purpose of the
corporate form and the nature of the right claimed.[40] Few general
statements can improve on Chief Justice John Marshall's in *Dartmouth College* two centuries ago: "Being the mere creature of law,
[the corporation] possesses only those properties which the charter
of its creation confers upon it either expressly or as incidental to its
very existence."[41] In effect, the proper analysis of corporate constitutional rights asks what rights are "incidental to its very existence."
A more modern summary of the problem comes in then-Justice
William Rehnquist's dissent in the 1978 case of *First National Bank
v. Bellotti.*[42] In *Bellotti*, the Court struck down state limits on corporate spending intended to influence voting on a state referendum.
The Court was protective of corporate spending (a holding later
limited in the *Austin* case, which was in turn overruled by *Citizens
United*). In his dissent Justice Rehnquist explained the question better than the Court did: "Since it cannot be disputed that the mere
creation of a corporation does not invest it with all the liberties
enjoyed by natural persons, . . . our inquiry must seek to determine
which constitutional protections are 'incidental to its very existence.' "[43]

This inquiry must begin with a discussion of the nature of corporations and what purposes they serve. There is much disagreement about whether corporations should be managed primarily to
serve shareholder interests or to serve a more robust set of stakeholder interests.[44] But there is broad consensus that corporations
are economic entities, created for the purpose of benefiting society
by creating wealth through the production of goods and services.

The constitutional analysis should begin with the presumption that corporations should receive the rights incidental to serving that economic purpose and should not receive those that are not germane to that purpose. This presumption may be overcome in specific contexts or to further other constitutional values, but that is the starting place for analysis.

Begin with the obvious point that corporations cannot vote or serve on jurics. It does not make any sense to think of corporations asserting those rights, both because of the nature of the right and the nature of the corporate entity. Service on juries and voting are rights that do not make sense to bestow on any collective body, whether it be corporate, charitable, or familial. Similarly, the Court has held that corporations cannot assert the Fifth Amendment right to be free of self-incrimination.[45] The exclusion makes sense because its purpose is to protect human beings from the coercive power of police authority. Corporations do not have psyches or emotions or fear, so they do not need such protection. The exclusion from the right against self-incrimination also makes sense because of the purpose of corporations to operate in a free and fair market. If corporations could "plead the Fifth," they could otherwise evade myriad disclosure obligations necessary to make markets work freely and fairly. It is easy to imagine the havoc created if, for example, General Motors had a constitutional right not to disclose safety defects in its cars.

A similar line makes sense in regard to the freedom to exercise religion. The right is to protect the freedom of conscience, and only actual human beings have a conscience. There should be allowances for genuine associations of religious people, such as churches. The Catholic Church is organized as a corporation.[46] But because of corporate separateness—that is, corporate personhood—it will be quite difficult for businesses to show that they are genuine associations of religious people since it will not be the shareholders' views that control. Courts should also be skeptical of corporate religious rights because when businesses win religious exemptions from regulation, the market is skewed in their favor and to the detriment of other market actors. Such exemptions undermine society's economic purpose of having corporations in the first place.[47]

Should corporations be able to claim First Amendment free speech rights? The answer is complicated. The short answer for now is: it depends. It will depend in part on whether the speech at issue is necessary for corporations to fulfill their economic purpose. Sometimes granting corporations a speech right would be inconsistent with their purpose. Securities laws, for example, routinely require corporations to disclose their financial well-being to the public. If human beings were required to reveal personal finances, they would rightly object to the requirement as coerced speech, a violation of the First Amendment. But corporations' arguments along those lines would fail, and they should. The Court recognizes the difference. In 2011, AT&T asked that information about its finances be excluded from Freedom of Information Act requests because the statute has an exception for "personal privacy." The Court unanimously rejected this claim—and Chief Justice John Roberts ridiculed it in his opinion. That exception, he wrote, "does not extend to corporations. We trust that AT&T will not take it personally."[48]

On the other hand, the best understanding of corporate speech rights would include the ability of the corporation to speak publicly about matters germane to its economic role. That is, speech that is "incidental"—to use language from the *Dartmouth College* case—to its existence in the marketplace should receive protection. This includes commercial speech at least[49] and presumptively even political speech concerning economic matters germane to the business.[50]

But the question of germaneness is not likely to do all the work we need in the free speech area. There are additional considerations at issue because of the nature of the right. Sometimes it is important to protect the speech rights of a corporation not because the communication is crucial to the economic role of the business, but because of the rights of human listeners to hear to what it has to say. The rights of listeners are what is actually at issue in many press cases, such as the Pentagon Papers case. But it is not limited to press cases and has often been used by the Court to explain commercial speech cases. On occasion, what a corporation says is relevant to public debate or is important for consumer decisions in the marketplace.

After *Citizens United,* one might think that this protection of corporations' ability to reach listeners is an ideologically conservative idea. But the idea that listeners have a right to hear the words of businesses began as a liberal one when, in the 1970s, Public Citizen brought a First Amendment challenge to limits on the commercial advertising of pharmacies.[51] It argued these laws violated the public's right to know. As Adam Winkler says, it is not unfair to say that Public Citizen's advocacy laid an important foundation for Justice Anthony Kennedy's reasoning in *Citizens United,* in which he rested the protection of corporate speech rights not on corporate "personhood" but on the right of the public to know what corporations believed.[52] Public Citizen now decries corporate constitutional rights, and its president declared after *Citizens United* that even the commercial speech cases should be overturned.[53] But its work forty years ago helped get us to where we are today.

Acknowledging corporate speech rights does not necessarily lead to the proposition that businesses should be able to spend money in elections, as the Court ruled in *Citizens United. Citizens United* all too simplistically extended speech rights to cover corporate spending rights. But the typical critique of that extension—that "money is not speech"—is as mistaken as the "corporations are not people" yelp. The Court's ruling in *Citizens United* that caps on spending are constitutionally problematic traces its origins to the 1976 case *Buckley v. Valeo,* where the Court struck down limits on individual (human) campaign expenditures as violations of free speech.[54] In neither *Citizens United* nor *Buckley*, however, did the Court say money is speech. Instead, the Court recognized that money is sometimes essential to make speech audible above the din. Giving it, too, can be an expressive act. Those notions are certainly correct. Imagine if a Republican-controlled Congress told citizens they could not contribute to Planned Parenthood or had to pay dues to the National Rifle Association. It would be inane to argue that the First Amendment would not be implicated because money is not speech.

Nonetheless, there are myriad reasons why a commitment to free speech rights—even corporate free speech rights—should not bar reasonable limits on independent campaign expenditures by both corporations and the wealthy. It is not hyperbole to say that without such limits, American democracy is at risk. The billions of dollars flooding the electoral process skew it—and the legislative process that follows—toward the moneyed and well-heeled. And the constant search for financial resources by candidates and elected officials perverts the nature of public service.

The Court has been so enamored with a simplistic, libertarian theory of free speech doctrine that it is blind to those risks. The crucial flaw in *Citizens United* was the same as in *Buckley:* the Court saw caps on spending not as crucial protections of democracy but as efforts to "restrict the speech of some elements of our society in order to enhance the relative voice of others." That, the Court said in *Buckley* and repeated in *Citizens United*, "is wholly foreign to the First Amendment."[55]

A sane Court could easily construct exceptions to otherwise applicable doctrine to protect the sanctity and fairness of our elections.[56] Canada's Supreme Court has done that very thing, ruling that limits on spending to create "a level playing field" were required by democracy rather than inconsistent with it.[57]

This belief that money is a genuine problem in our electoral politics does not mean, however, that *corporate* money deserves special attention. The worries touted by the corporations-are-not-people crowd have been, for the most part, overblown. For-profit corporations are not the main villain in Big Money's takeover of our electoral politics. By a large margin, most of the money flowing into Super PACs in both the 2012 and 2016 presidential election cycles originated not from the coffers of for-profit corporations but from the wallets and purses of the mega-rich and labor unions.[58] Corporations do appear on the disclosure statements of Super PACs, but most of that corporate money has come from private, closely held companies dominated by a handful of wealthy individuals. Most of the corporate entities listed as making political expenditures have been merely the conduits for the expenditures of rich individuals. Some of these corporations appear to have been created for that very purpose.

What's more, for-profit, publicly traded, non-ideological corporations are not big players in this space. For example, in the 2012 elections Chevron spent $2.5 million, which was the most spent by any single publicly traded company in that cycle.[59] This may sound like a large amount, but it was likely minuscule in terms of impact. It would not have been sufficient to purchase even a thirty-second commercial during the 2012 Super Bowl. (Ads in 2012 cost about $7 million per minute.)[60] Chevron's spending was minuscule also in relative terms. Sheldon Adelson, the casino owner, spent more than $90 million in the same cycle, and the Koch brothers ran a network of groups that together spent over $400 million.[61] Chevron's involvement was especially tiny by comparison to its size. Chevron had operating revenues in 2012 of $231 billion and net income of $26.2 billion. Its political spending was, therefore, about 0.001 percent of its revenues and 0.01 percent of its income. Campaign spending was hardly a blip in its cash flow; the company may have spent more on office supplies. And remember: Chevron spent more on electoral politics than any other company in the nation. (In 2016, it appears that Chevron sat out the presidential race entirely, though it donated $3.3 million to Super PACs supporting Republicans in congressional races.)[62]

In the 2016 cycle, too, publicly traded corporations were not active spenders.[63] According to data gathered by the Center for Responsive Politics, of the nearly three thousand instances of corporate contributions to Super PACs in 2016, only a tiny number came from publicly traded companies.[64] In fact, there were only twenty-six corporate donations of $1 million or more in the 2016 cycle and only forty-two of more than $500,000. Of the top fifty donations, only nine were made by publicly traded companies or their subsidiaries. Chevron made four, totaling $3.3 million; Devon Energy gave two, totaling $1.25 million; a subsidiary of Conoco-Phillips gave $1 million; NextEra energy gave $1 million; and a subsidiary of the parent company of R. J. Reynolds Tobacco gave $1 million. The other donations to Super PACs came from privately held companies, and, as noted, many appear to be mere conduits for contributions from their dominant shareholders. Totaled together, the top fifty donations from both public and private business entities amounted to just over $52 million. This is $30 million *less* than Sheldon Adelson and his wife gave in 2016.[65] What's more, of the large donations from public companies to Super PACs, only one—NextEra's $1 million—was spent in support of a presidential candidate: Jeb Bush, who dropped out of the race in February 2016.[66] That is worth emphasizing. In one of the most heated elections in modern history, only one publicly traded company contributed $1 million or more to a Super PAC supporting a presidential candidate in 2016. And that money went to a candidate who lost early. The remaining large corporate donations went to groups supporting candidates in Congress. Not a single large corporate expenditure went to support either candidate who won the nomination of the two major parties in 2016.

This is not to defend the efforts of corporations to skew and affect elections. But the focus on the idea of "corporations are not people" may be distracting us from the real and more fundamental general problem of money.

The power of corporations, to be sure, is frequently misused, usually to the advantage of the financial and managerial elite. Employees, communities, consumers, the environment, and the public interest in general are elbowed aside in corporate decision making unless the corporation can make money by taking them into account. Corporations are managed aggressively to maximize shareholder return. As a result, the risks they run—whether of oil spills in the Gulf of Mexico or financial crises erupting from Wall Street—are often unrecognized until too late. The executives who run American corporations do not generally think of themselves as having obligations to the public. The social contract of American corporations is thin. But these defects of corporate power, fundamental as they are, are not problems of constitutional law or corporate personhood. They are problems of corporate law, and they could be fixed by corporate law.

V. The Problem of Corporate Power: A Corporate Law Fix

The current conventional understanding of corporations and their obligations is that they should be managed primarily for the benefit of their shareholders. But that is not the only way corporations can be governed. A number of legal scholars have argued for decades that corporations should be seen as having robust social and public obligations that cannot be encapsulated in share prices.[67] Under current law and norm, executives are obligated to look after the interests of shareholders first and foremost. But progressive corporate scholars argue these fiduciary duties should be extended to employees and other corporate stakeholders.[68]

One way to make these obligations operational is to make the decision-making structure of the company itself more pluralistic. In a number of European countries, for example, companies have "codetermined" board structures that require representation of both shareholders and employees.[69] Even with these management structures, corporations continue their focus on building wealth— that is the core purpose of the corporate form—but not merely for a narrow sliver of equity investors. And it works. Germany, where codetermination is strongest, is the economic powerhouse of Europe. The CEO of the German company Siemens argues that codetermination is a "comparative advantage" for Germany; a senior managing director of the U.S. investment firm Blackstone Group said that codetermination was one of the factors that allowed Germany to avoid the worst of the financial crisis.[70]

These governance structure reforms make corporations more like persons, not less. Human beings routinely balance a multitude of interests—relationships, parenthood, friendships, careers, avocations. Only the rare oddball behaves as though accumulating money is the paramount and unitary good.[71] Humans have consciences; corporations do not. Left to their own devices, corporations will behave as though profit is the only thing that matters. The best way to constrain corporations is to require them to sign onto a more robust social contract and govern themselves more pluralistically—mechanisms designed to mimic the traits of human personhood within the corporate form.

If corporations had these traits of personhood, we could worry less about corporate involvement in the political arena. American corporations have become a vehicle for the voices and interests of a small managerial and financial elite—the notorious one percent. The cure for this is more democracy within businesses, more participation in corporate governance by workers, communities, shareholders, and consumers. If corporations were more democratic, their participation in the nation's political debate would be of little concern.

To cure the ills of *Citizens United*, we should stop fighting corporate personhood. Instead, corporations should be structured so they behave more like people.

TWO

Corporations and the "Damn Public"

"The public be damned," railroad magnate William Henry Vanderbilt snorted at a reporter in 1882. The impertinent scribe had asked
whether Vanderbilt ran his railroads with an eye toward public benefit.[1] At the time, Vanderbilt was among the most powerful men in
American business and by his own estimation the richest man in
the world. In an era when $1,000 a year was considered a decent
wage, his wealth was so great that it spun off interest income of $1
million *per month*. Not long before his death a few years later, he
remarked that he would not bother to cross the street for another
million dollars.[2] He knew how to run a railroad. Or several.

Vanderbilt was not, however, a careful cultivator of his public image. His damnation of the American public was big news,
appearing on the front page of hundreds of newspapers within
twenty-four hours.

The week before his comment, two trains had collided on his
railroad inside the Fourth Avenue tunnel in New York City, kill-
ing two passengers and injuring hundreds. Many New Yorkers

blamed the accident on Vanderbilt's unwillingness to cut into profits by spending money on safety measures. His "public be damned" tirade, spoken as he dined in his private train car on the way to Chicago, salted an open wound. The satirical magazine *Puck* ran a cover cartoon of a ballooned, profligate Vanderbilt wearing a diamond pin, smoking a stogie, and leaning back in a leather chair with a foot on the throat of an eagle dressed in Uncle Sam garb.[3] He is accompanied by two lapdogs on chains labeled "Congress" and "Legislature."

Impolitic as it was, Vanderbilt's comment embodied the business and political philosophy of the affluent classes of the Gilded Age. Many large corporations operated as if damning the public were a command both internally—as companies decided business policy and strategy—and externally—as companies became involved in politics and law. There was little separation between the way companies were run and how they manipulated the political and legal landscape. Gilded Age corporations, and the magnates who ran them, used all the tools at their disposal to aggrandize wealth. On the business side, workplaces were organized and run with ruthless efficiency and with little regard for the well-being of the workers, who could be quickly replaced from the hordes living in tenements in most American cities. Corporations routinely used outright bribery to control politicians and judges who protected them from intrusive legislation and untoward legal judgments.[4] Such influence also made it possible for corporations to use governmental power as their own, whether to open up swaths of land for railroads through eminent domain or to quash labor unrest with the help of police or militia.[5]

Corporate hegemony in politics was so pronounced that reformers worried that corporations enjoyed "systemic control" over government from "the lowest town offices" to "the executive officers of state and nation."[6] People feared that "the great business combinations, being the only centers of wealth and power, would be able to lord it over all the other interests and thus put an end to traditional American democracy."[7] The cartooned lapdogs resonated with *Puck's* readers because democracy itself was at risk.

In the same issue in which *Puck* published its cartoon, it also ran a blistering editorial about Vanderbilt and his ilk. "This man and the men like him have their heels upon you. . . . They keep you poor; they keep you under bad government. Your legislators are their tools." The evil perpetuated by the magnates came about because of how they acted in both the public and private spheres: "Almost every outrageous abuse in our social and political systems is traceable to the apathy of these men as citizens or to their vicious greed as monopolists."[8]

I. Jungle Freedom

For the most part, the law was a willing ally in corporations' damning of the public. There was little regulatory protection during the early years of the Gilded Age for workers, labor organizers, or the environment, and when legislatures began in fits and starts to offer some, courts came to the rescue of corporate interests. In 1905, the Supreme Court decided one of the most pivotal cases in its history when, in *Lochner v. New York*, it struck down a New York law establishing a sixty-hour maximum work week for bakers.[9] The case might seem at first glance to be inconsequential, but New York's law was a part of a broader effort of relatively meek legislative initiatives that also included minimum-wage laws. The Court's reasoning in *Lochner* undermined not only maximum hour laws, but also most other protections of employees and consumers.

The Court ruled that any such limits on the power of business were violations of their liberty interests, protected by the Constitution's due process clause. The Court's argument was that such legislation was an infringement on the right of each party to contract freely—"an illegal interference with the rights of individuals."[10] The implication of the ruling was that the so-called free market became presumptively constitutionally protected. In the years that followed, the Court would make occasional exceptions to the rule of the constitutionally protected free market—for example, with legislation that sought to protect women in the workplace because of their believed weaker physical and intellectual capacities.[11] But *Lochner* established the general rule: the prerogative and power of businesses were a matter of constitutional concern.

We can see now that the Court's assumptions about the freedom of the market were drastically misguided. The coercion inherent in the market—one characterized by the dominant power of corporations and other businesses, on the one hand, and the deadening crush of poverty and squalor on the other—was ignored in the legal analysis. That is not to say there was no logic to what the Court did, only that the logic was obtuse and distant from most people's genuine experiences and situations in the world. The analysis of the *Lochner* Court was simplistically libertarian. People choose their own situations—or at least choose their best options within their situations. Restrictions in the law are restrictions on their choices, and Choice Is Good—sufficiently good, in fact, to be protected by the Constitution.

Notice the irony. The Fourteenth Amendment and its due process clause were adopted after the Civil War to hold states to a national commitment to equality and liberty. Motivated by the need to protect newly freed slaves, the amendment's protection was not limited to them. The Fourteenth Amendment was, and continues to be, one of the most powerful tools to protect the marginalized and the oppressed. But with *Lochner*, the Court moved corporate interests to its core. In the skewed logic of *Lochner*, employers were the oppressed. They were oppressed by the restriction on liberty embodied in maximum hour or minimum-wage laws. The Constitution protected the free market; workers would have to protect *themselves* without the assistance of law. Instead of using the great promises of the Fourteenth Amendment to protect the powerless, the Court marshaled its protections in aid of businesses and the industrial and financial elites who ran them.

In the early twentieth century, Congress began to pass federal laws offering limited protections against the worst of corporate misdeeds, such as the employment of children in squalid conditions.[12] The Supreme Court found these regulations distasteful too. Because they came from the federal government rather than from the states, the Court did not have to rely on the due process clause but could strike them down as beyond Congress's enumerated powers.[13] Congress, said the Court, could legislate only pursuant to its authority to regulate commerce as given in Article I of the Constitution, and "commerce" was merely the transport of goods across state lines, not the manufacturing or farming that occurred before such transport. Thus the protection of children was outside Congress's powers; it would have to be done by the states if at all. But state laws that aimed at protecting workers or employees were, in the Court's view, contrary to due process. There was more room between Scylla and Charybdis.

The "*Lochner* era" of constitutional law lasted for nearly half a century and did significant harm. Attempts to protect consumers, children, and immigrant workers were thwarted by free-market ideology masquerading as constitutional law. The *Lochner* constitution was a social Darwinist law of the jungle. Upton Sinclair's *The Jungle*—a wilderness of unregulated greed and contempt for American workers and the public—was what we got.[14]

II. Corporate Law's Original Sin

But constitutional law was not the only problem. Corporate law, too, helped to keep corporations within a narrow set of obligations.

Still in its infancy, the law of corporations was faced with answering basic, fundamental questions. The most pivotal of these was to whom managers owed fiduciary duties. Are managers to look after all interested parties or just shareholders? Were there any obligations arising from corporate law toward employees? Communities? Creditors?

These questions were the same as those then being asked in constitutional law. Should corporations have public obligations, or should they be focused on the narrow and private? In constitutional law, the answer was emphatically that corporations should be insulated from public demands. They should run their businesses as their managers saw fit and should not be required to look beyond that narrow purview to take into account social welfare or other matters of public concern. In constitutional law, the answer to the question of whether corporations should be held to public duties was answered emphatically in the negative, and statutory insistence otherwise would raise constitutional implications. In corporate law, the general answer was the same, though it was couched in different language and posed in a different context.

A fight between Henry Ford and his rivals John and Horace Dodge gave rise to the pivotal articulation of the rule.

In the second decade of the twentieth century, Henry Ford was making money—an incredible fortune of money—making cars.[15] The Ford Motor Company, the company in which he was the dominant shareholder, was selling his masterpiece Model T as quickly as it could be produced. The popularization of the automobile was transforming the country, and Ford and his fellow shareholders were the main financial beneficiaries of the transformation. By 1916, the company had amassed a capital surplus of $60 million— not bad considering the company had been chartered with equity of $100,000 in 1903. Shareholders were receiving in scheduled dividends an amount equal to their initial investment *every month*.[16]

The company had also been declaring "special" dividends for several years—as much as $11 million in 1914.

Today, we are well aware of the dark side of Henry Ford's influence, which included his funding of anti-Semitic propaganda and his financial support for Hitler.[17] But in the 1910s and 1920s, Ford cultivated an image of a benevolent mogul, as different as one could imagine from William Henry Vanderbilt's obtuseness in such things a generation before. Ford made headlines in 1914 with his "Five-Dollar Day," when he doubled the wages of all his workers, explaining to the *New York Times* that companies had a direct role in improving the lives of the working class. His rhetoric sounded radical indeed: "I believe it is better for the nation, and far better for humanity, that between 20,000 and 30,000 people should be contented and well fed than that a few millionaires should be made."[18] This progressive stance played well with the public and even made Ford somewhat of a hero among American political radicals such as journalist John Reed.[19]

In 1916, Ford declared that special dividends had come to an end. He needed the money to build a new auto manufacturing facility that would be the largest in the world. (The factory that was eventually built, the River Rouge plant, built everything from Model As in the 1920s to Mustangs in the 2000s. A facility on the site assembles F150 trucks even now.)[20] Ford brashly claimed that his decision was motivated by a desire to do social good for the company's employees and customers, arguing that shareholder gain was not the *purpose* of a successful business but its byproduct. A business was about more than making money for shareholders, he said. It was about satisfying the obligations of a robust social contract to do "as much good as we can, everywhere, for everybody concerned . . . [a]nd incidentally to make money."[21] Ford seemed to demote the role of shareholders and promote the status of workers, saying in an interview with a local newspaper reporter that the profits earned by shareholders had been "awful" and that he wanted to drive down the price of his cars so more benefits could flow to "users and laborers."[22]

The shareholders were not amused. Particularly upset were the Dodge brothers, who owned 10 percent of Ford stock on the basis of a $10,000 investment in the first days of the company's history.[23] Though they had already made more than a 40,000 percent return, they sued for more, asking the Michigan courts to force the board of Ford Motor Company to declare a special dividend to distribute the capital surplus. It was a crafty demand. The brothers had started the car company that bore their name, a rival to Ford. An extraordinary dividend from Ford would both drain Ford Motor of financial surplus and provide cash to capitalize their own competing car company.

Henry Ford understood as much. He had no reason to fill the coffers of a competitor, and he had numerous solid business reasons to retain the capital in house and keep his customers and employees happy. Then as now, courts overseeing business disputes did not generally overturn the decisions of corporate executives in the absence of fraud or self-dealing. The dispute between the Dodge brothers and Henry Ford should have been no different. But instead of defending his refusal to issue special dividends as an exercise of his considered business judgment, a position that was both true and something that would have easily won the deference of a court,[24] Ford defended his actions by relegating shareholder interests and bringing workers' rights to the forefront: "My ambition . . . is to employ still more men, to spread the benefits of this industrial system to the greatest possible number, to help them build up their lives and their homes. To do this we are putting the greatest share of our profits back in the business."[25] The Dodge brothers seized on that rhetoric as evidence that Ford was using the company to further his own social agenda.

The case eventually made it to the Michigan Supreme Court. Ford's assertions of worker rights and shareholder subordination were too much for the court to endorse in an era when the Russian Revolution had already begun and socialism was on the rise in the United States. Legal scholar Todd Henderson explains that "if a firm as large and important to the American economy were permitted to pursue an overtly socialist strategy, the political impact and the effect on other firms could be enormous."[26] On the surface, the case was about whether shareholders were due some dividends. But more fundamentally it was a "test case of the foundations on which American capitalism would be built."[27]

The eventual decision was an iconic statement that corporations have no obligations beyond the bottom line. In one of the most famous passages in the history of corporate law, the Michigan Supreme Court announced the following:

> A business corporation is organized and carried on primarily for the profit of the stockholders. The powers of the directors are to be employed for that end. The discretion of directors is to be exercised in the choice of means to attain that end, and does not extend to a change in the end itself, to the reduction in profits, or to the nondistribution of profits among stockholders in order to devote them to other purposes.[28]

The court refused to enjoin the construction of the new car plant, but it ordered Ford Motor to issue an extraordinary dividend of $19 million.

Such judicial intervention into the internal disputes of a major corporation was odd then, and it would be almost unimaginable now. But Ford's rhetoric of worker and customer protection was sufficiently unusual and radical that it motivated the court to make clear that such motivation was out of bounds. *Dodge v. Ford* was a pivotal moment in the development of corporate law in that it defined the core purposes of corporations as being distinct from—even contrary to—the interests of workers, customers, and society. The case remains, a century later, one of the first opinions law students read in their introductory business law course. It is corporate law's original sin.

Rarely is *Dodge v. Ford* put into the broader context of what was happening in constitutional law at the time, but the trends conflate nicely. Courts were striking down state laws protecting workers as violations of a company's liberty interests under the Fourteenth Amendment. Courts were striking down federal laws protecting workers on the rationale that they went beyond Congress's commerce clause powers. When executives ran their companies to take into account the interests of workers, courts stepped in to rule such decisions unlawful under corporate law principles. These various assertions of judicial power arose in different contexts but together created and enforced a conception of the corporation as having a narrow set of obligations, focused on the economic gain of its financial investors. Law cemented the corporation as distinct and distant from government and bolstered its role as a tool for creating wealth for a sliver of financial and managerial elites. Employees, customers, or social welfare were not to be its concern.

Another way to describe this situation was that corporations were not required, or even allowed, to bear the responsibilities of citizenship. "The public be damned" had become more than a magnate's frustrated epithet. It had become the law's doctrinal touchstone.

III. A New Deal

This era of corporate legal hegemony endured for a couple of generations. In economic history, it was known as the Gilded Age; in legal history it was the *Lochner* era, after the bakery case. Regardless of the label, the era of corporate power did not weaken until the entire economy pitched into the abyss of the Great Depression.

The Depression provided the foundational shock that opened up the space for a profound intellectual and legal attack on corporate prerogative. It amounted to an intellectual turning point, as the economic upheaval caused people to reconceptualize the market itself as a creature of law rather than existing in a state of nature. In constitutional law, the Supreme Court reversed its previous fixation on the rights of corporations to be free from regulation. In a series of cases reviewing minimum-wage laws, the Court ruled that *Lochner* and its progeny had gone too far and that a business did not have a constitutional right to be free from regulatory obligations. The political impetus behind the change came when President Franklin Roosevelt threatened to enlarge the number of seats on the Court so he could pack it with appointees who would not obstruct his New Deal initiatives.[29] But the intellectual innovation that provided the basis for the switch was the insight that the marketplace was not natural or pre-political and that the "free" market was infused with coercion that needed government activity to counteract.[30] A failure by businesses to support the subsistence of their employees meant that society would be pressed into service to provide for their unmet needs. The Court channeled this insight in the case overturning *Lochner:* "The exploitation of a class of workers who are in an unequal position with respect to bargaining power and are thus relatively defenseless against the denial of a living wage is not only detrimental to their health and well being but casts a direct burden for their support upon the community."[31] The Court reasoned that a judicially enforced freedom of contract acted as a "subsidy for unconscionable employers."[32] The free market did not merit constitutional protection, and corporations could not claim constitutional protection from legally imposed obligations toward employees and communities.

The Court also repudiated its stingy reading of Congress's commerce clause authority, opening up the potential of federal regulation of the marketplace. The lead cases dealt with federal laws protecting the rights of employees to unionize, establishing a minimum wage and other worker protections, and regulating commodity prices.[33] The common theme in these cases was the Court's refusal "to shut our eyes to the plainest facts of our national life" or to "deal with the question" of congressional authority—and corporate freedom to be free from such authority—"in an intellectual vacuum."[34] Rather than interpreting the Constitution detached from any grounding in the real world of industrial power, the Court recognized the reality of what "recent economic experience had brought into a strong light": that corporations were simply too powerful to leave to their own devices.[35] Freed from constitutional limits, Congress adopted wide-ranging regulations of business, including the great securities acts of 1933 and 1934 (requiring disclosure and regulating fraud in the stock markets),[36] the labor protections in the National Labor Relations Act of 1935 (protecting the right to bargain collectively),[37] and the Fair Labor Standards Act of 1938 (creating a federal minimum wage).[38] Corporations were forced, through law, to act as if they had obligations to their employees, customers, and society in general.

Meanwhile, in corporate law too, intellectual innovation was occurring that reconceptualized the corporation and its relationship with the public. In 1932, a law professor, Adolf Berle, and an economist, Gardiner Means, published the most influential book in the history of corporate governance: *The Modern Corporation and Public Property*.[39] Berle and Means showed that industrial power was concentrated in the hands of the largest two hundred corporations and that shareholders—ostensibly the owners—had been disenfranchised to the benefit of company executives. Shareholders owned their shares, of course, but they had ceased to be owners of the corporation in any real sense. They enjoyed no genuine control over corporate decisions, whether small or large, tactical or strategic. Instead, a small group of interlocking and overlapping manage-rial elites controlled American business. (Means's statistical studies showed that fewer than eighteen hundred individuals controlled some two hundred corporations, presiding over one-third of the nation's wealth).[40] Berle and Means theorized that this "separation of ownership and control" undermined the traditional assumptions about the efficiency of free-market competition. Corporations, left to their own devices, would not perform according to the tradi-tional thinking that suggested the "invisible hand" of the market would maximize both private return and public benefit.[41] Managers might act in ways to maximize their personal benefit, but the con-nection to public benefit would be tenuous or haphazard. As legal scholar Dalia Tsuk has explained, "According to Berle and Means, the divergence between managers' and shareholders' interests indi-cated that managerial use of shareholders' property might be both self-interested and inefficient."[42]

Corporations had gained such power, both internally in regard to individuals working within them and externally in regard to markets and society at large, that Berle and Means argued that the corporation could "compete on equal terms with the modern state" and could potentially "supersed[e] it as the dominant form of social organization."[43] The problem for corporate governance, then, was how to ensure the responsible exercise of that power. Berle and Means argued that "power in economic organization shall be sub-jected to the same tests of public benefit which have been applied in their turn to power otherwise located."[44] With public benefit the test, they rejected both the notion of shareholder dominance and deference to managerial prerogative since neither would offer a genuine check on corporate irresponsibility.

Instead, Berle and Means argued the only way to check corporate power was through more systemic regulation and public oversight. The shareholders could not complain since "the owners of passive property, by surrendering control and responsibility over the active property, have surrendered the right that the corporations should be operated in their sole interest."[45] The "community," they posited, was "in a position to demand that the modern corporation serve not alone the owners or the control [that is, the controlling management] but all society."[46] For the corporation to survive, its management "should develop into a purely neutral technocracy, balancing a variety of claims by various groups."[47] And then,

> Should the corporate leaders, for example, set forth a program comprising fair wages, security to employees, reasonable service to their public, and stabilization of business, all of which would divert a portion of the profits from the owners of passive property, and should the community generally accept such a scheme as a logical and human solution of industrial difficulties, the interests of passive property owners would have to give way.[48]

This was a profound insight, amounting to an announcement that "all publicly held business corporations were public trustees," with powers to be exercised for the benefit of the community.[49] The responsibility of corporate citizenship flowed from the reality of corporate power. The assumptions and requirements of *Dodge v. Ford* would no longer hold.

The writings of academics are frequently ignored and often deserve to be. But Berle and Means's work was widely influential, providing the intellectual basis for greater regulation of business. Berle was a key adviser to President Franklin Roosevelt, and Roosevelt's New Deal used the space provided by the downfall of *Lochner* to take advantage of the contributions of Berle and Means.

The New Deal era is remembered as the American nascence of a more pervasive and comprehensive web of government regulations and protections. The target of most of these regulations was business. Minimum-wage laws operated as requirements on business payrolls. Protections for labor operated as limits on management. Disclosure mandates and fraud penalties operated as obligations on businesses to communicate—and to communicate the truth.

The New Deal embodied a completely different conception of the role of corporations in the economy and in society generally than had been dominant a few decades before. Corporations did not operate in their own insulated sphere but could be expected to play a broader role in society.

IV. Law and Economics, Shareholder Primacy, and a New *Lochner*

One can only understand corporate law—indeed all law—within the context of broader intellectual and ideological trends. It is not coincidental, for example, that the American Gilded Age of the late nineteenth century and early twentieth century saw an emphasis on the private nature of corporations as a rule of decision in both corporate law *(Dodge v. Ford)* and constitutional law *(Lochner v. New York)*. Similarly, it was not happenstance that the Great Depression brought about a fundamental rethinking of not only the nature of corporations, but also the place of the market itself and the role of government in regulating it.

In broad strokes, this was the state of play in both public and private law for the middle part of the twentieth century. On the public side, regulations required corporations to pay attention to their public obligations. Regulations of corporate behavior received only the gentlest judicial oversight. If Congress or state legislatures wished to constrain corporate behavior or channel corporate power toward certain ends, courts would not step in. On the private side, managers were held to duties of care and loyalty that had some teeth, but the obligations were not seen as being to shareholder value alone or even primarily to it. If corporations wanted to act as good corporate citizens, courts would not object.[50] To be sure, the vision of Berle and Means was never brought to fruition in that corporations were never forced to consider the interests of the public or non-shareholder stakeholders as a matter of fiduciary duty. And the structure of the corporation in the United States was never adjusted as it was in many European jurisdictions to require the representation of those interests within corporate governance. But the norm in the managerial class during the middle of the century was magnanimity toward those interests, and courts did not step in to enforce a strict shareholder primacy rule.[51] Managers were seen, and saw themselves, as a professional class, with professional obligations that could not be easily reduced to simple numbers on a balance sheet.

During the 1960s and 1970s, environmental scholars such as Rachel Carson and consumer activists such as Ralph Nader raised awareness of how the political influence, unsustainable practices, and global reach of corporations posed dangers to society.[52] On the regulatory side, environmental law, anti-discrimination law, anti-corruption law, and consumer protection law were all strengthened.[53] On the corporate side, we saw the rise of the so-called stakeholder statutes, which claimed to protect the ability of company management to look after the interests of companies' non-shareholder constituents.[54] Among academics, we saw an increasing skepticism about Delaware's status as the predominant provider of corporate governance law in the United States.[55] Congress held hearings on proposals to make corporate law a matter of federal rather than state law.[56]

Then, in 1980, something profound happened: Ronald Reagan was elected president of the United States. Reagan embodied a new Zeitgeist. He railed against government regulation, took pride in breaking up the power of public-sector unions, and ushered in an era in which people were encouraged to feel good about making money.[57] More broadly, he fostered a belief in, and a presumption in favor of, the market. Franklin Roosevelt had ushered in the New Deal saying, "The test of our progress is not whether we add more to the abundance of those who have much; it is whether we provide enough for those who have too little."[58] Reagan ushered in the 1980s proclaiming, "What I want to see above all is that this country remains a country where someone can always get rich."[59] One of Reagan's closest economic advisers, Nobel Prize winner Milton Friedman, famously said that the "one and only one social responsibility of business" is to make "as much money as possible."[60] The historical moment found voice in the 1987 film *Wall Street*, which featured the fictional corporate takeover artist Gordon Gekko proclaiming that "Greed . . . is good. Greed is right. Greed works."[61]

In the legal academy in the United States, this period saw the rise of the "law and economics" movement, whose scholars applied a simple version of neoclassical economic thought to law, arguing that individuals were rational maximizers of utility who acted with free will and that law should generally stand aside.[62] Law and economics scholars gained particular purchase in the corporate law field. The corporation was reconceptualized as a nexus of contracts, with the law needed only to establish presumably efficient default rules that the parties could otherwise negotiate around.[63] Corporate law was seen as emphatically *private* law, providing "off-the-rack" rules that were primarily enabling rather than prescriptive.[64] In this view, law should not dictate the details of the obligations among the parties because each party—including each of the various stakeholders of the firm—is assumed to know his or her own interests and protect them best through bargaining and exchange. If the parties disliked the terms of the "contract" between themselves and the company, they could leave. Not only could shareholders sell their shares, but employees could also quit, managers could find a different company to manage, suppliers could sell their goods elsewhere, and creditors could sell their bonds.[65]

This academic reconceptualization went hand in hand with a shift in emphasis among management. Duties to the company ceased to be seen as or enforced as a function of legal or moral obligation. Duties to the company were simply a function of the market, and the best way to ensure management's care and loyalty was not through fiduciary duty but through compensation mechanisms that aligned management interests with those of shareholders. Management began to care deeply about the maximization of share value, and the law—for the most part—stepped aside in enforcing fiduciary duties except in those cases where managerial self-interest polluted an obligation to maximize share price. It became more important for executives to understand finance than to understand the intricacies of their company's industry. CEOs could move around from one company to another, even if one company's business had little to do with the other. (One prominent example was Robert Nardelli, who was the CEO of a subsidiary of General Electric, then the CEO of Home Depot, then the CEO of Chrysler.)[66] Corporate health was equated with share price—or actually the positive movement of share price from quarter to quarter, then month to month, then day to day, then nanosecond to nanosecond. The managerial elite and the financial elite locked arms.

These trends revealed themselves in various ways over time. The 1980s saw a fixation on leveraged buyouts and hostile takeovers, driven more by the uber-competitive personality of celebrity CEOs than by business necessity or economies of scale. ("Winners" in the takeover battles mostly lost over time.)[67] In the 1990s, we saw an explosion of managerial compensation—most famously at Disney, where its president, Michael Ovitz, was paid $170 million to accept his firing after one ego-puncturing year in that role.[68] Charity stopped being seen as something done for the public. Charitable donations instead became a boon for management—a way to compensate elite managers by funding their pet projects or causes. The best example was the Armand Hammer museum in Los Angeles, an iconic tribute to the ego of Occidental Petroleum's CEO, funded by Occidental Petroleum.[69]

In the 2000s, as corporate leaders came to see themselves less as managers and more as financiers, those holding stock came to see themselves less as owners and more as investors, even speculators. Most stocks in the United States were owned by institutional investors, and most shares changed hands at least once a year. By 2008, U.S. stocks turned over four times a year.[70] The financial elite derived a host of new products, and the market came to depend more and more on derivative markets. The upside of betting on the markets became huge; the richest people in town were not the celebrity CEOs but the celebrity managers of hedge funds and private equity funds.[71] They made money because they maximized their incomes by way of leverage. But the risk—we now know in hindsight—was largely externalized to and borne by the economy as a whole, especially those who owned the underlying physical assets on which the financial elite was betting, derivatively.[72] Corporate executives were driven by this new market frenzy to care more and more about the short term.[73]

Another impact is almost so obvious that it tempts overstatement: the traditional dedication of the professional managerial class to a company's employees and communities decayed. Real wages stagnated or fell; job security eroded. Unions lost power; union membership in the United States fell to a historical nadir.[74] As companies became more international and finance became more global, workers' wages stagnated. Workers in Birmingham and Boston and Brisbane were competing with those in Bangalore and Beijing. As capital chased the highest returns, nations found it more difficult to maintain national regulatory boundaries.

This period of roughly thirty years—from the 1980s through the first decade of the 2000s—saw the ascendance of "contractarianism," a term that is simply a shorthand for the concurrence of three phenomena. First, in executive suites and board rooms: a fixation on share price. Second, in politics: a push for deregulation (sometimes called self-regulation), especially of financial markets.[75] Third, in corporate law and legal theory: a dependence on the notion of contract, rather than fiduciary duty, as the conceptual centerpiece.[76] These three phenomena together made it almost impossible to expect corporations to see themselves or to be seen as citizens. They had a very limited role, and being a citizen had absolutely nothing to do with it.

This contractarian model championed in the United States never gained complete hegemony throughout the world. Japan and much of Europe, for example, still believed in a broader conception of corporate duty.[77] Even the United Kingdom, usually the closest to the United States in its conception of corporate governance, recognized a more robust understanding of the social contract between corporations and the public in its Companies Act of 2006.[78] Among legal scholars, there were naysayers and Don Quixotes pointing out the structural flaws and the economic costs of the contractarian model and shareholder primacy while articulating some alternatives.[79] But for a generation, the mainstream view of corporations was that they existed to advance the interests of shareholders, and management would be handsomely compensated to make that a reality. *Dodge v. Ford* was not a legal commandment, but most executives and managers acted as if it were.

On the public side, the Supreme Court began rethinking the New Deal permissiveness toward economic regulation. Reagan promoted William Rehnquist from associate to Chief Justice, filling his associate chair with Antonin Scalia. Reagan also appointed Sandra Day O'Connor and Anthony Kennedy to the Court, and Reagan's successor, George H. W. Bush, appointed David H. Souter and Clarence Thomas. Each of these jurists replaced justices more liberal than they. By the mid-1990s, seven of the nine sitting justices had been appointed by Republican presidents.

The Rehnquist Court moved to reinvigorate limits on the power of Congress. For the first time since 1937, the Court struck down congressional acts on the grounds that they encroached on state power[80] or went beyond Congress's authority to regulate commerce.[81] In the lower courts, there was a reawakening of interest in using the "non-delegation doctrine" to strike down regulatory actions.[82] That doctrine had not been used by courts since 1936, but it provided a basis for courts to question the congressional delegation of regulatory authority to government agencies. These reassertions of constitutional limits on regulation caused many scholars to believe that we were on the verge of a new *Lochner* era, when government regulation of business would be subject to exacting judicial scrutiny.

In the end, these efforts mostly fizzled. The Rehnquist Court did create new limits to commerce clause power, but the limits were of only two stripes. The Court ruled Congress could not use commerce clause authority to regulate non-commercial activities or require individuals to enter the stream of commerce.[83] But neither of these limits was particularly pertinent to business. As for the non-delegation doctrine, when a case raising the issue made it to the Supreme Court, the justices balked. They decided unanimously that the non-delegation doctrine had been rightly laid to rest decades before.[84]

The efforts to limit the regulation of business shifted course to another area of constitutional law: the First Amendment.

One might not expect the First Amendment's guarantee of free speech to be a fertile ground for the anti-regulation efforts of American business.[85] The right of free speech has iconic beneficiaries— the political dissident giving out handbills, the religious minority refusing to say the Pledge of Allegiance, the civil rights leader marching in protest—that have little connection with corporations and their interests. Like the due process and equal protection clauses of the Fourteenth Amendment, the First Amendment has an anti-majoritarian attitude. It protects the speaker with unpopular views from being punished by the majority. But over the last couple of decades, American business has been brilliant in raising and winning First Amendment challenges to a range of regulations. This shift has come about because the Court increasingly thinks of the free speech right as ensuring a "marketplace of ideas." This free-market theory of free speech, like a free-market theory of economics, is all too often simplistically libertarian. The assumption is that truth will win in the marketplace of ideas by operation of the market itself, similar to how libertarian economic theory suggests that efficient outcomes will result from the unfettered operation of the economic market itself.

In the economic market, we have some understanding of how markets work—people pay more for things they prefer and less for things they don't. If you build a better mousetrap, the world will beat a path to your door. We have long recognized, however, that even "free" markets need regulation and fail without them. We punish fraud, restrict monopoly, ban market manipulation, and allow customers to sue the makers of products that harm them.

In the "free" marketplace of ideas, however, we have no pricing mechanism on which we can rely to identify ideas that are more or less preferred, nor do we enjoy regulatory protections against market defects such as fraud, monopoly, distortion, or latent harms. The end result is that a free speech doctrine based on a simplistic marketplace metaphor will be highly suspicious of any restriction on speech, in whatever context.

Corporations have been extraordinarily successful in using this libertarian free speech guarantee to protect themselves from regulation. Nike claimed the First Amendment protected it from fraud suits when it allegedly lied to consumers about whether its products were manufactured in sweatshops.[86] Pharmaceutical companies used the First Amendment to strike down a state law banning them from data-mining the personal health information of potential customers.[87] Cigarette companies used the First Amendment successfully to challenge proposed graphic warning labels on their packaging.[88] Companies make free speech arguments to challenge anti-discrimination laws, rules requiring the disclosure of sales of "conflict minerals," and even the reporting requirements of securities law.[89] And in *Citizens United*, the Court struck down restrictions on corporate political expenditures as contrary to free speech guarantees. According to Harvard professor John Coates, "Nearly half of First Amendment challenges now benefit business corporations and trade groups, rather than other kinds of organizations or individuals, and the trend-line is up."[90]

It is not unfair to say that the early years of the twenty-first century experienced a legal Gilded Age reminiscent of a century before. In corporate law, we saw a fixation on shareholder value and a dependence on the market to protect (or not) other stakeholders. On the constitutional side, we saw a dependence on a simplistic free-market understanding of the First Amendment to protect corporations from regulation. A new *Lochner* era was here.[91]

V. Three Shocks, and a Pushback

The pendulums on the private side and the public side historically swing together. Corporations are not allowed to care about the "damned public" as a matter of corporate law and are protected from public-regarding regulation as a matter of public law. Or corporations are allowed to act as good citizens toward their stakeholders as a matter of corporate law and practice and are subject to broad public-regarding regulation as a matter of public law. Such swings are hardly surprising since law is situated in a political, economic, and social context that defines the contours of debate and possibility.

Toward the end of the first decade of the twenty-first century, one could see signs that the corporate law pendulum was swinging back toward the more robust view of the citizenship obligations of corporations. The shareholder primacy framework of corporate law suffered three serious shocks in the United States—one economic, one environmental, and one legal.

The economic shock was the global financial crisis of 2008, which pulled back the curtain to reveal the Great Oz of the rational market to be a fraud, along with its subsidiary dependence on the rational actor model.[92] Even former chairman of the U.S. Federal Reserve Alan Greenspan, long a stalwart of the rationality school, was forced to admit that he had "found a flaw" in his theory of the free market driving the economy insulated from regulatory oversight.[93] As there are few atheists in foxholes, there are few libertarians in a market crash.

The second shock was the explosion and massive oil spill at the Deepwater Horizon oil drilling platform in the Gulf of Mexico in 2010. Occurring on the heels of the economic meltdown, the environmental catastrophe reminded Americans of the dangers inherent in trusting large corporations to regulate themselves. It was the perfect example of what can happen when corporations are driven by a short-term drive to make money while regulators are somnolent. The technology to make money will always outpace the technology to manage the risk and contain the damage.

The third shock was the decision in *Citizens United*. Federal and state laws limiting the political spending of corporations—laws that had been on the books in some instances for a century—were struck down.[94] The nation saw a massive inflow of money into the 2010 midterm elections and again in the presidential cycle of 2012, mostly by way of "Super PACs" organized for the purpose of collecting and spending the money of very rich individuals and unions. Independent expenditures exploded by a factor of ten, from less than $100 million prior to the ruling to more than $1 billion in 2012.[95] The climb continued in the 2016 cycle, with total independent expenditures approaching $1.5 billion.[96] Relatively little of this money originated from corporate treasuries, but corporations were blamed. Occurring hand in hand with the global financial crisis and the Deepwater Horizon spill, *Citizens United* impressed on the U.S. public that corporations were dangerous not only on the financial and environmental fronts, but on the political front as well.

These shocks seemed to push the pendulum back toward a more public-regarding conception of corporations and corporate law and governance. At the very least, a skepticism of the then conventional wisdom about the private and narrow nature of the corporation seemed to grow and take hold. An article in the *Harvard Business Review* proclaimed, "There's a growing body of evidence . . . that the companies that are most successful at maximizing shareholder value over time are those that aim toward goals other than maximizing shareholder value. Employees and customers often know more about and have more of a long-term commitment to a company than shareholders do."[97] An opinion piece in the *Financial Times* argued that "Companies need a bigger and better purpose than simply maximising shareholder value."[98] A *Forbes* article called shareholder primacy "the dumbest idea in the world."[99] A popular non-business essayist in the *New York Times* wrote that "it feels as if we are at the dawn of a new movement—one aimed at overturning the hegemony of shareholder value."[100] Another wrote in the *Washington Post* that the shareholder value "ideology" is "pernicious" and a "corrupting, self-interested dogma peddled by finance professors and money managers."[101] An essay appearing in a progressive policy journal calling for changes in corporate governance to require management to owe fiduciary duties to employees as well as shareholders was covered sympathetically by the *Washington Post*.[102] A group of international scholars issued a statement objecting to the traditional notion that shareholders own the corporation and that corporations have a duty to maximize return to shareholders.[103] These rumblings were sufficient to prod one prominent commentator to ask whether corporate governance was "on the brink of a revolution."[104]

VI. The Irony

The interplay between these two trends—a questioning of the nature and role of corporations in both the private and public spheres—may turn out to be the defining characteristic of our current historical moment. There is more openness to rethinking the roles corporations play in our markets, society, and politics than we have seen since the New Deal era. It is yet unclear, however, whether this questioning will result in any fundamental changes in corporate law and doctrine, constitutional law, or social and political theory.

One might imagine the rhetoric of *Citizens United* helping the arguments in favor of cabining corporate power. In the Court's reasoning, corporations act as "associations of citizens" that have rights of free speech.[105] It assumed that corporations both could and should be active in the public space.

It is a small step to then say, as some have, that if corporations are to be active in the public space, it is appropriate to ask them to act more like real citizens, with obligations that cannot be encapsulated in financial statements.[106] This is simply a remaking of the Berle and Means argument from eighty years ago. In this view, the best way to achieve that would be to broaden fiduciary duties and adjust the structure of company governance to include the views of more stakeholders. Rather than managerial centrism or shareholder supremacy, the two leading schools of thought within corporate governance, we could institute a system of real, enforceable fiduciary duties that extend beyond shareholders to the broader set of citizens that make up corporations in the real world.[107]

For a generation, members of the progressive corporate law movement have been advocating for a greater corporate participation in the public space. *Citizens United* could have been the genesis of a moment when the American left rallied around a call for corporations to be made more democratic and more pluralistically managed. The members of this movement might have used the broad, national skepticism of corporate power to call on corporations to act like what the Supreme Court assumed they were: associations of citizens. This moment might yet occur, though it faces a surprising and ironic obstacle. The biggest impediment to using *Citizens United* to change corporate governance for the better is the progressive left.

The prominent progressive critique of *Citizens United* has been to describe the Court's decision as bestowing personhood on corporations and describing corporate personhood as a great evil. Critics rail against corporate constitutional rights and want to end such rights by way of constitutional amendment. The irony is created when these critics argue against *Citizens United* by characterizing corporations as having a narrow social role and being obligated to shareholders to stay out of politics. A narrow role for corporations was conventionally the ideologically conservative view, embodied in the Milton Friedman statement that the social obligation of business was to make "as much money as possible."[108] After *Citizens United*, its ideologically progressive opponents began to push a similarly narrow view of business as a way to explain why corporations should be exiled from the public square. In order to fight corporate personhood, they bolstered shareholder primacy.

Take, for instance, Justice John Paul Stevens's dissent in *Citizens*

United itself. There is much to applaud in his opinion. He correctly pointed out the unnecessary breadth of the majority's ruling and rightly critiqued the opinion as activist in expanding the case beyond its original nature as an as-applied rather than a facial challenge to the law. He persuasively challenged the majority's insistence on sweeping large for-profit corporations into a case about nonprofit advocacy groups and accurately described the compelling justifications for limiting campaign expenditures in a democracy. But Stevens also, perhaps unwittingly, utilized and reinforced shareholder supremacy in his dissent. He considered shareholders as owners, as "those who pay for an electioneering communication," who "invested in the business corporation for purely economic reasons."[109] Corporate speech should be limited in order to protect shareholders' investments, Stevens argued. Corporate political speech did not merit protection because

> the structure of a business corporation . . . draws a line between the corporation's economic interests and the political preferences of the individuals associated with the corporation; the corporation must engage the electoral process with the aim to enhance the profitability of the company, no matter how persuasive the arguments for a broader . . . set of priorities.[110]

Even more revealing, Stevens cited as support for his dissent a set of corporate governance principles adopted by the prestigious American Law Institute almost twenty years before. Those principles were the product of compromise, both asking corporations to look after shareholder interests and allowing them to act with an eye toward "ethical" and "humanitarian" purposes. But Stevens quoted only the language embodying shareholder primacy: "A corporation . . . should have as its objective the conduct of business activities with a view to enhancing corporate profit and shareholder gain."[111]

Justice Stevens, at this point in his tenure, was the most liberal justice on the Court.[112] But in these passages, he described the role of corporations in a way that would fit comfortably within the "contractarian," law-and-economics, politically conservative view of corporate governance against which progressive corporate law scholars had been fighting for a generation.

Ever since the ruling, opponents of corporate personhood have followed Stevens into the shareholder rights trap. Common Cause—one of the nation's most reputable good government organizations—now has a "featured campaign" for "strengthening shareholder rights."[113] The Brennan Center for Justice—named after one of the liberal lions in the history of the Court—is supporting a "shareholder protection act" and calls shareholders "the actual owners" of corporations.[114] Professor (now Congressman) Jamie Raskin of American University, one of the brightest and most energetic voices of the progressive left in the United States, says that corporations should not be spending in elections because, "after all, it's [shareholders'] money."[115] This is all shareholder primacy language brought to bear in fighting *Citizens United*.

The irony runs the other way as well. In the *Hobby Lobby* case,[116] the Court granted corporations the statutory right under the Religious Freedom Restoration Act to avoid regulations on religious grounds.[117] One of the Court's leading conservatives, Justice Samuel Alito, wrote the opinion. He recognized that corporations need not maximize the bottom line:

> While it is certainly true that a central objective of for-profit corporations is to make money, modern corporate law does not require for-profit corporations to pursue profit at the expense of everything else, and many do not do so. For-profit corporations, with ownership approval, support a wide variety of charitable causes, and it is not at all uncommon for such corporations to further humanitarian and other altruistic objectives.

   . . . If for-profit corporations may pursue such worthy objectives, there is no apparent reason why they may not further religious objectives as well.[118]

Alito bolstered his point by noting that "over half of the States, for instance, now recognize the "benefit corporation," a dual-purpose entity that seeks to achieve both a benefit for the public and a profit for its owners.[119] Benefit corporations have been the darlings of many corporate law progressives;[120] *Hobby Lobby* marshaled their existence as an argument in favor of using corporate religious conscience to avoid regulation.

In these cases, corporations assert the ideologically conservative argument that they should be free from government regulation by using arguments often made by progressive stakeholder theorists. A lower court judge considering a companion case to *Hobby Lobby* voted to allow corporations to use religious reasons to avoid providing their employees health coverage required by law. His reasoning made the irony clear: "It is commonplace for corporations to have mission statements and credos that go beyond profit maximization. When people speak of 'good corporate citizens' they are typically referring to community support and involvement, among other things."[121]

The world is flipped. Progressives are championing shareholder rights. Conservatives are planting their ideological flag on the summit of corporate citizenship. To figure out how to get out of this mess, we should return to first principles and work up.

THREE

Should Corporations Have Rights?

No one believes that companies are actually people. Even when Mitt Romney famously said that "corporations are people, my friend," he did not mean that corporations themselves were living, breathing flesh.[1] Nor did he mean that corporations should receive all the rights and carry all the responsibilities of natural persons. Romney certainly did not believe, for example, that a corporation should serve on a jury or count as a passenger for purposes of traveling in an HOV lane.[2]

Instead, Romney was making the mundane point that corporations are inherently connected with humans—as managers, employees, investors, customers, and the like. But that is not what made Romney's statement so controversial. Romney got into hot water because his statement was seen as endorsing the *Citizens United* ruling that corporations could claim free speech rights. And people took him to be endorsing a view that corporations should be able to claim constitutional rights more broadly, either in their own right or on behalf of the people connected with them. This assertion of "corporate personhood" is problematic for the obvious reason that corporations are artificial entities, created by states. It seems strange to give such entities constitutional rights meant to protect people. But how strange is it?

The Court's decision in *Citizens United* was undertheorized, in the sense that it did not explain when corporations should be able to claim rights and when they should not. The Court did not say in the ruling that corporations were "persons" under the Constitution. Instead, the group bringing the case, and indeed all corporations, were "associations of citizens."[3] The next step was simple. The Court merely said the rights of the corporate entity deserved recognition to protect the citizens connected with the corporation and those interested in hearing what the corporation wanted to say.[4] The Court was making an instrumental claim—namely, that we protect corporations in order to protect persons.

This is not a strange argument at all. It is a straightforward argument used in scores of constitutional cases. Sometimes the Constitution protects groups—whether Planned Parenthood or the National Rifle Association—in order to protect the people in the group.

Corporations are not typical associations, however. The connection between corporate benefits and the well-being of the people connected with them can be tenuous and intermittent. But it can also be real and consistent. Sometimes it makes sense to protect corporations' constitutional rights; sometimes it does not. The *Citizens United* opinion by Justice Anthony Kennedy does not reveal deep thought about the difficult question of when corporations should have rights. But that is not surprising. The question of corporate constitutional rights has bedeviled judges and scholars for nearly two hundred years.

In figuring out when corporations should have rights, we have not advanced much beyond Chief Justice Marshall's statement in

Dartmouth College: "Being the mere creature of law, [a corporation] possesses only those properties which the charter of its creation confers upon it either expressly or as incidental to its very existence."[5] Corporations do not have all rights; nor do they have none. They have those explicitly granted to them and those "incidental" to their "existence."

What rights are incidental to the existence of corporations? This inquiry must necessarily begin with a discussion of what corporations are for and what purposes they serve. We don't need to agree on an understanding of how a corporation should be managed or answer the question, salient in corporate law, of to whom managers owe their fiduciary duties. We don't have to decide, for example, whether corporations are to be governed under the conventional U.S. view that shareholder value is the ultimate goal or under the conventional European view that corporations have obligations to a broader set of stakeholders. But to analyze the constitutional questions, the theory we need is one that places the corporation into its institutional role in society and the economy. Why do we have corporations? Why do we incentivize their creation and development? What do corporations add that we do not obtain from our other central institutions: families, churches, associations, universities, governments?

The answer is clear. Corporations are created to be the economic engine of society with the task, individually and collectively, of building wealth over time by selling goods and services for a profit. To do this, they collect a range of inputs from various sources—employee efforts and expertise, financial investment, management guidance and decision making—and put them together to produce something more valuable than the sum of the inputs.

This description is necessarily vague. But it describes the core function of corporations (indeed, of business in general). It distinguishes corporations from other core institutions. A family, university, or government need not produce economic gain for society to be successful. A corporation is a failure if it does not. Societal economic gain may be an ancillary benefit of some family activities, governmental actions, or university projects. But that is not the core purpose of those institutions. By the same token, some corporate activities may engender education, protect familial bonds, or even serve to praise a god or two, but these are not the core functions of a corporation.

Deep disagreement remains about the organization of internal corporate governance and whether shareholder primacy is the lodestar for managerial decisions. But broad consensus exists for the notion that is crucial here: for-profit corporations are economic entities, created for the purpose of benefiting society by creating wealth through the production of goods and services.

This description of the corporation's core function helps orient the discussion of corporate constitutional rights. A first cut on the constitutional analysis should begin with the presumption that corporations should receive the rights necessarily incidental to serving that economic purpose and should not receive those that are not germane to that purpose. This presumption will need more nuance in certain circumstances and might be set aside in some contexts to further other constitutional values. But that is the starting place for analysis.

I. Constitutional Rights for Things?

Much of the energy behind the "corporations are not people" effort springs from the notion that rights are for people, not corporations. Indeed, the "People's Rights Amendment," introduced in Congress to overturn *Citizens United*, would turn this notion into constitutional text. The text of the proposed amendment states that "we the people . . . intend the rights protected by this Constitution to be the rights of natural persons." And "people, person, or persons as used in this Constitution does not include corporations."[6]

At the level of first principle, no one doubts that human beings are, and should be, the ultimate beneficiaries of constitutional limits on government actions. If a limit on government has no benefit for natural persons, then one should be skeptical of a claim that the government has overstepped its bounds. For example, it is not persuasive to suggest that the free exercise clause, which warns that Congress "shall make no law . . . prohibiting the free exercise [of religion]," should be interpreted so as to serve God. Similarly, it would not be persuasive to argue that the takings clause should be interpreted in a way to protect the environment divorced from any benefit that protection would provide for natural humans, present or future (though it is difficult to imagine what environmental deregulation would not eventually have an impact on humans. Pollution on Mars, perhaps?) The ultimate beneficiaries of any constitutional limit on governmental prerogative must be human beings.

But that does *not* mean that only human beings can be constitutional claimants. Often, it makes sense to allow groups, associations, or institutions to assert constitutional rights. A church can bring a free-exercise claim if a state aims a statute to limit its rites of worship.[7] To say so is not to say the church itself has a soul. A group of law schools can claim they have a free speech right to exclude military recruiters from their campuses.[8] To say so is not to claim the group has a physical mouth. As Chief Justice Marshall wrote two centuries ago, a university can assert a constitutional defense to an effort by a state to transform it from a private college into a public one.[9] To protect its contractual rights is not to say the university has a brain necessary to form contractual intent. To say all of these things—that churches, law schools, or universities can claim constitutional protections—is not to say these entities are natural persons. It is to say, instead, they have constitutional "personhood" in order to protect natural persons.

The legitimacy of group-based claims springs from several sources.[10] The group could be bringing a claim on behalf of its members if the group is a conduit for, or a holder of, the claims of the human beings in the group. A church is an example, as are the Boy Scouts.[11] If a government restriction burdens the rights of the individual members in their association as a group, the best way to vindicate those rights is often by recognizing the group as the constitutional claimant.

Another source of legitimacy for a collective claimant is the notion that some rights themselves are collective in nature. The right of association, long seen as a component of the rights to free speech and free assembly, is an example. Humans gain meaning in and through their identification with groups, whether it be their bowling club, the Audubon Society, or the Republican Party. The groups can assert rights in their own name to protect not only the rights of individual members to join, but also to voice the rights of the humans joined collectively.

There is another kind of institutional constitutional claim—one that is based on the rights of the group itself. The *New York Times*, for example, does not have members in the way the Boy Scouts do. Yale University does not have members in the way the Audubon Society does. Planned Parenthood does not have members in the way the local Baptist church does. (Planned Parenthood has contributors, but they do not go to meetings or gain privileged access to Planned Parenthood facilities.) Yet each of these organizations may have legitimate claims against the government despite not being membership organizations. Their claims will be on their own behalf and not as stand-ins for human claimants, even if the ultimate beneficiaries will be natural persons who read, study, teach, or seek medical care.

When the *New York Times* and the *Washington Post* won the right to publish the Pentagon Papers in 1971, no one suggested that they, as corporations, did not have standing to bring a constitutional claim. Their victory did not mean that the Court thought of the *Times* and the *Post* as human persons. Nor was their claim based on an assertion that they were claiming rights on behalf of members; neither paper had any. Nor were the papers suing to protect the rights of their shareholders. The newspapers sued to protect *themselves* against government censorship. The ultimate beneficiaries were readers—and indeed all citizens—but they were not required to be parties to the suit.

In 1992, Planned Parenthood—organized not as a membership organization but as a corporation—won a hard-fought battle to have the Supreme Court reaffirm *Roe v. Wade.* More recently, health clinics organized as corporations are challenging increasingly stringent and arbitrary restrictions on their ability to provide abortions.[12] No one suggested in 1992 that Planned Parenthood had no standing to object to limits on its ability to provide abortions, and no one objects now that the incorporated health clinics are somehow barred by their corporate status from bringing their contests. These entities bring suit in their own names in order to defend their ability to provide certain kinds of medical care to women. These women were not and are not required to be part of these suits, even though they are the ultimate beneficiaries. The regulations at issue in 1992 and those at issue now restrict the activities of clinics themselves; to allow the organizations themselves to bring the claim makes sense.

This discussion prompts a clarification about what it means to have a constitutional right. A right is simply a way to describe a limitation on government behavior. The Bill of Rights was adopted after the main body of the Constitution because of a fear that without an articulation of rights the government would become too powerful. A list of rights was important as a constitutional limit on the illegitimate assertion of government power.[13]

To assert that groups and institutions are able to claim constitutional rights is another way of saying that the government should be stopped from asserting illegitimate power against them. Saying rights are for natural persons only is an enormous grant of space for government to exert power of constraint or punishment against groups or institutions. Imagine what the world would look like if such were the rule. Individual human reporters might be able to publish the Pentagon Papers but not through any institutional conduit, whether the *New York Times, Washington Post,* CNN, *Fox News,* or a blog on the Internet. Individual women would have an abstract right to an abortion but would not be able to gain access to one at any institutional provider—whether Planned Parenthood, a hospital, or a health clinic. Individuals could assert a right to worship the god of their choice, but their parish or synagogue or mosque could be seized, sold, or taxed out of existence. The opposite of a constitutional right is a government power. If corporations have no rights, then governmental power in connection with corporations is at its maximum. That power can be abused, and corporate personhood is a necessary bulwark.

The rhetoric around the assertion that "corporations are not people" is thus both obvious and obviously wrong. At the level of the obvious, corporations are not human, gravity pulls you down and not up, and cigarettes are not great for your lung capacity. But the claim that the rights intended to be protected by the Constitution are the rights of "natural people" alone is obviously wrong. It makes sense—at least sometimes—for corporations to claim constitutional rights.

The best argument one could make in favor of restricting corporate rights is a textual one. The protections of both the Fifth and Fourteenth Amendments explicitly flow to "persons." The Fifth

Amendment says "nor shall any *person* . . . be deprived of life, liberty, or property, without due process of law." The Fourteenth Amendment says "nor shall any State deprive any *person* of life, liberty, or property, without due process of law, nor deny to any *person* . . . the equal protection of the laws." The Second Amendment's right to bear arms is described as a "right of the *people*." Fourth Amendment rights to be free of unreasonable searches are premised on "the right of the *people* to be secure in their persons, houses, papers, and effects."

Not all constitutional provisions are so limited. The First Amendment, for example, says that "Congress shall make no law . . . abridging the freedom of speech" without limitation of such right to persons. The takings clause is textually agnostic about who might claim its protections: "Nor shall private property be taken for public use, without just compensation." The Sixth Amendment's protections in criminal cases reference the rights of "the accused," without limiting it to persons. The Seventh Amendment's guarantee of a jury trial is stated in a passive voice without a limit on who—or what—can claim it: "The right of trial shall be preserved." Nor is the Eighth Amendment's ban on cruel and unusual punishments, "excessive bail," and "excessive fines" limited to persons or people.

A strict textualist might say that the inclusion of the words "person" or "people" in articulating some of the most important rights must have been intentional. One could also say that the First Amendment's omission of a "person" limitation is no longer crucial since the protections of the First Amendment are applied to the states by way of the Fourteenth Amendment's protection of "liberty," which is indeed limited to "persons." The argument against corporate rights is, perhaps ironically, based on the interpretive methodology of strict textualism, which is typically associated with a conservative judicial philosophy. The progressives pushing the anti-corporate personhood movement must necessarily adopt the interpretive methodology of conservative jurists such as the late Justice Antonin Scalia and his jurisprudential acolyte and successor, Justice Neil Gorsuch.

But let us set aside the irony and ask: Does the language of constitutional provisions stating that rights flow to "persons"—where such limitations exist—mean that corporations should be barred from claiming those rights? The answer can only be no. There are several reasons why.

If corporations are not protected, then neither are associations, groups, churches, universities, hospitals, unions, advocacy groups, or charitable organizations. None of these entities is a natural person and would not thus be covered by a literal reading of the text. All of these groups would be subject to government overreach, unreasonable searches, arbitrary violations of basic due process, and unlimited censorship. They would all be at the mercy of mean-spirited bureaucrats and judges. The capacity of these groups to defend themselves from government action would depend completely on the good will of government actors. Such a legal framework would be bizarre, even Kafkaesque. Indeed no one on the Court, even the strictest of textualists, now or ever, has advocated for such a proposition.

The kind of strict textualism necessary to reach such a bizarre result is not required by constitutional law. In fact it is inconsistent with it. Chief Justice Marshall reminded us that our Constitution should not be read like a contract or statute: "We must never forget that it is a *Constitution* we are expounding."[14] Constitutions are meant to survive over time, and thus their language must allow for elasticity and evolution.

One simple example is the question of the constitutionality of the air force. The Constitution gives Congress the ability "to raise and support armies" and "to provide and maintain a Navy." Does the absence of explicit authority for creating an air force mean that the U.S. Air Force is unconstitutional? Of course not. Airplanes did not exist at the time the Constitution was drafted and ratified. The framers authorized Congress to create a military force to the full extent of what was possible at the time. One can either say that Congress's authority should be interpreted in light of the principle that the grant of power should be interpreted as broadly today as it was then, or one can say that "armies" and "navy" should be interpreted to include implicitly an air force. Either method leaves the explicit text behind but is more loyal to the document (and the framers) than a strict interpretation would be.

The same is true with the use of the word "person." Corporations hardly existed at the time of the drafting of the Fifth Amendment and were still scarce by current standards at the time of the Fourteenth. There is no indication at all that the use of the word, where it exists, was meant to limit the kinds of claimants who can sue to validate the right in question. What really matters in the articulation of these rights is the constraint on government power, not the identity of the rights holder. An interpretation of the provisions to exclude non-mortals is actually *disloyal* to the Constitution's purpose of limiting government power and authority. To be loyal, one must say that the provisions should be interpreted in light of their purpose. And that means that corporations are "persons" and "people" at least some of the time.[15]

That is not to say that corporations should get all rights included in the text. It simply means that we cannot figure out which ones they should be able to claim by looking at the text.

All in all, the argument that corporations have no constitutional rights is simply unsustainable. The difficult questions are which rights should they be able to claim, which they should not, and when. Let us begin answering those questions by looking at some easy cases.

II. The Easy Cases: Takings, Due Process, Power

Corporations are collective economic enterprises with the institutional role of creating wealth for society, broadly defined. A corporation that does not make money is a failure for its employees, investors, and society in general. A corporation that makes money for its employees and investors by externalizing costs onto society (by polluting the environment or selling dangerous or defective products, for example) may not be a failure for its internal stakeholders but is nevertheless a failure from society's perspective.

Let us test the following notion: corporations should be able to claim constitutional protections consistent with their institutional role. How would that notion play out in practice?

The easiest cases under this rule would be those springing from the Constitution's protections of economic rights. The takings clause of the Fifth Amendment, for example, says that "private property [should not] be taken for public use, without just compensation." That this provision restricts the government from taking the property of a for-profit corporation should be obvious. Similarly obvious is that these protections need not be derived from a view that shareholders are the owners of corporations. Agreement on a theory of corporate ownership is not required to protect corporations from unconstitutional takings. In fact, institutions without owners can bring these claims as well. A takings claim can be brought by a university, which does not have shareholders, or a church, whose members have no property interest in the church. The constitutional right is a limit on government encroachment into private property, regardless of the property holder's personhood or lack thereof.

The protection against uncompensated takings is especially important for corporations because of their economic purpose. No persons or entities contributing to the collective enterprise would do so if their contributions could be expropriated by the government. Or more precisely, if the government could take corporate property at whim, every investor would demand more in exchange for a contribution, undercutting the economic viability of the collective enterprise.

This is not to say that it is impossible to run a country without a takings clause or that the right to be free of uncompensated takings is some kind of natural right. But in a constitutional regime that protects natural persons from uncompensated takings, there is no reason to refuse those protections to groups, institutions, and corporations.[16]

The very same argument can be made for the Constitution's protections of procedural due process. The Fifth Amendment announces that the federal government shall not deprive "life, liberty, or property, without due process of law." The Fourteenth Amendment extends this restriction to states. The due process clause is perhaps the most important protection against government tyranny. (Note that here we are discussing *procedural* due process.) Arbitrary or mean-spirited government actions are corrosive to the legitimacy of government and oppressive to citizens. As Justice Felix Frankfurter once wrote, "The history of liberty has largely been the history of observance of procedural safeguards."[17] Justice William O. Douglas went further, saying, "Procedure . . . spells much of the difference between rule by law and rule by whim or caprice."[18]

Nothing makes one feel more powerless than to be the object of a capricious governmental act, whether it be a criminal charge, a loss of a license, or even a parking fine. Without protection against procedural irregularities, every interaction with government could be an opportunity for oppression, unfairness, and arbitrariness. In such a world, the governed resent and ultimately resist the government. With procedural protections, even those who lose their disputes nonetheless tend to accept the legitimacy of the outcome.[19]

Without such protections, losers in disputes will refuse to accept their losses, and government will find it increasingly difficult to enforce its decrees.

Is there any reason to restrict this ban on government arbitrariness to human beneficiaries? Without such protection, the government could bring civil or criminal actions against unions, churches, or associations without satisfying procedural obligations. The space for government arbitrariness would expand, and no one could do anything about it.

These due process protections are particularly important for profit-making corporations. Like protection against uncompensated takings, due process protections are essential to encourage corporate stakeholders to make or continue their various investments. If the government can act arbitrarily toward a corporation, the corporation's ability to succeed in satisfying its institutional purpose will be in jeopardy. Worse, government officials could act unfairly or hostilely toward specific businesses and do so with impunity, hurting some and boosting others. Such inequality would be corrosive not only to the marketplace, but to democracy as well.[20]

Takings claims and procedural due process claims are easy. Corporations should be able to bring both. Each right is essential for corporations to perform their institutional role of building wealth, and each is an essential check on government power.

Another category of easy cases is not about rights but about authority—for example, whether the president can seize steel mills in a time of war;[21] whether Congress possesses the power to require Americans to purchase health insurance;[22] whether a state can preference in-state companies at the expense of out-of-state companies.[23] These cases ask if specific government actions are beyond the powers authorized in the Constitution. If about the president, they concern the scope of the executive power. If about Congress, they usually concern the contours of the commerce clause. If about the power of states, they often concern the so-called "dormant" commerce clause—the limitation on states' abilities to discriminate against commerce originating in other states. These are important cases, asking the courts to articulate the edges of government power. In a sense, they are about rights, for the analogous reason why cases about rights are necessarily about power. Authority not given to the government means that private action is unconstrained; a right to engage in private action means that government is constrained. Rights and powers are the opposite side of the same coin.

Regardless of how corporations are characterized, there is no question that they should be able to bring these claims. Indeed, some of the leading cases in this area were brought by corporations and other businesses. The foundational case on executive power challenged President Harry Truman's seizure of steel factories in anticipation of a work stoppage during the Korean War. That case was brought by Youngstown Sheet & Tube Co., suing in its own name. The 2012 case challenging the Affordable Care Act (Obamacare) on commerce clause grounds had as its lead plaintiff the National Federation of Independent Business, an association of for-profit companies. Challenges to state laws on dormant commerce clause grounds have been brought by milk producers, railroads, and trucking companies.[24]

A refusal to allow corporations to bring such suits would be bizarre. The suits complain that a government entity is acting beyond its constitutional power and petition courts to intervene. If corporations could not bring these challenges, government could overreach with impunity. Or more precisely, it could overreach vis-à-vis *businesses* with impunity, putting at risk businesses' ability to satisfy their institutional and social obligations.

These are the easy questions—takings, process, power. Our presumptive rule—that corporations should be able to assert constitutional claims that fit with their institutional role of building social wealth—decides these questions well. And notwithstanding the powerful rhetoric of "corporations are not people," few people seriously contest the notion that corporations have the right to be free of uncompensated takings, to receive fair process, and to not be the victims of government misuse of power.

III. More Difficult:
Corporations and Criminal Procedure

A trickier set of questions surrounds the issue of when corporations can assert rights meant to constrain law enforcement officials. Do corporations have a right to be free of unreasonable searches and seizures? Can they claim a right to remain silent when under official questioning?

These are more difficult questions than those covered in the previous section, both because of the nature of the rights and the nature of the corporation. On the one hand, the importance of restraining arbitrary government power is high, whether corporations or humans are the focus of prosecutorial attention. On the other hand, the private interests to be weighed in the balance— privacy and autonomy—appear at first glance to be more important with persons than with corporations. But because businesses do have privacy interests worth protecting, working out the correct balance here will demand some attention.

Let us start with current law. The Fourth Amendment right to be free of unreasonable searches and seizures can be claimed by corporate entities.[25] The Fifth Amendment right of "any person" not to "be compelled in any criminal case to be a witness against himself," however, cannot be asserted by corporations.[26]

Does this taxonomy make sense, given the presumptive rule announced above? That is, do Fourth Amendment rights protect the corporation's ability to achieve its institutional and social role while the right to "plead the Fifth" does not?

74

A complete absence of Fourth Amendment rights would make it quite difficult for corporations to conduct business since they could be subject to warrantless, unreasonable searches at the whim of government officials. Google could be required to submit to a search of its servers; Barnes and Noble could be required to hand over its list of who bought which book. Kentucky officials could demand to search the interior of the vault where the secret, hand-written recipe for KFC's fried chicken is kept hidden. Corporations need privacy to develop products, serve their customers, protect intellectual property, and guard against the misuse of financial data.

At the same time, corporations should not have privacy rights coextensive with natural persons. Corporate interests in privacy, as significant as they are, are unlikely to be as weighty as the legitimate needs of humans to keep away from the prying eyes of government officials. There has been a long-standing respect for the right of human beings to maintain a private sphere, outside the scope of government oversight. This is not a blanket protection against government intervention. If you are making a bomb in your basement or abusing your spouse, you have every reason to fear a knock at your door. But humans want and need a private realm. In contrast, corporations by their very nature are engaged in the marketplace, a very public place. Their institutional purpose is to interact in economic transactions with public effect. Too much privacy would allow corporations to avoid the necessary and legitimate regulation necessary for the market to work. Food inspectors, for example, need access to grocery stores to ensure that the food being sold is safe. Capital market regulators need access to the financial information of businesses to ensure that the securities they sell are not fraudulent. The difference between the public nature of corporations and the private (or less public) nature of humans should make a difference in constitutional analysis.

As a matter of doctrine and Supreme Court precedent, the

Fourth Amendment protects claimants' "reasonable expectation of privacy."[27] The origin of this formulation is the notion that the government should not have to prove probable cause to search something that is not private. It is not a government search to look at something that is public. If you are selling drugs on your front stoop, it is not a search when police officers observe those sales as they drive by in a squad car.

Whether someone has an "expectation" of privacy is variable, however, and can be manipulated by the government itself.[28] If the government were to announce, for example, that everyone using public transportation is subject to search, then no one boarding a bus or subway would expect to be free of such searches. This formulation of the Fourth Amendment right has been criticized as circular. It makes available to the government an argument that people lose their expectation of privacy whenever they engage in behaviors the government has previously announced would subject them to search. This explains a host of things we see in everyday life, such as signs at the entrance to government buildings or at airports announcing that every person crossing the threshold is subject to search or video surveillance. The Court has also allowed government officials to require people to waive their expectation of privacy as a condition of receiving something else. For example, a high school student's participation on a sports team may be conditioned on a drug test, even though the test would otherwise constitute a government search.[29]

Related to the notion of waiver is the principle of consent. If a person agrees to a search, the Court has said that it is, by definition, reasonable. This holds even if the consent is won within a context of power disparity. One case deemed a search to be consensual when an interstate bus passenger agreed to a search even though a refusal would have caused him to be thrown off the bus in the middle of the night.[30]

Assuming an expectation of privacy that is reasonably held, and absent waiver or consent to search, the usual rule is that a government officer must obtain a warrant prior to a search. To highlight the Byzantine nature of Fourth Amendment law, there are exceptions even to this rule. Searches incident to arrest, searches of cars, and "pat down" searches are all examples of searches that can legally occur without a warrant.[31]

Another quirk in Fourth Amendment law bears mention here. So-called "administrative searches" are a category of searches where government officers are excused from a warrant requirement. The paradigm administrative search is a building inspection. Safety code violations are not typically obvious from the outside of a structure, and entrance to the interior of a building should not wait for a catastrophe or depend on the consent of the owner.[32] A strict warrant requirement would frustrate the purpose of the search since warrants depend on a particular suspicion about a specific place. Routine, periodic building inspections must occur without such particularized suspicion in order to be useful.

Administrative searches have for this reason presented a puzzle to the Court since they do not fit easily into the traditional Fourth Amendment analysis. The Court's solution has been twofold.[33] The first has been to identify a handful of "heavily regulated" industries, where the Court has simply assumed consent to search. The pervasiveness of government involvement in the business of gun sales, for example, is taken to mean that gun sellers have implicitly consented to searches as a condition of participating in the business. The second has been to require government inspectors to obtain a warrant for an administrative search but with a lower level of proof needed than for a search warrant in a criminal case. The inspectors only have to show a reasonable basis to gain a warrant for a typical administrative inspection.[34]

We need not venture deeper into the weeds to see the broader point. The Fourth Amendment protection against unreasonable searches does and should apply to corporations as a presumptive matter. As the same time, the doctrine provides a number of ways for courts to be attentive to the different privacy interests of humans and businesses. Private residences receive more deference in Fourth Amendment cases than business locations, mostly because people have a greater expectation of privacy at home than businesses have in their facilities. Administrative searches, mostly applicable to businesses, are subject to Fourth Amendment scrutiny but at a level lower than courts would apply in run-of-the-mill criminal cases. Highly regulated businesses are deemed automatically to have consented to warrantless searches.

Without any Fourth Amendment protections, the danger of government overreach is real. When the amendment was drafted, the framers had fresh in their minds the abuses of the British soldiers enforcing the Stamp Acts in colonial America by searching businesses with little or no cause.[35] If businesses were subject to warrantless, unreasonable searches, they would find it difficult to conduct business. Imagine if, say, a Trump administration official decided to curry favor with the President by ordering searches of companies competing with Trump's various business interests. Those searches would undoubtedly be an abuse of government authority. They would also be a perversion of the free market.

Moreover, the privacy harms caused by such searches would be felt by humans. Consider the case of *City of Los Angeles v. Patel*, in which the Court struck down a Los Angeles city ordinance—quite common in other parts of the country as well—requiring hoteliers to hand over their hotel registry to police on demand.[36] The Court could easily have said that the ordinance itself gave fair warning to hotels that they had no reasonable expectation of privacy. Or the Court could have ruled that hotels are a pervasively regulated industry and thus subject to warrantless searches. The Court instead insisted on the importance of constraining government power. A better analysis would have focused on the reality that the real beneficiaries of the Court's ruling were hotel guests—real humans. But the end result was the same: in order to protect the privacy of the persons staying in the hotel, the Court had to recognize the constitutional personhood of hotels.

The bottom line is that corporations should get some Fourth Amendment protection but not as much as natural persons. This is essentially where the Court is now as a matter of doctrine. The cases might come out incorrectly here or there, but the doctrine is generally fine, and the doctrinal tools the Court has developed —the reasonableness of the privacy expectation, implied consent, waiver, and lower levels of probable cause for administrative searches —allow the Court to calibrate the protections as necessary and appropriate.

The Fifth Amendment right to not be compelled to be a witness against oneself protects a privacy interest quite different from the Fourth Amendment's right to be free of unreasonable searches. The right to "plead the Fifth" springs from the desire to avoid the practice, prevalent at the time the Constitution was drafted, of officials building criminal cases on the basis of coerced confessions. Such coercion makes police investigators lazy, increasing the risk of mistake and error. And the legitimacy of the entire criminal system wanes if neither the process nor the results can be trusted.

At first glance, these rationales would seem to apply as powerfully to corporate defendants as human ones. The legitimacy of criminal prosecutions is crucial regardless of the humanity of the defendant. But on reflection, one can see that the nature of a corporation makes the right less important and more difficult to assert. Human beings stand to lose their physical freedom as a result of a criminal conviction, a punishment impossible to impose on a corporate defendant. The interests of the corporate defendant will therefore weigh less in the constitutional balance than the interests of a human defendant. Moreover, the Fifth Amendment's protections are most closely attached to oral testimony, which humans have the physiological ability to perform but corporations do not. Documents are not generally protected by a Fifth Amendment plea; a human has to produce relevant documents or answer to a subpoena *even if* such demands include incriminatory evidence.[37] But since corporations cannot physically speak, the corporate act analogous to a person's oral testimony would be a documentary or textual production. To allow corporations to "plead the Fifth" to insulate documents would give corporations *more* rights than humans. Given that corporate interests are less than human interests in this area, such an outcome would be nonsensical.

Also, the likelihood of coercion is much greater with natural persons than with institutions. The risk of government actors imposing psychological or physical pressure to induce a confession is profound for human suspects—humans are quite sensitive to situation and interpersonal power dynamics. But corporations are only legal persons; they do not have a psychology that can be influenced and pressured. The need to create prophylactic rules to protect them from government coercion is much lower than for natural persons.

Also, giving corporations the capacity to avoid testimony would undermine the social purpose of corporations. Markets depend on truthful information. The potential for mischief arising from a corporate right to hide illegalities from regulators, investors, customers, and employees is significant.

The need to protect corporations from self-incrimination is lower, and the potential costs of such a right are higher. It thus makes sense that the Supreme Court has refused to extend to corporations the Fifth Amendment right to not incriminate oneself. As the Court ruled over a century ago, "While an individual may lawfully refuse to answer incriminating questions ... it does not follow that a corporation, vested with special privileges and franchises, may refuse to show its hand when charged with an abuse of such privileges."[38]

Corporations may be "people" but not in ways that matter for every right. They should be able to claim the rights essential to keep the government in check or those necessary for companies to fulfill their institutional role of building wealth in the marketplace. They should not be able to claim rights based on human characteristics or rights that, if asserted, would undermine the operation of the marketplace.

Let us now turn to even more difficult cases, starting with cases having to do with equality, religion, and fundamental rights.

FOUR

Corporations and Fundamental Rights, Equality, and Religion

The heart and soul of constitutional law are the questions of fundamental rights, equality, and religion. Herein lie those of abortion; affirmative action; assisted suicide; immigrants' rights; marriage equality; religious freedom; voting; and discrimination on the basis of race, sex, sexual orientation, and sexual identity. Supreme Court eras are defined by these questions. Presidential campaigns revolve around them.

The protection of fundamental rights and the promise of equality spring from the due process clauses of the Fifth and Fourteenth Amendments and the equal protection clause of the Fourteenth. The Fifth promises that "no person shall . . . be deprived of life, liberty, or property, without due process of law." The Fourteenth uses a more active voice: "No state shall . . . deprive any person of life, liberty, or property without due process of law." It continues, saying a state may not "deny to any person within its jurisdiction the equal protection of the laws." Religious freedom finds its textual bases in two clauses of the First Amendment, one protecting free exercise of religion and the other prohibiting government from establishing an official religion. "Congress shall make no law respecting an establishment of religion, or prohibiting the free exercise thereof." These religion clauses are nominally aimed only at Congress but apply to the entirety of the federal government and have been extended to the states by way of the Fourteenth Amendment.

The due process clauses might appear at first glance to be merely about ensuring fair process. But "due process" has long been interpreted to protect certain substantive rights that pertain not to process but to core, fundamental principles thought to be "essential to the orderly pursuit of happiness,"[1] relate to "choices central to personal dignity and autonomy,"[2] or are "implicit in the concept of ordered liberty."[3] The right to raise one's children,[4] the right to marry,[5] the right to engage in intimate relationships,[6] the right to obtain contraceptives or an abortion,[7] the right to make one's own medical decisions[8]—these are all fundamental rights protected by the due process clause. (Though there are two due process clauses, discussions of due process usually talk about the two clauses as one.)

The equal protection clause is a promise that the government will treat its citizens equally. The architects of the Supreme Court building in Washington, D.C., etched the words "Equal Justice Under Law" over its portico. These words do not appear in the Constitution itself, but they encapsulate the promise of equal protection quite well. The government is under an obligation to treat its citizens equally.

In operation, the difficulty is what "equal" means. Government makes distinctions among people all the time—and should. Obese people should not serve in the Navy Seals; elite public schools can legitimately be populated with students who are intellectually gifted; police officers may give citations to drivers who exceed the speed limit. The job of government cannot be done without treating people differently and without some kinds of classifications among citizens.

The doctrine of equal protection, then, has focused on whether the government uses certain classifications that are "suspect." Race, for example, is a suspect class that is almost always illegitimate to use as a basis for government decision making. Sex is a classification that is "quasi-suspect"—meaning that it can be used in rare cases but usually will be illegitimate. The Court has never said so expressly, but its rulings imply that sexual orientation also fits in this intermediate category.[9] But most other classifications are appropriate and can be used to make distinctions among people as long as a rational connection exists between the classification and a legitimate government interest.

The religion clauses help ensure a freedom of conscience. They do so by ensuring that the government does not "establish" a religion and that individuals can "exercise" their religious beliefs or lack thereof. Both clauses have been the sources of scores of Supreme Court cases, but the main contours are straightforward. Government may not "establish" a religion by adding its authority to bolster a particular faith or religion in general. Prayers in public schools are unconstitutional establishments,[10] for example, as is direct government funding of religious schools.[11] The difficult cases arise around the question of how much establishment is too much. Does a school voucher program violate the establishment clause even when some of the money ends up in the coffers of religious schools? The Court has said no.[12] Does a city's decision to display the Ten Commandments in public schools constitute an establishment? The Court has said yes.[13] What about a display in a public square outside a courthouse? The Court has said no.[14]

A government ban on a particular religious observance would not be an "establishment" but a violation of free exercise rights. The Court struck down, for example, a Florida law punishing the use of animals in the religious ceremonies of Santería.[15] The law burdened the exercise of that religion. The most difficult cases pertain to situations in which laws are not aimed at religious exercise but nevertheless have negative effects on it. When a state law punishes the use of a hallucinogenic drug, for example, can such a law be applied to those who use the drug as a part of religious ceremony? The Court has said yes.[16]

Should these rights of substantive due process, equal protection, and religious freedom be available to corporate entities? The question at first seems easy, almost ridiculously so. Corporations do not marry, have sex, raise children, or get pregnant. Substantive due process claims, then, look like they are off the table. Similarly, corporations do not have race, ethnicity, sex, or sexual orientation. So the equal protection clause does not seem to offer any heightened judicial scrutiny to corporations either. Corporations also do not have consciences and do not typically exercise religious beliefs or engage in religious behavior. So constitutional protections for religious freedom would appear to be irrelevant to corporations as well.

But this is not yet a complete analysis. The answer is more complicated and demands a more thorough evaluation. Let us begin with substantive due process and then turn to equal protection and finally to religion.

I. Corporations and Fundamental Rights

More than twenty-five years ago, Planned Parenthood sued to challenge Pennsylvania's strict abortion restrictions. The laws imposed serious obstacles on women who wished to terminate their pregnancies, including a duty to notify their husbands. Most Court observers at the time believed the case would be used as the vehicle to overturn the 1973 case of *Roe v. Wade*, which had announced abortion as a fundamental right protected by the Fourteenth Amendment.[17] In the end, *Planned Parenthood of Southeastern Pa. v. Casey* did not overturn *Roe.* A famous plurality, authored jointly by Justices Sandra Day O'Connor, Anthony Kennedy, and David Souter, re-affirmed abortion as a fundamental right.[18]

Planned Parenthood was and is a corporate entity, albeit a non-profit one. It provides abortion services but—to state the obvious—does not ever need one itself. Planned Parenthood was neverthe-less an appropriate plaintiff in the lawsuit because the government's regulations made it difficult for the organization to provide abor-tions. Without Planned Parenthood's ability to provide them, its patients' rights to obtain abortions were abstract and difficult to fulfill. Protecting the corporation's ability to sue was necessary to vindicate the rights of the human patients harmed by the restric-tions. Whether one sees its ability to sue as arising from "third-party standing" to assert the rights of others or from its *own* right to provide abortions free of the restrictions at issue, the fact remains the corporate entity was properly before the Court to challenge a law on substantive due process grounds.

What this means is that there is nothing in the corporate status of a plaintiff that in itself bars that plaintiff from raising a substantive due process challenge to a government regulation. If protecting a corporate entity is necessary to protect the substantive due process rights of human beings, then the constitutional analysis can simply ignore the corporate status of the plaintiff. This is what the Court did in *Casey.* In the five separate opinions of the various justices in that case, not a single one questioned the ability of Planned Parent-hood to bring the claim. Every opinion simply ignored the fact that a corporate entity was the named plaintiff, and all the opinions—even those in dissent—argued on the merits of the claim as if the named plaintiff were a woman in need of an abortion rather than a corporate entity providing it.

This makes sense. Imagine, for example, a state that barred commercial establishments from providing services to same-sex couples wishing to get married. Those establishments would be able to bring a substantive due process claim to challenge those restrictions, based on the fundamental right to marriage. The fact that the entities themselves could never get married would be immaterial, as would be their status as corporate entities.

Substantive due process claims brought by commercial entities can thus exist. But they will be rare. The fundamental rights recognized in American jurisprudence are quite narrow compared to those of other nations that offer constitutionalized promises of education, health care, and even economic subsistence and water.[19] In the United States, fundamental rights are few, and most have to do with intimate relationships, marriage, child rearing, and medical decisions. What's more, these rights are "negative"—protections against government restriction—rather than "positive"—affirmative claims on government resources.

The nature of the rights at issue means they will not be exercised by corporate claimants very often. Corporations do not get married, raise children, have sex, or need medical care. But in those situations in which government restrictions on corporations restrict the ability of natural persons to marry, raise children, have sex, or secure medical care, corporations can legitimately raise substantive due process claims to challenge those restrictions. And a court's analysis can safely ignore the corporate personality of the plaintiff.[20]

A further illustration can be found in the set of cases from the so-called *Lochner* era of the early twentieth century. The Supreme Court spent a generation protecting businesses from government regulation on the basis of an aggressive, activist reading of substantive due process that equated constitutional liberty with laissez-faire economics. A libertarian notion of the freedom of contract became constitutionally protected. The *Lochner*-era Court threw up obstacles to beneficial government protections for workers and consumers for more than a generation.

The Court was mistaken about the nature of constitutional freedoms and the scope of substantive due process. But in a legal framework that protected economic liberties as substantive due process rights, it made no difference whether the claimant was a person or a corporation. The *Lochner* Court was wrong about a great many things. But it was not wrong about that. Nothing imbedded in substantive due process itself stands in the way of corporations bringing such claims. Whether they can assert rights in a particular case depends on the nature of the claim, not the nature of the claimant.

The discussion is not affected by our earlier presumption that corporations should be able to claim those rights that help them satisfy their institutional role of building wealth. After *Lochner* was repudiated, due process ceased to have anything to do with economics, one way or the other. In fact, economic regulations are now subject to the lowest level of constitutional scrutiny—"rational basis." If there is any rational basis for an economic regulation, substantive due process will not pose a limit on it. Economic "liberty" might be the centerpiece of libertarian thought. But in our constitutional framework it receives only the lowest level of judicial oversight unless it violates other constitutional provisions such as equal protection, the First Amendment, or the commerce clause.

One could still say that corporations have the same ability as natural humans to bring a "rational basis" substantive due process claim challenging an economic regulation. But like mortals, corporations will lose those cases—and should.

II. Corporations and Equality

In the late nineteenth century, California's constitution contained a provision awarding tax benefits to individuals and certain corporations but excluded railroads.[21] The railroads sued, arguing that their exclusion violated the equal protection clause. Lower courts ruled against the railroads, but the railroads took the case to the Supreme Court.

The case, *Santa Clara County v. Southern Pacific Railroad Company*, arose less than twenty years after the adoption of the Fourteenth Amendment. The breadth of the equal protection clause was still up in the air. The Court would not articulate its notion of "suspect classifications" for decades. It was wrestling less with the question of what kinds of classifications affected equality than with the question of who could bring a claim in the first place. The railroad case depended on the question of whether railroads, and corporations in general, had standing to bring an equal protection claim. As we have discussed, the text of the clause uses the term "person": "No state shall . . . deny to any person within its jurisdiction the equal protection of the laws." The argument that corporations are not "persons" is straightforward. Corporations are not people, one might say.

But in *Santa Clara*, the Court believed the opposite view to be sufficiently obvious. When the lawyer for the railroad stood to begin his argument before the Court, Chief Justice Morrison Waite said, "The court does not wish to hear argument on the question whether the provision in the Fourteenth Amendment to the Constitution, which forbids a State to deny to any person within its jurisdiction the equal protection of the laws, applies to these corporations. We are all of the opinion that it does."[22] The Chief Justice's statement was dutifully recorded by the official court reporter, Bancroft Davis, who just happened to be a former president of a railroad company.[23] He later included it in the opinion's unofficial introduction and summary (called the headnote) when the opinion was released. The Court's opinion decided the case on a different ground, based on the reading of the California statute, and did not say anything about equal protection. But the reporter's headnote—

which included the quote of Waite's statement at oral argument—
has since been taken to stand for the notion that corporations are
"persons" for purposes of the equal protection clause. In the rogues'
gallery of opinions most despised by the "corporations are not people" crowd, *Santa Clara* ranks as high (or low) as *Citizens United.*

In figuring out whether *Santa Clara* was wrong, one should first
remember that modern equal protection law focuses on "suspect"
classifications such as race or sex. Distinctions in the law arising
from some other criteria—size, age, height, or whether a corporation is a railroad or not—would receive only rational basis review.
That means that after the downfall of *Lochner* and its libertarian
assumptions, economic regulations are upheld if rational. That has
not been a difficult standard to meet since a "law need not be in
every respect logically consistent with its aims to be constitutional.
It is enough that there is an evil at hand for correction, and that it
might be thought that the particular legislative measure was a rational way to correct it." The Court does not strike down laws just
because they "may be unwise, improvident, or out of harmony with
a particular school of thought."[24]

The Court has never cared whether these rational basis challenges to economic regulations are brought by corporations or
natural persons. The Court merely looks at whether there is any
plausible justification for the law. The question of corporate personhood is immaterial. The vast majority of equal protection challenges to economic regulations will lose, whether it is a person or
corporation that brings suit.

As to whether corporations can raise equal protection challenges on the basis of suspect classifications, like race or sex, the
answer might appear easy. Corporations, even if legal persons, do
not have a race or sex or sexual orientation. It would appear that
corporations could never claim unconstitutional discrimination on
such a basis. But there is a lurking difficulty: the Supreme Court

has recognized this very kind of claim. One example was a 1995 case challenging so-called "minority set-asides." The federal government had a practice of giving preferential treatment, including additional compensation, when awarding construction contracts to companies controlled by racial minorities. The case concerned the government's award of such additional compensation to a contractor using the Gonzales Construction Company, which the government had certified as a minority business, as a subcontractor. Under federal law, companies could receive that certification if they were "owned and controlled" by individuals who were "Black, Hispanic, Asian Pacific, Subcontinent Asian, [or] Native American." Another contractor, Adarand Constructors, Inc., not so certified, sued to stop the government from offering advantages to minority businesses. The claim? The law violated Adarand's right to equal protection.[25]

Adarand was in effect saying it had a race and that its race worked to its disadvantage in competing for government contracts. The winner of the contract, Gonzales Construction, also had a race, and its race worked to its advantage. This is a paradigmatic equal protection claim: the claimant alleges that the government is imposing burdens and bestowing benefits on the basis of a suspect racial classification. The only oddity was that the claim was brought by a for-profit corporation. The federal statute simply assumed the corporation had the race of its shareholders.

The oddity was not noticed by the Court. Nowhere in the opinion was it even raised whether a corporation has a race or borrows the race of its shareholders. Adarand's brief in the case is silent on the point; its lawyers did not worry the case would be thrown out because it was not a "person"—with a race—under the equal protection clause.

Did the Court get this correct? Do corporations have a race? The correct analysis, perhaps surprisingly, leads to the answer that corporations do *not* have a race but *can* bring equal protection claims. This deserves some explanation.

Here is a place where corporate law insights are important to the constitutional analysis. Because of corporate separateness—corporate "personhood"—corporations are not the alter egos of their shareholders. You will recall that a number of corporate law professors filed a friend-of-the-court brief in *Burwell v. Hobby Lobby Stores, Inc.*—the case about whether corporations can claim religious freedom rights—arguing that corporations should not be able to put forward the religious rights of their shareholders. The corporation is separate and distinct from its shareholders, and the company should not be deemed to hold the religious views (and claim the religious rights) of its shareholders. This is true, the brief argued, even when the shareholders are few, are in the same family, and have similar religious views. Corporate personhood means that the corporation should not be deemed to have automatically adopted the views and traits of its shareholders.

In *Hobby Lobby*, that argument lost. The court believed that corporations could indeed adopt the views of their shareholders when it came to matters of religion. Though it might seem odd that a corporation can be seen to have a religion or a conscience, the court essentially made the same assumption about the nature and the identity of corporations in *Hobby Lobby* as it did in *Adarand*. During oral argument in *Hobby Lobby*, Chief Justice John Roberts pointedly asked the government lawyer whether corporations could have a race.[26] The assumption was that if a corporation could have a race, then it also must be able to have a religion. Or more precisely, the Chief Justice was pushing the assumption that the corporation should be deemed to have both the religious views and the race of its shareholders.

The Chief Justice was incorrect, as a matter of corporate law, to equate the corporation with its shareholders. Indeed, a commitment to corporate personhood should have led the Court to deny the corporation's ability to assert the religious views of its shareholders. Roberts was also incorrect to imply that the result in *Adarand* determined the result in *Hobby Lobby*. The two cases raised fundamentally different kinds of claims, and the differences help illustrate why corporations do not have a race but should be able to bring equal protection challenges.

When thinking through the nature of corporate rights, we need to look not only at the nature of the entity, but also at the nature of the right and the nature of the government action thought to violate it. In the case of a government entity giving preferences to certain companies based on the race of their shareholders, the classification itself is the problematic act. Government is putting its finger on the scales of the marketplace, based on the judgment that the benefits of the market should flow to one race more than the other. ("Minority set-asides" deserve support as a policy matter, as do affirmative action policies and race-conscious remedies for generalized societal prejudice. This discussion takes as given the current rule that remedial and invidious uses of race must both satisfy strict scrutiny. This was the important holding in *Adarand* itself.) The government's preference for companies whose shareholders are a certain race is constitutionally problematic whether one believes shareholders "own" the corporation or not.

It is also important to remember that equal protection law focuses on "disparate treatment" rather than "disparate impact." A law intended to treat people differently on the basis of suspect classifications is highly problematic and subject to the strictest of judicial scrutiny. A neutral law that is not based on bad intent but nevertheless has differential effects on people correlated with suspect classifications is not considered a violation of equal protection.[27] In *Adarand*, the Court saw the law giving preferences to some companies because of their shareholders' race as a case of "disparate treatment." It was not a case in which some companies were especially burdened or benefited from a neutral law.

To say that such intentional preferences are problematic is not the same as saying the corporation has a race. Courts can respect corporate "personhood"—they can consider corporations distinct from their shareholders—while simultaneously believing it to be constitutionally illegitimate for the government to distinguish among corporations on the basis of the race of their shareholders.

The case should have come out the same way if the preferences had been based on the race of the employees or customers and even if we did not consider employees or customers the owners of the business. The question of "who owns the corporation" does not determine whether a corporation can bring an equal protection challenge to a regulation that classifies it based on the race of a stakeholder. The classification itself is the problem.

To illustrate, consider a town filled with white supremacists who elect their own to important town posts. If that town refuses to conduct business with a company whose majority shareholders are African American, it would be a violation of equal protection, and the business would be within its rights to bring the case to court. The same would be true if the town refused to do business with a company whose *employees* were African American or whose *customers* were predominantly African American. To say that a company can bring an equal protection claim only when it is targeted because of its shareholders' race, but not that of its employees, would be nonsensical. It would elevate conventional wisdom about shareholder primacy to constitutional doctrine. And it would allow government actors to get away with highly problematic racial biases as long as they aimed their prejudice at the employees or customers of businesses rather than at shareholders.

What this means is that corporations may raise equal protection claims when a state action makes distinctions among corporations on the basis of the race—or by extension sex, alienage, or sexual orientation—of their stakeholders. To be a proper constitutional plaintiff, corporations need only show they have been injured by the distinction and that the government's act is illegitimate.

III. Corporations and Religion

As with equal protection doctrine, religious claims must point to an intentional governmental act burdening belief or exercise. In the 1990 case of *Employment Division v. Smith*, the Court ruled, in an opinion by Justice Antonin Scalia, that neutral laws do not violate religious freedom even if they have disparate effects on religious observances or belief.[28] In effect, *Smith* made the law of religious exercise analogous to that of equal protection in that laws that target on the basis of religion must satisfy heightened scrutiny. Laws that are not motivated by racial, sexual, or anti-religious animus are not constitutionally problematic even if they have disparate effects on the basis of race, sex, or religion.

The hypothetical white supremacist town mentioned above can be used as an example here as well. If the town refused to do business with companies whose majority shareholders were Catholic, a company could challenge the town's action as an unconstitutional restriction on religious freedom. This is *not* because the company borrows the religion of the shareholders any more than it borrows their race. As under equal protection law, the governmental act would be problematic regardless of whether it was aimed at a company's shareholders or a different stakeholder. The corporate status of the claimant would be constitutionally unimportant. A contrary result would be nonsensical.

Similar results would flow from claims of religious establishment. If a state required businesses to close on Sunday out of respect to the religious observances of mainstream Christians, a business would have standing to complain the law impermissibly established religion. The government act would be beyond its rightful power; the corporate entity status of the plaintiff would be immaterial. If the corporations could not sue to redress such government missteps, some number of such missteps would go without remedy.

One question remains to be considered: the kind of religious claim raised by Hobby Lobby in its case against the Affordable Care Act. The company complained that the "contraceptive mandate" that required it to provide employee health insurance that included contraceptive care violated its beliefs. Corporate separateness— corporate personhood—should have led the Court to rule against the corporation because it should not be deemed to hold the religious views of its shareholders.

This seems inconsistent. Corporations are able to bring equal protection claims and free exercise and establishment claims but should have lost in *Hobby Lobby*?

The main difference in the *Hobby Lobby* case was that it did not concern a targeted governmental act intentionally infringing religious beliefs or making religious classifications. The contraceptive mandate to which the company objected was neutral vis-à-vis religion and belief. Hobby Lobby was not being singled out for hurtful treatment. All that was required was to provide the same health insurance its competitors were providing. Under *Smith*, Hobby Lobby had no free exercise claim at all.

Hobby Lobby based its claims of religious exercise not on the Constitution but on the Religious Freedom Restoration Act, which Congress passed after *Smith*. RFRA requires that the federal government show a compelling justification any time a federal law imposes a significant burden on the religious beliefs of any "person."[29] The law need not be targeted at religious belief or exercise; RFRA covers even those laws neutral toward religion. In operation, RFRA offers religious persons a way to be exempted from otherwise applicable federal laws. (RFRA does not apply to state law.)[30] So Hobby Lobby was not complaining about being singled out. It *wanted* to be singled out to receive an exception from having to obey a law that applied to other similarly situated employers. Hobby Lobby's argument was that because RFRA protected religious "persons," and because corporations are persons, it should be exempted.

But the fact that corporations are "persons" should have led to the opposite conclusion. Corporations are separate from their shareholders. The central characteristic of the corporate form is a separateness of legal status from its investors and other stakeholders. The law professors' brief in *Hobby Lobby* did not contest that corporations could be "persons" under the statute; it challenged the notion that the views of shareholders penetrated the separate legal status, the personhood, of the corporation. The personhood of the corporation meant that RFRA should not apply to a situation in which the corporation's claim is really a shareholder claim brought in the corporation's name. For Hobby Lobby to win, the Court had to assume both that the corporation was a "person" under RFRA but was not a person—was not separate—under corporate law. Both cannot be true.

One might say that *Hobby Lobby* was a narrow case about a small set of companies run by religious people who objected to one provision of the Affordable Care Act. But it certainly felt like a case that had broader implications. It has been roundly criticized as creating another aspect of corporate "personhood" that protects corporations from government oversight and regulation. The rationale that corporations should be assumed to embody and carry the religious views of their shareholders is deeply problematic and could have implications for many laws beyond RFRA, including anti-discrimination law.

So let us face the question squarely. Even if shareholders' views are not to be projected onto corporations, can corporations nevertheless have religious views or a religious identity that deserves some amount of government deference or respect?

At first glance, the question might seem easy to answer. Corporations do not have consciences or souls. Religious belief is something in a mind or heart, which corporations cannot claim regardless of how we might anthropomorphize them. The question is not so easily dismissed, however. Organizations have cultures and value systems, and it is possible for an organization to have a culture or value system defined in religious terms. It is not meaningless to speak of "corporate conscience," and it is not meaningless to speak of religious organizations. Many universities, hospitals, and charitable entities hold themselves out as religious in nature, with commitments and values that flow from that nature.

Can for-profit corporations make the same claims? Of course. There is nothing inherently inconsistent with religious commitments on the one hand and the drive to make money on the other. The view that religion requires financial charity or selflessness is certainly commonly held. But that notion is a product of certain kinds of religious norms, not shared by all. And it is certainly possible for companies to claim, and operate in accordance with, a set of religious commitments while still engaging in the day-to-day work of manufacturing tires, providing tax services, or selling chicken sandwiches. And like all aspects of corporate culture, a religious corporate culture can be a product of top-down strategic management or bottom-up, organic organizational life. And like other aspects of corporate culture, a religious corporate culture can be either oppressive or empowering to employees, customers, and other stakeholders.

A company can be like Malden Mills, which helped employees after a factory fire in part because of the religious sensitivities of the CEO and majority shareholder.[31] Or a company can be like Hobby

Lobby, refusing to offer employees health insurance coverage they want and need in part because of its purported religious sensitivities. Sometimes religiosity will cause corporations to act as better "corporate citizens" and with more care toward their stakeholders. Sometimes it will cause them to be worse on both fronts. But that does not matter in the constitutional analysis.

The real question is not whether corporations can have religious values. They can. The question is what to do about that.

This is an instance in which the analysis is affected by the fact that we are discussing a corporation, not a natural person. A human being with a religious belief that is sincerely held generally suffers economic or personal hardship because of it for the single reason that religion imposes obligations on its adherents. There are exceptions of course, but in the run of cases it is not difficult to determine whether someone has a sincerely held religious belief. You can simply observe how that person behaves. While there are occasional examples of humans who falsely claim a religious belief in order to make a point or game the system (like the Massachusetts woman who, claiming to be a "Pastafarian," won the right to have her driver's license photo show her wearing a pasta strainer),[32] those will be rare. Courts generally do not inquire deeply into the veracity of religious claims by humans. When human beings assert RFRA claims—that their sincerely held religious beliefs are burdened by a federal law—the courts generally take them at their word.

But such deference to a corporation's bare assertion of religious belief would be mistaken. Because of the economic purpose of corporations, they have an incentive to avoid regulation. Since RFRA affords this very possibility, corporations will have incentives to claim religious belief to gain a competitive advantage over non-religious companies. And if such assertions are not questioned by courts, company boards will simply assert whatever belief they need to avoid regulation. This may have been the case in *Hobby*

Lobby. The company previously provided health insurance that included contraceptive coverage. Only when the ACA made it mandatory did the company raise religious objections, conjuring its RFRA claim to avoid providing an employee benefit their competitors were required to provide.[33]

It might be possible for corporations to raise valid RFRA-like claims. But several conditions would have to be met. First, the company should not be assumed to hold the views of its shareholders. Because of the personhood of the corporation, there is a separation between shareholders and the company. It would have to be the company *itself* that holds religious beliefs. That is not impossible, but a corporation would be put to its proof. There are simply too many incentives for corporations to engage in subterfuge on this front.

That leads to the second condition: a corporation should have to prove its religious views have been long-standing and consistent. The corporation should have to show how its beliefs limited its activities in ways that imposed economic obligations or competitive disadvantages on it.

Third, the regulatory exception gained by the corporation should not be so great that it gives the corporation a material advantage in the marketplace. In other words, the importance of ensuring the fairness of marketplace competition should count as a compelling interest to justify not extending RFRA protection.

Sometimes it is essential to offer corporations constitutional protections under the due process, equal protection, and religion clauses. Corporations' rights are not always coextensive with those of human beings—most notably in the religion context—but both because of the nature and importance of these rights and the nature of corporations themselves, it is sometimes important to use these constitutional tools to constrain government's power.

FIVE

Corporations and Speech Theory

For decades, cigarette packages in the United States carried warnings about the dangers of smoking. But they were on the side of the package, were notoriously easy to ignore, and had little impact. In an effort to make the dangers more salient, Congress passed a law in 2009 requiring cigarette packages to carry graphic images as warnings. According to scientific studies, such depictions of the risks of smoking help bolster the resilience of smokers trying to quit, saving thousands of lives.[1] The images eventually proposed by the Food and Drug Administration ranged from depictions of a dying cancer patient to a baby crying as smoke billows around her.[2] Even though the proposed labels were nowhere near the grotesque depictions of cancer, lung disease, and death required in other countries, U.S. tobacco companies raced into court to stop the law, arguing the warning labels violated their right of free speech.

To back up their argument, the cigarette companies cited the 1943 Supreme Court ruling that the government could not force Jehovah's Witnesses schoolchildren to recite the Pledge of Allegiance at the beginning of the school day. In *West Virginia State Board of Education v. Barnette*, Justice Robert Jackson wrote for the Court in favor of the children. He penned some of the most famous words in the nation's first amendment jurisprudence: "If there is any fixed star in our constitutional constellation, it is that no official, high or petty, can prescribe what shall be orthodox in politics, nationalism, religion, or other matters of opinion or force citizens to confess by word or act their faith therein."[3] This remains one of the most important free speech cases in the history of the Court because it made clear that the freedom of speech means not only the freedom to speak, but not to speak as well.

The cigarette companies sued to stop the warning labels using this argument. Multinational conglomerates not wanting to warn customers about addictive and toxic products argued they stood in the constitutional shoes of religious schoolchildren refusing to recite the Pledge of Allegiance. This might strike most Americans as a reach. But the tobacco companies won a judgment in their favor in the federal trial court and on appeal.[4]

Are corporations protected by the free speech clause as the rest of us are? Can we require warning labels on cigarette packages? Can we limit corporations' political spending? Can newspapers publish classified documents leaked by a whistleblower or be sued for stories critical of a presidential candidate? Can states regulate violent video games? Can federal regulators require companies to disclose their complicity with human rights violations in their supply chains?

Under current law, the entity status of a free speech plaintiff is neither here nor there. What generally matters to the Court are the merits of the claim, not the nature of the claimant. Up until 2010, there was a single doctrinal niche where the corporate status of the claimant made a difference in free speech law: the area of campaign finance. But *Citizens United* did away with that distinction, holding that corporations—whether profit or nonprofit, closely held or publicly traded—had the same rights to spend money to influence electoral outcomes as individuals had.

Jeff Clements, one of the leaders of the anti-corporate personhood movement, wrote that the notion that corporations have the same speech rights as people would strike most Americans as "bizarre."[5] Legal scholar Tamara Piety argues that there is no "good reason" that a corporate "entity, as such, needs protection for freedom of expression."[6]

Corporate speech rights are not bizarre or without reason. But there is little doubt that the theory of corporate constitutional rights, in regard to both speech and beyond, is undertheorized. Supreme Court Justice William O. Douglas once admitted that the extension of constitutional rights to corporations was undertaken "without exposition or explanation."[7] According to political scientist David Ciepley, "remarkably, the Court has never offered a sustained argument as to why corporations merit constitutional rights. . . . Strictly speaking, the question has never been decided but merely presumed decided."[8]

The problem of corporate speech is particularly acute, timely, and complex. There are reasons to protect corporate speech in a host of contexts. At the same time, there are reasons to believe corporations are situated differently from humans vis-à-vis free speech rights. Unless the best constitutional answer is that corporations should receive the same speech rights as humans, or none of those rights, the reality is that new lines will have to be drawn. And the placement of those lines should make sense.

First, we need to look at the purpose of the right in question and ask whether such purpose is furthered by extending it to corporations. For example, the Fifth Amendment right to be free of self-incrimination is a distinctly human right. It protects individuals from giving oral testimony in a situation where they might be under terrific psychological pressure to capitulate to law enforcement officials. Such a right does not easily translate to the corporate form, where there is no oral testimony to give and the entity is not subject to psychological bullying.

Second, we look at whether the right is important for the corporation to achieve its institutional purpose of building wealth by producing goods and services. The protection of religious exercise, for example, is neither here nor there when protecting most companies' economic endeavors, and religious waivers undermine marketplace fairness. In contrast, constitutional protections for procedural due process are essential in protecting corporations from governmental arbitrariness that would undermine the investor and stakeholder confidence necessary for companies to survive.

This two-step analysis is especially difficult in the area of free speech because of the vast disagreement about the purpose of the free speech right and the vagary of the nexus between speech and a corporation's purpose. More than anywhere else in constitutional theory, one's theory of the role and nature of corporations is more material in this analysis than elsewhere.

So what is the purpose of protecting free speech? Much of the disagreement about corporate speech is a product of disputes and lack of certainty about this simple question. While the free speech clause did not receive much attention from litigants, judges, or scholars during the first century of our nation's constitutional history, few provisions have been litigated more in the second and beginning of the third. While disagreements abound, starting at the level of first principle and cascading from there to specific cases, there is a remarkable agreement about the notion that speech is valuable. We may disagree about why we protect it, and there is inevitable disagreement about individual cases on the edges. But the present-day United States is the political jurisdiction most protective of speech anywhere in the world and indeed any time in history. When it comes to speech, we are the most libertarian society that has ever existed.[9]

When we consider the phenomenon of corporate speech, then, those who want to expel corporations from the protection of the free speech clause have a heavy burden. To argue that corporate speech does not fit within the broad range of protections offered by the First Amendment is going against a powerful trend.

Scholars turn to three principal theories to explain the constitutional importance of speech: the marketplace of ideas; human autonomy; and democratic governance. Each provides good reasons to protect corporate speech but also reasons to regulate it.

I. Marketplace of Ideas

In the early twentieth century, Supreme Court Justices Oliver Wendell Holmes, Jr., and Louis Brandeis were the first jurists to take seriously the idea that the free speech clause contained meaningful constraints on government behavior. They were hardly absolutists—for example, they voted to uphold the conviction of Eugene Debs, the famous socialist, for speaking out against World War I.[10] Holmes also famously opined that the First Amendment "would not protect a man in falsely shouting fire in a theatre and causing a panic."[11] Holmes and Brandeis nevertheless labored to develop a workable theory of when speech should be protected and when it should not be.

Their efforts highlight the crucial preliminary point one must recognize in thinking through free speech problems. No one thinks all speech should be protected. Perjury, though an act of speech, is punishable as a crime. Defamation of a private person, though an act of speech, is a civil wrong. Conspiracy to commit a crime, though engaged by way of whispers at the local pub, can get one thrown into jail. A telephoned bomb threat, an offer to sell a security founded on a misrepresentation, a fraudulent sales pitch for a new gadget, a spoken offer of employment in exchange for sex—all of these are verbal in nature but nonetheless subject to legal regulation and punishment—and rightly so.

The pervasive question for free speech theorists, then, is how to draw the line between speech that is protected and speech that is not. Most scholars and jurists who have taken this task seriously have "reasoned down": they have started with a theory of why speech is important and deduced outcomes in specific cases. A theory can be tested against iconic, touchstone cases in which consensus about an outcome is high. But for free speech questions, theory drives outcomes as much or more than any area of constitutional law.

When Holmes and Brandeis were working through the first steps of developing the rationales for speech freedoms, their areas of agreement outweighed their disagreements. But in hindsight, their disagreements are more helpful in teasing out the various possible theoretical bases for protecting—or not protecting—speech.

Holmes, for his part, fathered what has become known as the "marketplace of ideas" theory of free speech, which posits that the purpose of speech and communication is the search for truth or, more precisely, that the purpose of protecting speech is to advance the search for truth. In a case in which the Court upheld the convictions of Jewish anti-war protestors, Holmes dissented (and was joined by Brandeis).[12] "It is only the present danger of immediate evil" that "warrants Congress in setting a limit to the expression of opinion."[13] Attempts to persuade cannot be punished since "Congress certainly cannot forbid all effort to change the mind of the country." Persuasion should be protected because "the ultimate good desired is better reached by free trade in ideas—that the best test of truth is the power of the thought to get itself accepted in the competition of the market."[14]

"There is no such thing as a false idea," Justice Lewis Powell said several decades after Holmes.[15] We know this to be wrong—the idea that Earth is flat was false, as was the idea that Jews deserved to be gassed in ovens. But the point Powell was making was Holmesian. Protecting the pronouncement of ideas—even ideas that turn out to be false—helps us discover which are false and which are true. Ideas are vetted by those who hear and consider them. Over time, ideas that contain more truth will win out over those containing less. In this theory, the principal remedy for incorrect ideas is not a limit on their communication but the communication of better ones. As Brandeis said a few years after Holmes created the marketplace theory, "If there be time to expose through discussion the falsehood and fallacies, to avert the evil by the processes of education, the remedy to be applied is more speech, not enforced silence."[16]

The marketplace analogy is apt. Like products in the consumer marketplace, ideas compete against one other for "buyers." Quality ideas, like quality products, will attract more "buyers" over time and squeeze inferior ones out. Competition will improve the quality of ideas over time. We march forward, little by little, toward a more perfect understanding of our world. The theory suggests that competition subjects ideas to something like the scientific method. Propositions are tested, and those that are falsified lose. Those not falsified survive and form a part of our collective understanding.

Notice a couple of things. First, the theory focuses on the value of speech at a social, cultural, or political level. The value of speech is weighed by those who hear or read the communication and decide whether it is valid and conducive to truth. Second, because the theory focuses on the effects of speech over time, the interests of listeners weigh heavily in the balance of which speech is protected and which is not. But the theory does not particularly care about the interests of *specific* listeners. Rather, the focus is on listeners collectively, much like economic analysis cares about the atomistic purchasing decisions of individuals in service of understanding economic behavior generally.

This has become the dominant theory of free speech in the United States. The Supreme Court routinely cites it almost by rote. For example, in his opinion for the Court in *Citizens United*, Justice Anthony Kennedy asserted that restrictions on corporate speech "interfere[] with the 'open marketplace' of ideas protected by the First Amendment."[17] The Court's embrace of the theory is understandable. There is certainly something to the notion that discourse about ideas advances our understanding of those ideas and their competitors. The alternative to protecting the free market in ideas—government picking among ideas—is highly problematic. The government would have to be quite certain of the correctness of an idea to regulate or ban its competitors.

Just as a laissez-faire economic theory results in a high level of protection for economic activity, the marketplace of ideas theory results in a high level of protection for speech. It is quite libertarian in its results. Hands off, it says to those who want speech to be regulated. We have "a profound national commitment" to "uninhibited, robust, and wide-open" discourse.[18] In the long run, this will make us better off. Proponents of the marketplace theory would have us trust Adam Smith's invisible hand to work with ideas as it does with markets.

The analogy with markets illustrates the theory's power but also its weakness. Products and ideas are not the same. Products are more easily comparable than ideas and can be tested more readily. The consumers of products have a mechanism to translate their preferences into a form the marketplace can understand: money. If you like a new gadget and think it beats your old gadget, you can buy the new one. The market responds by raising the price of the preferred gadget and depressing the price of the rejected one. Eventually, unless the rejected gadget improves, it will be squeezed out.

No similar pricing mechanism exists for ideas. One does not buy an idea with money, and good ideas do not cost more than bad ideas. It is nonsensical to think in such terms. It is costless to move from one idea to the next, and there is no way to reveal my preferences about ideas to the public in a way that squeezes out bad ideas. There is little similarity in how ideas and products compete. Bad ideas will linger longer than bad products, and the arc of competition among ideas—if it bends at all—will be long. As a theoretical matter, then, the presumption against government intervention in the free market of ideas should be less than in the free market of economic exchange.

This leads us to another flaw in the theory. In economic markets, we recognize the reality of failures and the necessity of government intervention. Product markets sometimes fail in providing for the success of good products over bad. Markets are "sticky"; better products do not always win when people are intransigent in their preferences. Such intransigence leads to "path dependence," the notion that early designs gain permanence over time, not because of efficiency but because of inertia. The example often used is the modern keyboard with the standard QWERTY layout. It was invented in the early days of the typewriter, when the devices could not keep up with fast typists and frequently jammed. The keyboards had to be designed to make typing awkward, with oft-used letters in odd positions. Despite its inefficiency, the QWERTY keyboard has survived not because it is better but because humans do not like to change.[19]

When it comes to economic markets, we are aware of their benefits and their limits. We know preferences are shaped not only by the characteristics of the products and services for sale, but also by influences unrelated to quality or services, such as advertising and peer pressure.[20] We punish lying and fraud since we understand that they can skew competition. We limit monopolies since we know that the domination of a market by a small number of suppliers can make it impossible for competitors to gain a toehold.

And when products or services cause harm, those responsible for their manufacture or sale must compensate those harmed. When risks are latent and harms go uncompensated, dangerous products are overproduced.

It is odd, then, that the marketplace theory of free speech has created a free speech doctrine that is so libertarian in its attitudes when laissez faire economics is widely discredited. The same defects we find in markets for goods and services will also appear in ideas markets. Psychological inertia exists with ideas as with products, so people are not always persuaded by better ideas. The attractiveness of ideas is affected by irrelevant influences such as advertising and peer pressure. Untruths and misrepresentation can distort competition. Monopolies can exist and make it difficult for new ideas to elbow aside the old. And, like products, ideas and speech can cause harm. Sometimes the harm can be psychological—as with threats or hate speech—and sometimes physical—as with incitements to violence.[21] And any under-compensation of victims will mean that harmful speech will be overproduced.

Widely understood limitations on economic markets are rarely acknowledged in free speech doctrine. But the Court could recognize that, like in economic markets, the marketplace of ideas does not work perfectly and is subject to knowable defects and flaws. The marketplace theory's dependence on counter-speech, for example, could take into account whether counter-speech is genuinely possible or whether a monopoly in a speech market has erected such barriers to entry—to use an economic term—that make counter-speech less possible and robust.

One way to think about this is that even if a marketplace theory is the best way to analyze the reasons why speech is protected, it need not result in the level of blanket protection one typically finds in cases applying this theory. One could recognize the benefits of competition among ideas and the value of counter-speech while also acknowledging the reality of "market defects." The doctrine could be less simplistically laissez-faire and be more nuanced in its analysis of speech regulation.

For example, in *Buckley v. Valeo*, the 1976 case that struck down federal limits on individual campaign expenditures as violations of free speech, the Court depended on a simplistic version of the marketplace of ideas theory. It held that unrestrained election spending was necessary to secure "the widest possible dissemination of information from diverse and antagonistic sources" and "to assure unfettered interchange of ideas for the bringing about of political and social changes desired by the people."[22] The Court was not persuaded by the argument that a stark unbalance in expenditures would skew the idea marketplace, as a monopoly or oligopoly might in an economic market. The Court said balancing was beyond the pale: "The concept that government may restrict the speech of some elements of our society in order to enhance the relative voice of others is wholly foreign to the First Amendment."[23]

Buckley has long been criticized as creating the notion that "money is speech." The Court never said this, however. It said, instead, that the regulation of money often has free speech implications. That part of *Buckley* is correct. People spend money to express viewpoints, and limitations on how one spends money can burden speech interests in material ways. But *Buckley* does deserve criticism for its obtuseness about balancing. A sophisticated understanding of how markets work should have led the Court to be more open to the idea that a deluge of independent expenditures on one side of an election could dangerously skew the marketplace of ideas. And if we believe that democratic rule should be based more on ideas than on money, then such imbalance can harm democracy. In other words, the Court could have adhered to a marketplace of ideas theory of free speech—albeit a more sophisticated one that understands monopolies—and come out the other way in *Buckley*.

A constitutional amendment is not required to get rid of *Buckley* or its jurisprudential descendant, *Citizens United*. All that is required is a court more sophisticated in its understanding of free speech and less obtuse about the real-life implications of money in politics.

Marketplace Theory and Corporations

How does the marketplace theory deal with the problem of corporate speech?

The theory does not care about the source of speech. An idea deserves protection whether uttered by a human, an association of like-minded advocates, an incorporated business, or a robot. Nor is there a hierarchy of the substance of ideas. Ideas about tax policy or a proposed constitutional amendment are protected, but so are those about whether climate change is real, which Stephen King novel is the best, or what brand of jeans provides a good fit for middle-aged men. A hierarchy would be inconsistent with the theory's agnosticism about untested ideas since it would be based on a notion that some categories of speech are more important than others.

That is why the outcome in *Citizens United* flowed so easily from a simplistic application of the marketplace theory. The views expressed in the anti-Hillary movie sponsored by Citizens United merited exposure and vetting in the marketplace of ideas. The fact that the creator of the film was a nonprofit corporation rather than a human being was immaterial. And it would have made no difference if the creator had been a for-profit corporation. Within the theory, the Court could decide the case at hand and expand its reasoning to all corporations, whether for-profit or nonprofit. Without a more sophisticated understanding and application of the marketplace theory, the Court's decision in *Citizens United* was virtually certain.

There was a way for *Citizens United* to come out differently within the marketplace theory, but the Court would have had to be willing to evaluate the marketplace of ideas as if it were a real market, with defects and limitations that justify regulation. The Court might have ruled as it had in the 1990 case *Austin v. Michigan Chamber of Commerce*, upholding a state ban on corporate expenditures advocating for specific candidates for office.[24] Writing for the Court, Justice Thurgood Marshall explained that corporate speakers are more likely than individual actors to exert an oligarchic influence on political debate. Marshall cited "the corrosive and distorting effects of immense aggregations of wealth that are accumulated with the help of the corporate form and that have little or no correlation to the public's support for the corporation's political ideas."[25] Marshall was not saying that corporations do not deserve free speech rights because of their status as corporate entities. The reasoning instead was that the wealth that corporations amass can skew the marketplace of ideas by exerting what are essentially monopolistic influences. This argument takes corporate personhood as neither here nor there but looks instead at corporations' potential to slant the debate because of their economic power. This is market analysis that one would find straightforward in an economic realm and should fit comfortably within a sophisticated application of the marketplace of ideas theory. And for twenty years, it did.

By the time *Citizens United* got to the Court in 2009, however, government lawyers were no longer willing to press the argument that corporate speech should be regulated because it skews public debate. As a tactical matter, that adjustment was probably smart. The Court showed no inclination to re-endorse that view. The conventional wisdom at the time was that the Court granted review of *Citizens United* to overturn *Austin* and its rationale. In fact, after the Court first heard arguments in the case, it notified the parties that it wanted them to argue it again and explicitly address whether

Austin and its progeny should be overturned.[26] In the second hearing, Solicitor General (now Justice) Elena Kagan focused her argument for the government on shareholder rights and the appearance of corruption caused by corporate spending.[27]

Within the marketplace of ideas frame, neither argument was likely to be particularly persuasive. Worries about shareholders—or other stakeholders for that matter—do not have much traction in the marketplace theory. What matters is the idea, not how it is created or vetted within the group or entity that espouses it. Worries about shareholders are akin to the concerns that arise when any member of an association disagrees with the collective views of that association. The remedy in such a situation is for the member either to fight within the organization to change its views or to leave the association. The *Citizens United* Court assumed that shareholders have these same remedies of voice or exit. And as long as shareholders can voice their dissent or sell their shares—actions the Court simply assumed they could do—there was no reason to gag the voice of the corporate collective. Justice Kennedy, writing for the Court, believed there was "little evidence of abuse that cannot be corrected by shareholders 'through the procedures of corporate democracy.'"[28] The reality of shareholder influence over corporate political spending is much different, as a number of scholars have pointed out.[29] But as a matter of theory, the Court was on firm ground—within the marketplace theory—to dismiss the concerns of shareholders.

As for corruption, that worry provided no basis to distinguish corporate speakers from human ones. The appearance of corruption arises from the flow of money to political figures. It does not matter if the source of money is an individual or a corporation unless there is reason to believe that a corporation spending a given amount is more likely to demand something in return than an individual is. And while this may be true in some circumstances, the Court did not seriously grapple with the possibility. Its view of "corruption" is exceedingly narrow, essentially limited to *quid pro quo* understandings.[30] Most corporations are not so ham-fisted.

The hard reality is this: once the government abandoned *Austin's* rationale that corporations distorted the marketplace of ideas, the outcome in *Citizens United* was preordained. There was little reason to distinguish corporate speakers/spenders from similarly situated human speakers/spenders. The Court could see no reason to treat corporations any differently from individuals. The marketplace of ideas theory wielded by the Court was more simplistic than necessary and insufficiently sophisticated to make that distinction. A marketplace theory nuanced enough to capture the notion that sometimes a marketplace needs regulation was beyond the ken of the Court.

II. Autonomy and Self-Fulfillment

The second rationale for protecting speech is not about a general search for truth or the advancement of understanding for society. Instead, it argues that speech is protected to give individuals the space to develop and pursue their own identity and autonomy. Speech is protected to provide the mechanism for individuals to fulfill their potential as human beings, both by developing the capacity to speak and communicate as they see fit and to be exposed as listeners to the views and perspectives of others. As in the marketplace theory, speech is protected in the autonomy theory for instrumental reasons: it creates worthwhile effects. The effect that matters in the marketplace theory is the societal march toward truth; in the autonomy theory, it is the development of the capacity of individuals. But the autonomy theory goes further in that speech is also protected for intrinsic reasons. Speech *in itself* is a good thing because it represents the way individuals express their identity and pursue their version of the good life.

Justice Louis Brandeis championed these notions of autonomy and self-fulfillment: "Those who won our independence believed that the final end of the State was to make men free to develop their faculties. . . . They valued liberty both as an end, and as a means. They believed liberty to be the secret of happiness."[31] This description of the value of speech from almost a century ago aligns with much popular assessment of the value of free speech today. If you believe music, art, poetry, tattoos, or erotica should be protected from government regulation absent a compelling reason, you probably think so because these expressions are vital to human enrichment and because speakers and listeners use them to express their identities. A Jackson Pollock painting, Robert Frost poem, or Beyoncé ballad may advance society toward truth in some vague and tangential way, but the more central reason to protect them from governmental regulation is their "deep relation to self-respect arising from autonomous self-determination without which the life of the spirit is meager and slavish."[32] How we express ourselves is centrally important to us, in both exposing who we are and developing who we are becoming.

This rationale also takes seriously the interests of those hearing speech or receiving the communication. You exercise your autonomy and work toward self-fulfillment by writing blogs, singing at the subway station, or taking a photograph. But you also exercise your autonomy and work toward self-fulfillment by *reading* blogs, *listening* to someone else's song, or *looking* at a photograph. The theory has a public aspect to it, but it is not based on a search for some absolute truth or an exploration of matters of public interest. Instead, it acknowledges that the benefits of speech—in autonomy terms—flow to both the originators of the speech and its recipients.

Despite this theory's many attractions, it has serious difficulties. Perhaps the most fundamental is that it has no obvious limitation. If we are to defer completely to each individual's own view of what advances his or her autonomy and what does not, then the theory simply acts as a mechanism to protect every kind of communication imaginable. You could claim that lying about a product you want to sell is a way of expressing that you are a lout. You could claim that burning down your neighbor's house is a way to express your hatred of him. You could claim that offering your employee a raise in exchange for sex is your way to express the enjoyment of your power. A theory that counts all such communication as protected speech subject to the most serious judicial scrutiny does not help much in drawing the difficult lines that a theory is supposed to help draw.

This suggests another difficulty. The two bases of the theory—a respect for autonomy and a protection of a space for self-fulfillment—are often at cross-purposes. Autonomy, in the sense of a deference to the bare preferences of the individual engaging in the speech, is not always consistent with self-fulfillment. For example, you may enjoy playing video games. A respect for your autonomy would lead a judge to strike down limits on violence in video games.[33] But it is probably correct to say that your video game habit is not conducive to your self-fulfillment within a fully realized human life. The same could be said for any number of pursuits, whether they be reading trash novels, watching trash television, or surfing trash Internet sites. In other words, if one takes a libertarian view in regard to the value of autonomy, one has to be very skeptical, or at least agnostic, toward the theory's prioritization of self-fulfillment. If one instead takes seriously the importance of self-fulfillment as a goal for the free speech clause, one cannot take as given each individual's autonomous choices when it comes to expression.[34]

Finally, the theory does not explain how to decide cases in which one person's autonomous choice infringes on the autonomy or self-fulfillment of another. Consider so-called hate speech in this context. To pick one example from the last few years, a celebratory chant of frat boys at a university campus claiming they would rather lynch African American students than allow them membership in their fraternity would certainly be protected speech under the autonomy theory if we looked only at the autonomy of the chanters themselves.[35] But such speech most likely encroaches on the autonomy and self-fulfillment interests of African American students on that campus by marginalizing them, forcing them to speak up in their own defense, and causing them to fear for their safety. Whose autonomy trumps: that of the speakers or the listeners? On the one hand, a theory that protects only speech that does not affect others is a weak one indeed. On the other, if autonomy and self-fulfillment are the goals, the theory needs to grapple with the instances in which the interests of speakers and listeners are in conflict.

The implications of the autonomy theory in campaign finance regulation turn on whether, in the general parlance, money is speech. If so, then it will presumptively be protected by the free speech clause. ("Protected" means that its regulation must survive judicial "strict scrutiny"—that is, be justified by a compelling governmental interest and carefully tailored to achieving that interest.) If it is not, then campaign contributions and expenditures can be regulated more easily and with a less important governmental purpose.

The oft-cited conventional wisdom on this point—that "money isn't speech"—is jaw-droppingly simplistic. The aphorism is true as a statement of basic physicality: spending twenty dollars does not require the movement of vocal cords. But the free speech clause protects more than just audible voices. If speech is protected because of its ability to assist humans to fulfill and exercise their autonomy, there is nothing categorical that would exclude the spending of money from this class of protected communicative activity. You can spend money to express your identity, whether by contributing to

Planned Parenthood, buying a photograph for your office, or purchasing a new car. An autonomy theory would treat these decisions as any other communication that expresses identity. And that makes sense. Imagine if a government regulation prohibited contributions to Planned Parenthood or the purchase of photographs. A person who believes the First Amendment protects the expression of one's identity would be justifiably troubled by those types of restrictions, despite that fact they all target the use of money.

In other words, the spending of money is neither here nor there in the autonomy theory. It does not in itself make an act communicative in ways that would make it protected speech. But the fact that a communicative act is performed through the use of money does not exclude it from protection either.

Autonomy Theory and Corporations

At first glance, the autonomy theory would appear to be quite helpful to those who believe corporations should not benefit from constitutional speech protections. Corporations may be (legal) persons, but they are not human. A theory that prioritizes the self-fulfillment and autonomy of human beings would not protect the speech of corporations since they have no human capacity to fulfill or human autonomy to exercise. But a difficulty arises when one remembers that the autonomy theory protects the interests not only of speakers but also of listeners. It should not "count" within the autonomy theory if a corporation wishes to communicate. But the wishes of human beings who care what a corporation says *do* count. One thing is certain about our society: some people self-identify using the communication of corporations. We often pay extra for items—whether basketball shoes, handbags, or sports coupes—that brand us with a corporate logo. For-profit publishing companies sell nonfiction books from which humans learn and novels in which humans lose themselves. Giant for-profit conglomerates produce music that offers enjoyment to human listeners and opens up emotional depths that are otherwise difficult to plumb.

Another difficulty within the autonomy frame for those who want to exclude corporations from speech protections arises from the reality that humans often exercise their autonomy and gain fulfillment by organizing in groups.[36] We join the National Rifle Association, Planned Parenthood, and the Boy Scouts. Those entities are organized as corporate forms, though they embody a collective effort of their members to exercise their points of view or develop their abilities and knowledge. Groups are the mechanism by which people exercise their autonomy. To exclude those groups from speech protection under an autonomy theory would be awkward.

One might argue that the groups that fall into this category are primarily membership organizations and corporations are different. But humans choose to associate with groups organized in the corporate form as well. A university, for example, is typically organized as a corporation and is not a membership organization as one usually thinks of that term. But the people who choose to associate with it—professors and students mostly, but also staff and even fans of athletic teams—frequently do so because they identify with the culture, mission, or goals of the institution. A rule that sets aside the speech interests of universities as beyond constitutional protection would be *inconsistent* with the autonomy and self-fulfillment of humans. To protect that autonomy, sometimes the speech and associational interests of corporate entities need to be protected—not because the institution itself has an interest in self-fulfillment, but because protecting the institution's speech rights is instrumental in furthering the self-fulfillment of those who voluntarily associate with it.

Should the rule for for-profit companies be any different? The answer depends on the nature of the corporation in question. Within the autonomy frame, the corporation would not have a cognizable speech right on its own behalf because it is not a human being. But even setting aside the interests of listeners, it is certainly possible, even likely, that the speech rights of certain corporations should be protected because some humans express themselves by associating with those companies. Companies have cultures and institutional commitments, and sometimes people choose to work at a company or buy from a company or purchase stock in a company because of what it says about them. Someone who works at, buys from, or invests in Patagonia, for example, might do so because he or she supports the company's efforts to be environmentally conscientious. (Patagonia is chartered as a "benefit corporation" to ensure its environmental commitments are an organic part of its corporate identity and governance.) Someone might work at, buy from, or invest in Google because he or she identifies as a hip techie. And, yes, someone might work at, buy from, or invest in Hobby Lobby because he or she wants to be a part of a company that wants to serve Jesus. It would be wrong to say that most companies can claim that kind of group identification. Most employees, customers, and investors do not perform a First Amendment–relevant act when they work for, buy from, or invest in companies. But some do, and it would be incorrect to suggest that no company can claim the protection of an autonomy-based free speech doctrine.

At the same time, the autonomy frame can also accommodate *regulation* of corporate speech. Because its reasons to protect corporate speech are instrumental in nature, a sophisticated version of the theory would allow for the regulation and limitation of corporate speech rights when necessary to protect human beings. Corporate speech that is misleading or manipulative would not have a claim of protection, even if a lie uttered by a human being might.[37] Listeners are not assisted by such lies or manipulation, and there is no autonomy interest on the part of the corporation to put in the balance. No one's autonomy is advanced by being lied to by a corporation in a market transaction. And even if it were advanced in the odd case, such lies would adversely affect the market in such a way as to undermine the ability of other corporations to fulfill their social and institutional role of building economic wealth.

One type of regulation that a sophisticated version of the theory would allow would be requirements that corporations disclose certain facts about their business activities. A prominent example from recent years was the provision in the Dodd-Frank Act requiring companies to disclose their use of "conflict minerals" mined in the Democratic Republic of the Congo or one of its neighboring countries.[38] The Court of Appeals for the District of Columbia Circuit struck down the rule, saying it operated to coerce speech from those corporations contrary to the First Amendment.[39] The court equated the disclosure with a government effort to "compel" a company to "confess blood on its hands."[40]

That court decided incorrectly from the perspective of the autonomy frame. The company itself has no claim to be free of coerced speech since companies themselves have no autonomy interests violated by such a rule. And the rule would have operated to give more information to market participants who would use such information to decide whether to associate with the companies in question. In other words, a disclosure requirement would have been autonomy *enhancing* to human beings, and that is all that matters.

Another example of a distinction the autonomy theory would make that does not appear in current law arises in campaign finance regulation. Under this frame, corporations should receive only those speech protections instrumental in protecting the interests of listeners and those who self-identify by associating with the company. If this rationale had guided the Court's reasoning in *Citizens United*, the interests of the corporation itself would not have counted in the constitutional calculation. What would have counted was whether the expenditure of corporate funds in support of a candidate or cause advanced the autonomy interests of those on the receiving end of the communication or those who voluntarily associated with the company. This would mean that the Court could have taken into account considerations as to whether the communication was misleading or duplicative of material or points of view already available. Neither would be appropriate if the communication were coming from a human being, but both *would* be appropriate in a situation in which the speaker's interests do not count but the listeners' do. Moreover, when considering the associational interests of listeners, the importance of disclosure is increased: how does one decide whether to associate with a company unless the company's political expenditures are known?

One crucial takeaway from this discussion of corporate speech is this: even the autonomy theory—which prioritizes the interests of human beings—would protect corporate speech some of the time. It would also allow it to be regulated some of the time. Like the marketplace theory, it requires lines to be drawn.

III. Public Debate and Self-Governance

The final prominent rationale for protecting speech is to protect debate about issues of public importance. The free speech clause, the argument goes, is meant to protect the mechanism of democracy. Democracy depends on a well-informed population making decisions to govern itself based on thorough public debate. The right to free speech is not based on a search for truth nor founded on a belief about the nature of human beings. Rather, it is about democracy. Justice Brandeis articulated this theory when he said:

> Those who won our independence believed . . . that freedom to think as you will and to speak as you think are means indispensable to the discovery and spread of political truth; that,

without free speech and assembly, discussion would be futile;
... that public discussion is a political duty, and that this should
be a fundamental principle of the American government.[41]

In this view, the core of the First Amendment is discussion about
politics and public issues. The closer we are to that core, the more
protective the Constitution becomes. As Cass Sunstein has described, under this theory "The First Amendment is principally
about political deliberation."[42]

A number of prominent scholars from across the ideological
spectrum have supported this view of free speech,[43] but it is most
closely associated with the work of Alexander Meiklejohn. Meiklejohn's famous metaphor to explain the theory is the town meeting,
"called to discuss and, on the basis of such discussion, to decide
matters of public policy."[44] In such a meeting, a commitment to
free speech would not require "unregulated talkativeness" but a
fair opportunity to discuss the important matters at hand.[45] Self-
governance requires an exploration of competing views on issues of
public importance but does not require each speaker to receive an
unlimited right to chatter on. The allocation of the right to speak
would not turn on who pays for the microphone but would depend
on who has a right to participate, most likely based on membership
in the governed polity and with some kind of equality norm in play.

Many advocates for limitations on campaign finance depend explicitly or implicitly on the self-governance theory. While protecting political speech is central to the free speech clause, this theory
acknowledges that some regulation of speech can be consistent
with the furtherance of self-governance. What is important is that
views are heard and vetted, not that each person gets to speak as
much or as loudly as he or she would like. As megaphones are not
permitted in a town meeting, the theory is attentive to the problem of some voices drowning out others. As the right to speak at a

meeting is allocated according to rightful presence in the meeting rather than willingness to pay, it is more open to limits on campaign contributions and expenditures. As good self-governance at a town meeting depends on the hearing and consideration of a range of views, the theory is more open to the possibility of ensuring that all viewpoints are heard even if it means subsidizing some.[46]

Another way to conceptualize these notions is to consider free speech protections as informed not only by a liberty norm, but an equality norm as well. The libertarian tendencies of the other two theories are mitigated in the self-governance theory by a dedication to the equality of citizens taking part in the democratic process.

Occasionally, the Supreme Court will make reference to political discourse being at the core of free speech protections.[47] But for the most part, this theory is respected more as a matter of rhetoric than of jurisprudence. The Court will use it as an additional reason to protect political speech but is skeptical of using it to refuse protections for non-political speech. The key reason for this skepticism is that if taken seriously, the theory would mean that novels, scientific inquiry, music, poetry, and entertainment could be censored with a low level of governmental justification. That is, with only a rational justification, a town could ban the sale of *Lady Chatterley's Lover* (as Boston once did),[48] a state could stop children from buying violent video games (as California once tried to do),[49] or local drugstores could be prohibited from advertising prices (as Virginia tried to do).[50] In other words, if a self-governance theory restricts its protections to discussions of matters that roughly fall into a class of "political speech," a huge swath of communication—much of which strikes many of us as quite fundamental and important—becomes regulable. Lines are fairly easy to draw, but the lines feel uncomfortable to many.

Two answers arise to this dilemma. The first is that the self-governance theory protects not only political speech, but also communication necessary to build good citizens. As Meiklejohn himself announced after his theory was criticized, "There are many forms of thought and expression within the range of human communication from which the voter derives the [necessary] knowledge, intelligence, [and] sensitivity to human values. [These], too, must suffer no abridgment of their freedom."[51] The second is that many forms of communication that do not *appear* to be about politics are, in fact, about politics or other matters of public interest. Pornography, for example, can be seen to contain a point of view about the role of women and the propriety of sexuality; music often raises very poignant questions about the human condition; comedy—even when it is not explicitly about politics—necessarily asks whether laughter is the best medicine.

The problem with these two answers is that they erode the distinctiveness of the theory and its capacity to make the necessary distinctions. If everything is politics, then nothing is not. If everything helps us make political decisions, then nothing does not. When discomfort around where the line has been drawn causes us to blur the line, the benefit of a clear line is lost.

Self-Governance Theory and Corporations

The self-governance theory is often used to bolster the arguments against corporations receiving the benefit of free speech protection. Under this theory, corporate participation in democratic self-governance has both a "who" problem and a "what" problem. The "who" problem is that corporations are not citizens. They do not have the right to vote, and they are not a part of "we the people," the source of authority and legitimacy for democratic governance.[52] The "what" problem is about what corporations do with their voice. The claim is that their participation skews the debate in predictable ways, weakening the ability of real citizens to self-govern.

Both the "who" and the "what" problems are serious. In the Meiklejohn town meeting, it is difficult to imagine how a corporation takes part. A corporation is not a "who"—it does not have a human form to occupy a seat or a physical mouth to proclaim a point of view. Moreover, to allow a corporation to argue a point of view within a political debate duplicates the views of those human beings within the business, in effect giving the business two turns at the microphone. And as Meiklejohn explained, the self-governance theory does not value unfettered talkativeness and does not allow participants more turns than are necessary to have all points of view heard and vetted.

As for the "what" problem, opponents of corporate involvement in politics point to concrete evidence of its pernicious impact within democratic debate. After *Citizens United,* Uber spent \$600,000 on a voter referendum in Seattle;[53] a Super PAC funded by coal companies and other corporations spent \$2.6 million on a 2016 judicial election in West Virginia;[54] various companies spent \$30 million to fight a California referendum mandating labels on genetically modified foods.[55] Chevron spent \$2.5 million in support of Mitt Romney in 2012; Trump's inauguration was bankrolled by energy, telecommunications, and tobacco companies.[56]

The critics say these efforts are not public-spirited. Because of the profit orientation of business, one can assume these expenditures are intended to pay off for the companies. Some corporate decision makers may be mistaken or even self-interested, but there is little doubt that most corporate expenditures are *intended* to affect politics.[57] This fact alone is enough to provide corporate skeptics with a basis for opposition to corporate political speech rights. Corporate speech in the political sphere is seen as illegitimate because it is intended to skew the debate in its favor and comes from an entity that does not have a right to participate.

Usually implicit—and frequently explicit—in these critiques is the assertion that corporate input has an ideologically conservative effect on political debate. Corporate speech is used to oppose progressive candidates, environmental protections, increases in the minimum wage, and additional disclosures to employees or consumers. The bias is predictable, significant, and, because of the nature of corporations, likely to endure. Humans change their mind and sometimes act in their role as citizens from altruism, patriotism, or self-sacrifice—that is, in some way contrary to self-interest. But because a corporation is always going to be oriented toward business success, it is much less likely to be persuaded to change its position by way of public debate. Though there may be an occasional exception, corporations as a group should never be expected to act except pursuant to self-interest, enlightened or not.

These are strong arguments. But neither the "who" problem nor the "what" problem is enough to exclude corporations from political debate completely. The "who" problem is not as intractable as it might at first seem, simply because groups and associations are not typically excluded from political debate. The PTA is not a citizen or even a person, but it is not unimaginable for a town meeting to recognize its spokesperson to make a statement. The same goes for the Kiwanis Club or the local chapter of the Daughters of the American Revolution. As we have discussed, sometimes human beings gather together for various reasons—including politics—and it would be an odd self-governance theory indeed if those groups were excluded from the democratic conversation. When in *Citizens United* Justice Kennedy equated corporations to "associations of citizens," this was what he was getting at.[58] Not all corporations are rightly seen as such associations, but *some* are.

The "what" problem is less damning than it might seem as well. Even if we assume that all corporate speech is in service of the corporation's self-interest, that fact alone does not make it an illegitimate addition to the self-governance discourse. Humans advocate for their own self-interest quite often—the town meeting is not necessarily a collection of altruists—and those self-interested views are relevant to public debate. My advocacy for a new park in my neighborhood is not out of order at the town meeting even if my kids are among those who will enjoy it. Similarly, the question of what hurts or helps business interests is a valid element in public debate. The fact that a corporation has a selfish point of view in such matters does not in itself make it an illegitimate part of the discussion. And even setting aside self-interest, corporations at times have expertise that is valuable in public discourse. Should the town finance its new road project with current income or with a bond issue? Perhaps a banker—or a bank—would have insight.

What's more, because corporations have perpetual existence and must plan for the long term, they often have a longer time horizon than individual human beings. Natural persons often incorrectly prioritize the near term, whether by way of miscalculation or selfishness.[59] Corporations, in contrast, cannot do that if they expect to survive. Humans do not need to take the long view and are often swayed by emotions and ideological commitments that would be odd indeed in the corporate setting. General Electric may be keenly interested in seeing a president elected who will appoint regulators kind to its business interests. But it is unlikely to spend hundreds of millions of dollars on campaigns aimed at advancing conservative views on social issues such as abortion, as the Koch brothers do, for example. Taking the corporate viewpoint into account in the metaphorical town meeting can indeed bias the debate—but this biasing might be a helpful corrective to expected biases among the human actors. Corporations can take the long view, setting emotions and prejudice aside even when humans cannot.

When companies do involve themselves in the political sphere, it is not always with the ideologically conservative angle that many opponents assume. When affirmative action in college admissions programs was challenged at the Supreme Court in 2015, forty-five major corporations—including Apple, Shell Oil, Johnson & Johnson, and Pfizer—filed a brief asking the Court to continue to allow race-conscious policies.[60] After the Supreme Court's ruling allowing same-sex couples to marry, several states responded by adopting "religious freedom" laws that purported to expand the right of people and businesses to object. Some of the most vocal opponents of these bills were corporations. Walmart, for example, spoke out forcefully against the bill proposed in its home state of Arkansas and is credited with almost singlehandedly bringing about its defeat.[61] When North Carolina passed a law in 2016 requiring transgender students to use the bathroom of their biological sex markers, the outcry from the business community was forceful. Bank of America and American Airlines, two large employers in the state, were among scores of major businesses who spoke out against the law.[62] President Trump in late 2017 sharply reduced the size of two national monuments in Utah by over two million acres, the largest rollback of federal land protection in the nation's history. Statements of opposition erupted from Patagonia, REI, and other outdoor outfitters.[63] "The President Stole Your Land," read a banner that popped up on Patagonia's website. As one commentator explained, "Big business tends to be more enlightened than smaller business interests rooted in only one place, because the broader your perspective, the bigger your market, the less tolerant you can afford to be of idiosyncratic regional prejudices."[64]

Finally, the dire warnings about corporations buying elections are overblown. The amount of corporate money in play in elections is quite small in comparison both to the amount of spending from individuals and to the total cost of campaigns.[65] Spending by publicly traded corporations appears to have accounted for less than 1 percent of the total independent expenditures in the 2012 presidential cycle,[66] and data indicate that corporate spending in 2016 was in the same ballpark.[67] If spending from private corporations is added, then the impact might be somewhat larger. But much of that spending was through shell companies as a conduit for the contributions of wealthy individuals. Such use of shell corporations is problematic, but it does not mean that corporations were trying to influence the election. It meant that *individuals* were trying to influence the election.

We may have a "dog that didn't bark" question.[68] One might expect corporations to care quite a bit about who is elected president of the United States. The difference between Mitt Romney and Barack Obama or Donald Trump and Hillary Clinton is likely to be material in a range of industries from financial services to energy. One example is the Keystone pipeline project. It was clear during the 2016 election that Trump was a supporter and Clinton was not. For energy companies, that political difference was likely to create real economic differences, perhaps to the tune of billions of dollars. But we did not see significant levels of independent spending in the 2016 cycle by such companies.[69] The dog did not bark.

Why not? Perhaps the difference between Trump and Clinton on that issue was mitigated or outweighed by differences leaning the other way. Perhaps the companies did not want to run the risk of public relations problems if their efforts to influence politics were brought to light. Perhaps the rational economic calculus was to stay on the sidelines: the expected value of a dollar spent to influence the outcome of the election was less than the expected value of a dollar spent other ways. Perhaps because a company has to consider the long term, it is better for it to stay disengaged in any given election. Even if the calculation on a specific election is clear, perhaps it is better over time to be (and be seen as) a company that remains on the electoral sideline. Companies have every reason to be risk averse; one bad decision in the short term can impose lasting costs. Target, for example, still labors with the image of being the company that supported an anti-LGBT gubernatorial candidate in Minnesota some years ago.[70] All of this is to say that it is highly unlikely that corporate spending has materially influenced any presidential election in the modern era. The amount of corporate spending has been a paltry slice of all spending, and its influence has very likely been swamped by other factors.

That is not to say that worries about corporate involvement in politics are not valid. The *potential* for outsized impact is there, and corporate spending does seem to have had material effects in scattered down-ballot races and referenda.[71] For example, according to Public Citizen, in the 2016 cycle there were thirty-seven ballot initiatives in seventeen states where at least one side was mostly funded by corporate interests. In contests in which the corporate-backed side faced opposition, the corporate-backed side outspent the opposition by 33–1. And the side supported by corporations ended up winning 62 percent of the time.[72]

This is worrisome to be sure. But these instances of corporate successes in politics are merely a subset of the larger problem of money in politics; they do not pose a distinctive problem of *corporate* spending. And focusing on corporate spending, ironically, lets the big individual spenders, such as Sheldon Adelson and the Koch brothers, off the hook. The public-discourse theory should lead us to worry just as much about the Kochs' money as Coke's money.

This discussion of corporate speech within the self-governance theory reveals a proposition that aligns with what we saw with the previous two theories. Corporate speech is not excluded by force of the theory, though there may be reasons to limit some corporate speech some of the time. Lines must be drawn.

In our thinking about corporations and speech, the choice of animating theory will make a difference in how we analyze the various regulations of corporate speech. None of the theories would exclude corporate voices from the protection of the free speech clause, but none—if properly understood and applied—would protect corporate speech from all regulation.

Understanding how these theories apply to corporate speech helps us discern which limits on corporate communications deserve skepticism and which merit deference. But we cannot make final decisions until we look at the purpose of corporations and ask which kinds of corporate speech regulations advance that purpose and which inhibit it.

SIX

Speech and Corporate Purpose

In all of the theories of the First Amendment, one must make distinctions between speech receiving the highest level of judicial protection—what courts call "strict scrutiny"—and speech receiving less. Each theory protects speech for a reason. And each theory offers rationales to be marshaled to restrict speech. Under the marketplace theory, speech can presumably be regulated to protect against market "defects." Under the autonomy theory, speech can presumably be regulated if the speech conflicts with the autonomy of another or is not conducive to the building of a fully realized human life. In the public-discourse theory, courts should uphold regulation of speech that is not about matters of public concern or skews the nature of public debate outside permissible bounds. As becomes obvious even from merely stating these basic understandings, it becomes clear that these lines can be exceedingly difficult to draw. How much of a market "defect" should count? How does a court know if speech conflicts with the autonomy interests of another? How much skewing of public debate is too much? It's complicated. And this is even without adding the complexity of the question of corporate status.

The corporate question is also difficult. There are reasons to protect corporate speech under each construct but also reasons under each to be skeptical of unbridled corporate speech. An honest judge or scholar would be hard-pressed to explain why corporations should receive no speech rights. By the same token, the judge or scholar would be hard-pressed to explain why corporations should be able to claim the same speech rights as natural persons. A jurisdiction that limited corporate speech rights in some way would not, by that reason alone, necessarily butt up against the best understanding of free speech principles. The best understanding of free speech principles would suggest that corporations should receive some, but not all, of the free speech rights of natural persons.

As we evaluate how to make these distinctions, one half of our initial proposition remains to be discussed. The question of corporate speech turns not only on the purpose of speech, but also on the purpose of corporations. Corporations should receive those speech rights necessary in order to achieve their institutional and social role. That is, corporations as a class of institutional speakers should be able to speak on the questions that arise about that role, and individual corporations should be able to speak on matters that are germane to their own business. The further afield a corporation roams from those areas of focus, the less persuasive its claim to First Amendment protection will become.

A necessary corollary to this is that the speech rights of corporations may be constitutionally curbed to ensure that they—both as a class and individually—satisfy their institutional and social role. Requirements that corporations disclose financial and other information material to those who engage with them, for example, should be unassailable even if such requirements might be constitutionally problematic if applied to natural persons.

The theoretical justification for this construct is straightforward. Under any of the theories of free speech, corporations should be able to claim some, but not all, rights of natural persons. To draw the lines required, we also need to consider the connection and relationship between the corporation and the speech in question. The corporation's claim will be strongest where the speech is necessary to pursue and satisfy its social and institutional goal of producing economic well-being through the sale of goods or services.

This general proposition makes sense from both sides of the analytical construct used through this book, from the perspectives of both speech theory and corporate theory. In the former, the closer the speech hews to a corporation's business, the stronger the claim that the corporation's expertise and point of view are valuable additions to the marketplace of ideas, the robustness of public debate, and the ability of natural persons to achieve and act on their autonomy. From the perspective of the latter, the closer the speech hews to a corporation's business, the stronger the claim that the speech is an important component of its efforts to satisfy its social role. Also, because truthfulness and the availability of material information is so crucial to the working of the marketplace, the First Amendment will not be offended by an insistence on corporate disclosure and the truthfulness of corporate statements.

Speech that is further afield—less germane to a company's business—has less of a claim of value since it will be less distinctive and depend less on the expertise that the corporation can bring to bear. Such corporate speech will also more likely duplicate speech already present. Speech that does not relate to the core purpose of the corporation is more likely to be motivated by managerial overreach than advancement of corporate purpose. Such managerial overreach is disfavored regardless of one's theory of the corporation. That is, one need not believe that shareholders own the corporation to believe that managerial overreach is inappropriate.

Let us apply this categorization to specific corporate speech problems and see if it derives results that make sense.

I. Commercial Speech

Much of what a corporation communicates relates to the products and services it sells, whether it be automobiles, smoothies, or speedy deliveries of your most recent Internet purchase. The Supreme Court ruled four decades ago that this "commercial speech" receives a level of constitutional protection, and it was correct to do so.[1] Such communication is essential for businesses to satisfy their institutional role. If the government could stop businesses from telling purchasers about their goods and services, it would be a death knell. A company must be able to engage in the communication necessary to exist.

The Court does not grant commercial speech the highest level of constitutional protection, however, but instead applies something akin to intermediate scrutiny in equal protection cases. For example, the Court recognizes that the government can require truthfulness in commercial communication. For other substantive restrictions of commercial speech, the government must show the regulation is based on a "substantial interest" and that the regulation is no broader than necessary to serve that interest.[2] This is a greater level of judicial inquiry than the review of non-speech economic regulations, which typically receive only "rational basis" review, requiring the government to show a mere "legitimate" interest.[3] But it is less than the strict scrutiny provided to most content-based restrictions on speech, which requires the government to show the regulation is narrowly tailored to serve a "compelling" interest.[4]

This intermediate level of protection seems correct under the analysis proposed. Companies need protection for speech necessary for them to do the work they are supposed to do. At the same time, markets do not work without a number of restrictions on speech.

There is no institutional or market reason, for example, to protect the right of a company to lie or mislead about the goods or services it sells. Economic markets depend on truthfulness. A company that lies will survive longer than it should, thwarting the market process of forcing out inferior products and services and undermining the institutional role and purpose of corporations and the free market more generally. The Court is correct when it says that commercial speech should be subject to a higher obligation of truthfulness than non-commercial speech.

Note that the obligation of truthfulness for commercial speech is based on the content, not the entity status of the speaker. If an individual is participating in the market to buy or sell, then an obligation to speak truthfully can be attached to that individual's communications without offending the Constitution. The rationale for such an obligation springs less from the nature of the speaker than the nature of the marketplace. But most commercial speakers are corporate entities and agents of those entities. A rule that would allow individuals to lie in the marketplace but prohibit corporations and other business forms from doing so would create disincentives to create those legal entities. So even if one would believe that lying about proposed commercial transactions as an individual would advance the marketplace of ideas or enhance the speaker's autonomy, a rule allowing such would undermine the marketplace and the ability of corporations to fulfill their institutional purpose.

One problem that arises within commercial speech doctrine is the difficulty of distinguishing between speech that is commercial and speech that is not. The general rule is that if speech is in regard to a transaction of some kind, then it is commercial. But there are myriad examples of corporate communications that skirt the line between commercial and non-commercial speech. For example, Clint Eastwood's *It's Halftime in America* commercial for Chrysler during the 2012 Super Bowl struck many viewers as an endorsement of the Obama administration's automobile industry bailout.[5] If an endorsement, then it would probably best be seen as political speech. If an advertisement to build the brand and sell cars, it would be commercial speech, worthy of a lower level of constitutional protection and thus subject to a higher level of government regulation of its truthfulness, among other things. Those kinds of shape-shifting ads may be the exception rather than the rule, simply because most businesses will not want to cloud their commercial messages with political ones. But in other instances, businesses may want to build a brand awareness by opining—or appearing to opine—on a host of public issues, and courts will need to determine whether such ads are commercial or political speech. Courts typically look at the dominant purpose of the communication, and while there may be judicial mistakes in particular cases, such an inquiry is not only appropriate, but also unavoidable.[6]

One could argue that *all* communication by for-profit entities should be deemed commercial speech, even if the apparent topic of such communication is political or social. Some serious scholars have suggested this, and the argument is not frivolous.[7] A corporation is always acting in furtherance of its profit-making nature, the argument goes, even when it engages in communication that does not appear on its face to be about buying or selling products. A company may be talking about abortion, affirmative action, or which presidential candidate it prefers, but its ultimate goal in those communications is to survive as a profitable company. And even when profit is not its goal *in fact*, we should assume it to be as a matter *of law*.

There is much that is attractive about this view. It would recognize the difference between corporations and natural persons based on the limited, profit-making purpose of the former. And while it would offer some (intermediate-level) protection for corporate speech, it would cordon off the highest level of free speech protection from corporate speakers. This line would be fairly straightforward to adjudicate.

In the end, however, defining all corporate speech as commercial speech is not the correct doctrinal answer, because of both the nature of corporations and the value of their speech. The central social role of corporations is to create and build wealth. That requires more than the mere buying and selling of products and services or the mere communication about the buying and selling of products and services. Corporations can and should be players in the public space in ways that go beyond that.

Corporations must depend on infrastructure, employees, an effective financial system, and a regulatory framework that protects them and holds them accountable. Corporations may and should weigh in on public debate concerning these things, all of which are germane to the business of individual companies and the social role of corporations in general. The points of view of corporations on these topics are important to the public debate because of their importance not only to corporations themselves, but also to the individual human beings who are members of the citizenry.[8] To lower the protection of all corporate speech to an intermediate level of scrutiny on the basis of the corporate status of the speaker is to offer insufficient protection for some important speech.

II. Fraud

There is one area of commercial speech doctrine that should be applied more generally to the speech of all for-profit corporations, no matter the topic: an insistence on truthfulness. Outside the business context, the Court has been reluctant to uphold laws that punish individuals for lying because of the notion that "there is no such thing as a false idea" and a worry that enforcing veracity would chill speech.[9] The Court assumes that counter-speech, rebuttal, and reputational constraints should do whatever is necessary to hold liars accountable. This reluctance to punish falsehoods has not extended to commercial speech, however, and should not extend to corporate speech generally. Because of the economic nature and purpose of the corporation, the First Amendment should not prohibit jurisdictions from insisting on a higher degree of truthfulness and disclosure for corporations than for natural persons.

Laws have long punished businesses for fraud in the sale of products or in the issuance of financial securities. There is no constitutional problem with these rules, as the success of the market—whether for consumer goods, securities, or even labor—depends on the existence of truthful information.[10] Lies and misrepresentation pervert the market, allowing inefficiencies to survive longer than they otherwise should. Punishing companies that lie about their products or their financial well-being does not raise particularly difficult questions for free speech law.

The difficult cases arise when the speech at issue is both material to the business enterprise of the company and also related to political and social issues. These cases can be constitutionally tricky. The most famous one was *Nike, Inc. v. Kasky*, a Supreme Court case about the truthfulness of statements Nike made regarding the labor practices of its manufacturing contractors in Southeast Asia.[11] Nike had been accused of complicity with its contractors' violations of labor and human rights. In response, Nike issued a series of statements in press releases, letters to newspapers, and letters to colleges and universities defending its practices. Californian Mark Kasky sued Nike under California consumer protection law, alleging the company's statements were misleading.

The case was poised to be, in the words of *New York Times* reporter Linda Greenhouse, "the most important ruling in years on the constitutional contours of commercial speech."[12] The California Supreme Court had ruled that Nike's statements were commercial speech, and as such, they were subject to liability for being misleading or false. Nike, for its part, argued that the statements amounted to political speech "belong[ing] at the very core of . . . First Amendment protections."[13] If political speech, they would be protected from run-of-the-mill fraud law. Nike's allies—which included the ACLU, industry groups, and even the AFL-CIO— argued that holding such statements to be commercial speech would make the definition so broad as "to include virtually every corporate utterance."[14]

In the end, the case fizzled. The Supreme Court dismissed it as "improvidently granted," meaning the Court discovered a procedural defect that allowed it to avoid the merits of the free speech arguments.[15] Perhaps the constitutional questions were too complex. In any event, the questions raised by the case were left unresolved.

In my view, neither side in *Nike* applied the correct analysis. The communications at issue were not commercial speech as traditionally understood. Nike was trying to protect its brand, to be sure, by defending itself against allegations of labor abuses. But the letters and press releases were not advertisements selling shoes. The speech at issue was not pure political speech either. The speech concerned matters that pertained to how Nike's products were produced. Even though the company's positions concerned matters of political import, they related to the company's operations. Such information was material to consumers' decisions about whether to purchase the product.

Once we recognize the materiality of the information, the corporate-purpose analysis leads us to recognize that there is no legitimate reason why the Constitution would stand in the way of a public insistence that the company tell the truth about these matters. Just as an untruth in an advertisement about a product or fraud in a prospectus for an issued security skews the marketplace, so does a company's statements about its own behavior. In fact, this is the kind of misrepresentation that has multiple skewing effects. Many consumers are more likely to purchase shoes from, and many investors are more likely to invest in, a company that does not mistreat its workers. Business partners are more likely to enter into agreements with a company less likely to embarrass them. And even if the effect on the marketplace is not always in those directions (perhaps some investors would bid up the price of companies that exploit workers), there is little doubt that the information is material. From an economic perspective, a company's misrepresentations about its labor practices are no less harmful to the market than misrepresentations about its products or the bonds it issues.

Nike argued at the time that it was unfair for its statements about these matters of public concern to be subject to fraud standards. But this is a situation in which the nature of the corporate entity makes a difference in the analysis. Corporations are money-making entities that, left to their own devices, will tend to bend the truth to gain a competitive advantage. We acknowledge this fact when we institute broad protections against corporate fraud in the consumer and securities markets. But this tendency to bend the truth to gain a competitive advantage is not restricted to those markets or venues. The answer to Nike's argument about unfairness, then, is to ask, "Compared to what?" The playing field is not level in the *absence* of regulation. Companies that can gain competitive advantage by engaging in fraud and misrepresentation in regard to matters of public concern will have an economic incentive to do so. Human beings do not have the same set of incentives and are unlikely to have the same impact with their words. It is not offensive to the First Amendment to recognize the difference between corporations and human beings on this ground.

Another worry behind the reluctance to punish fraud and misrepresentation on the part of natural persons is a more general concern about discouraging or "chilling" speech. The Court fears that if individuals can be held responsible for any white lie or inaccuracy, whether "made in a public meeting" or in "personal, whispered conversations within a home," they will be less willing to speak in the first place.[16] But these concerns do not apply with the same weight to corporations. A corporation does not "speak" as constantly as natural persons for the mundane and obvious reason that it typically "speaks" through agents and after some kind of internal decision-making process. The statements of a handful of executives are attributable to the company for purposes of corporate liability, and those executives are accustomed to taking care when they speak publicly to avoid allegations of securities fraud. The only speech that would likely be "chilled" by a broader obligation of truthfulness would be messages that are strictly true but so close to the line of misrepresentation that cautious corporate decision makers would judge them not worth the risk. Such speech is unlikely to be so important to risk the significant market-skewing effects arising from allowing untruthful corporate communications.

The "chilling" effect is a phenomenon that arises from the nature of legal line-drawing. Under typical free speech thinking, it is better to overprotect speech—even lies—because of the worries that individuals will self-censor when they get close to the legal line. But corporations have less reason to self-censor. A corporation's desire to build its brands and influence current and potential customers, investors, and employees will likely overcome any potential chilling effect.

Moreover, when considering corporate speech, one must recognize that a protective rule allowing businesses to lie and make misrepresentations will impose costs on consumers, employees, shareholders, and the economy generally. These harms count in the constitutional calculus when we are talking about entities whose very purpose is to advance economic well-being. Because of their economic nature and purpose, corporations can be held to a higher level of truthfulness than natural persons without raising constitutional problems.

A duty to speak truthfully will attach to information that is "material," a concept that has a long doctrinal history within corporate and securities law. "Materiality" has a well-settled definition when it comes to securities law—whether the information has a "substantial likelihood" of affecting the decision making of the "reasonable" investor.[17] Over time, this inquiry has collapsed into a question of harm: if investors can show harm, then the misrepresentation was material; if they cannot, then it was not.

For purposes of our constitutional analysis, materiality would not be limited to information important to investors but would extend to other stakeholders. Even where shareholders are the focus of corporate law duties to disclose, constitutional law need not be so narrow. If, for example, a piece of information is material to the "reasonable" employee, customer, bondholder, supplier, or other stakeholder, then a governmental entity can require the company to be truthful in its disclosure. The Constitution would not pose an obstacle for the same reason it would not pose an obstacle to holding Nike liable for lying about its labor practices. If the market cares about the truthfulness of a statement, then it is not unconstitutional for a corporation to be required to be truthful. This is not to say that the government *must* punish such misrepresentations (though as an economic matter it almost certainly should), but only that the Constitution would allow such punishment.[18]

III. Disclosure and Coerced Speech

Companies have long been subject to a wide range of disclosure obligations, from financial reports, to nutrition information on food packages, to safety announcements about the chemicals present in the workplace. Even though these disclosure obligations are in a strict sense "coerced" in that they arise from government requirements, they generally have not been seen as raising First Amendment difficulties. The public interest in accurate information is strong, and the speech interests are slight whether one uses a marketplace-of-ideas, autonomy, or public-discourse framework. Forcing a company to disclose the amount of saturated fat in its peanut butter is not the same as forcing a child to recite the Pledge of Allegiance. Our free speech theory and doctrine has never been so ham-fisted as to see them as identical.

Under our corporate purpose analysis, these disclosure obligations are easily justified. On the one hand, corporations exist to advance economic goals; an obligation to disclose meaningful information to those who interact with them in the marketplace furthers those goals. On the other hand, corporations will have legitimate property-based claims to the confidentiality of information they need to survive. For example, the interest in disclosure is not enough to force Coca-Cola to make public the secret formula of its eponymous product.

While most disclosure obligations have been unproblematic, two kinds of cases pose tricky constitutional issues. The first are laws that mandate affirmative disclosures on non-financial matters. The second arise under programs mandating corporate contributions to government-sponsored advertising campaigns. The latter are not really disclosure cases but have been seen as raising issues of coerced speech.

An example of the first class of cases is the recent controversy over the federal government's proposal that companies disclose their use of "conflict minerals" from the Democratic Republic of Congo, which is rife with violence, civil war, and human rights violations. The Securities and Exchange Commission's rule would require "publicly-traded corporations that use certain minerals in their manufacturing to either certify their products as 'conflict-free,' or disclose the countries and mines that are the source of the raw materials."[19] The National Association of Manufacturers sued to stop the rule, saying that such a requirement was a violation of the

First Amendment's limits on coerced speech. The organization claimed that forcing companies to disclose their use of minerals not certified as "conflict free" was akin to branding them with a "scarlet letter."[20] The Court of Appeals for the District of Columbia circuit, usually seen as the second-most-important court in the country, agreed that the rule forced a company "to confess blood on its hands."[21]

This case and others like it should come out differently under the corporate-purpose analysis. These disclosures do not pose existential difficulties for the companies involved—this is not like a forced disclosure of a piece of intellectual property crucial for the company's survival. Moreover, the information required is germane to the companies' work and business. The proposed rule would not have required a company to opine on broad issues of public interest unrelated to the company, and the disclosures relate only to factual matters pertinent to those interacting with the company in the marketplace. In other words, the information sought is material in the marketplace, and having the information easily available allows the marketplace to work more smoothly and efficiently.

It is easy to understand why companies did not want to disclose this information. If a company is taking advantage of human suffering to bring a product to market at a low price, of course it would prefer to keep that fact hidden. It may indeed be a "scarlet letter" in the sense that a company is forced to admit something that will cause reputational harm. But as an economic matter, there is no difference between these disclosures and the requirement that Hershey disclose the amount of sugar and fat in a candy bar, that Goldman Sachs disclose a downgrade in the value of its portfolio of mortgage-backed securities, or that Pfizer admit Viagra can cause vision loss. These disclosures bring truthful information to the marketplace that is vital to stakeholders when making decisions about a company's products, investments, or employment opportunities. Under the corporate-purpose analysis, these kinds of affirmative, truthful disclosures raise no serious First Amendment problem.

Nor does the First Amendment care whether the disclosures are for the benefit of shareholders or other stakeholders. Courts sometimes seem to assume that disclosures material to the securities markets are less problematic for the First Amendment than disclosures to consumers or employees. The federal court struck down the conflict mineral proposal in part because the rule was, according to the Securities Exchange Commission, "quite different from the economic or investor protection benefits that our rules ordinarily strive to achieve."[22] The court emphasized the rule was "not 'intended to generate measurable, direct economic benefits to investors or issuers.'"[23] The commission's intention to achieve "overall social benefits" and "a humanitarian purpose" was disfavored, even though those benefits would flow to market participants (such as individuals in the supply chain) and arise from market forces (such as consumer avoidance). The benefits would not flow to investors, so the court applied special scrutiny.

That reasoning is terribly flawed. Nothing in the First Amendment prioritizes the interests of equity investors over the interests of consumers, employees, communities, bondholders, or other stakeholders. That hierarchy is a function of corporate law—a very contentious one, in fact—not free speech law. As a matter of free speech law, what matters is the social and institutional role of corporations, and there is no reason to prioritize one set of stakeholders over others.

These cases reveal a difference between corporate speakers and natural person speakers. Typically, the free speech clause protects speakers from coercion because the Constitution creates what the Court has called a "general rule, that the speaker has a right to tailor the speech" and such right extends to "statements of fact the speaker would rather avoid."[24] It would certainly be a violation of the First Amendment if, for example, a city required humans to display on their doorpost their total annual income or a list of recent charitable contributions. But in this respect, corporations are differently situated, and it is simplistic for courts to transpose the holdings of the coercion cases from situations concerning humans to those concerning corporations. Humans have privacy concerns that are not as salient for corporations since corporations are by nature public entities that voluntarily engage in the public space in order to satisfy their reason for existing in the first place. The coerced speech doctrine—quite important in protecting human beings from oppression by the state—should not be used to allow corporations to hide information that is necessary or helpful for the market to work.

Yet corporations do have an interest in not being forced to state *opinions* with which they disagree. As Justice Robert Jackson said over seventy years ago in the Pledge of Allegiance case, "If there is any fixed star in our constitutional constellation, it is that no official, high or petty, can prescribe what shall be orthodox in politics, nationalism, religion, or other matters of opinion or force citizens to confess by word or act their faith therein."[25] Jackson's statement describes the rights of "citizens," but it makes constitutional sense to extend it to corporations—although not for the same reason. For individuals, the harm of coercion is primarily one of autonomy, which is not an interest shared by corporations. But it makes sense to extend the right to corporations because of the importance (again) of truthfulness in the marketplace. Consider a hypothetical law requiring companies to fly a flag or display a photo of the president. If corporations can be made to appear to support points of view with which they disagree, then current or potential stakeholders will be unable to discern whether those views should be attributed to the companies or not. A rule against coerced speech protects corporations from being forced to make statements that can be, in many cases, misleading. It is one thing to force companies to disclose truthful information helpful to stakeholders' decisions; it is quite another to force companies to say things that make stakeholders' decisions more difficult. Thus a state could not mandate a company fly a rainbow flag because it might be misleading for a company to claim solidarity with LGBTQ people when it is not in fact supportive. But the company could be required to post a notice to employees of their right to file discrimination complaints on the basis of sexual orientation. That is truthful information relevant to a stakeholder. The conflict minerals case is more akin to the latter than the former. It should have come out the other way, upholding the SEC rule.

Another set of tricky cases that raise questions of coerced speech springs from the genuinely odd laws that impose taxes on certain businesses to subsidize industry-wide advertising efforts. The best-known example is the National Beef Promotion and Research Act, which requires all beef producers to contribute $1 per head of cattle sold to the "Beef Checkoff Fund" to promote the sale and consumption of beef and veal.[26] You may remember the ad campaign "Beef: It's What's for Dinner," with the gravelly voices of Robert Mitchum and Sam Elliott extolling the American virtues of a good steak or burger. Those ads were funded by the beef checkoff. Other agricultural products have similar advertising campaigns financed with mandatory contributions from members of the industry. "The Incredible Edible Egg," "Pork: The Other White Meat," and "Got Milk?" are all creatures of these checkoffs.

These checkoffs seem like particularly bad public policy, especially since the government ends up imposing costs on producers (and presumably consumers) to advertise competing products. The end result is generally a higher cost of food, and the more prevalent the checkoffs, the less likely any industry will gain an advantage.

And any advantage is likely to be haphazard and inefficient. But are they flawed as a constitutional matter?

For a while, the Supreme Court said yes. Checkoffs were the subject of numerous attacks on First Amendment grounds, with dissenting producers claiming that they were being coerced to subsidize messages with which they disagreed and that undermined their own efforts to distinguish themselves within the industry. The first time the Court considered these checkoffs, it ruled in favor of the dissenters in a case about the mushroom checkoff, saying "First Amendment values are at serious risk if the government can compel a particular citizen, or a discrete group of citizens, to pay special subsidies for speech on the side that it favors."[27] A few years later, however, the Court changed its mind. Upholding the beef checkoff, the Court explained that the advertising at issue should instead be considered "government speech" since the Secretary of Agriculture had ultimate control over the content of the campaign. And "Citizens may challenge compelled support of private speech, but have no First Amendment right not to fund government speech" even "when the funding is achieved through targeted assessments devoted exclusively to the program to which the assessed citizens object" rather than through "general taxes."[28]

These are difficult cases. If the Court is correct in the beef checkoff case that the ad campaign is government speech, then there is no constitutional problem with a tax to fund it. The government can have a point of view on issues ranging from the healthfulness of smoking to the need to recycle soda cans to the importance of driving sober. Government speech on such issues, like all government activities, needs to be funded. It is not a violation of the free speech clause to require individuals or companies to pay their share.

The problem, however, with these checkoffs is that the ads do not look like government speech and are not disclosed as such. Indeed, most of the ads mislead about the source of the speech. The beef ads, for example, often ran with a tagline "Funded by America's Beef Producers."[29] From the standpoint of the targets of the campaigns, they appear as though they are advertisements from the industry itself about the virtues of beef, pork, mushrooms, or eggs. These ads are misleading in two ways: with regard to the source of the "voice" and to the undifferentiated nature of the product. These ads skew consumers' decisions away from dissenting producers who wish to distinguish their product from the crowd. This skewing can have existential implications for small producers already suffering a disadvantage in the marketplace.

These checkoff cases are different from the forced disclosure cases discussed above. The key is not whether companies are being forced to communicate things they would rather not communicate. That is a quite common and unproblematic implication of a range of disclosures necessary for the marketplace to work. But when the forced communication is misleading and poses existential implications for dissenters, the dissenting businesses have a serious constitutional claim. For these reasons, the Court was likely correct to strike down the mushroom checkoff and wrong to uphold the beef checkoff.

Finally, a word about the cigarette warning cases discussed in the previous chapter. Given the discussion so far, a requirement that cigarette companies disclose the risks of their product to their intended consumers is entirely unproblematic. The market is assisted by a requirement that businesses warn about the risks of their products, and a failure to warn can be misleading to consumers. Just as gas stations must warn about the flammability of gasoline, pharmaceutical companies must warn about possible allergic reactions to ibuprofen, and lawn mower manufacturers must warn about the risk of propelled gravel, cigarette manufacturers cannot normally raise complaints about the constitutionality of requirements to warn about the latent risks of smoking.

Cigarette companies know this. Their arguments raised in response to the Food and Drug Administration's more graphic warnings proposed in 2009 assumed the propriety of the old, textual (and largely ineffectual) warnings that had appeared on packages since the 1960s. Their arguments against the new warnings were that the new ones were *too* graphic for the companies to be required to carry them.

If the cigarette companies were individuals, their arguments might carry significant weight. There should be a difference under the First Amendment between forced speech that is slight—a requirement to put a license plate on your car, perhaps—and forced speech that is more salient—a requirement to put a license plate on your car that proclaims the state motto as your own.[30]

But here again is where the corporate status of the claimant should make a difference. Companies selling products should not be able to claim a First Amendment defense to forced speech about those products unless that speech is misleading. Are graphic warnings about cigarettes misleading? Not in a strict sense—the proposed warnings stated known scientific truths about the dangers of smoking, such as "smoking can kill you" and "cigarettes cause strokes."[31] The only way the warnings could be misleading would be if the visual, photographic additions to the textual warnings were so salient as to mislead consumers into believing cigarettes were more dangerous than they are. That is not an impossible argument to make—just a difficult one.

IV. Corporate Political Spending

Now the most pressing question: How and to what extent can corporate political spending be curbed? Ought corporations have the same right as individuals to spend money in elections?

The level of spending in political campaigns is almost undoubtedly a significant problem for our democracy. In the absence of a meaningful public financing option for campaigns at all levels of government, the advantages offered by the availability of money will be significant.[32] A system of electoral politics that depends on private money tends to skew results toward those who have resources—not in every case but enough of the time to matter. Candidates need money and will implicitly or explicitly offer access in exchange for that money. That access will, in turn, skew policy results since candidates with greater exposure and adherence to the views of the moneyed interests will have more resources and thus tend to win more often. The dominance of moneyed interests in politics will delegitimize the results of elections for those below the top tier of the economic ladder who feel systemically disadvantaged by the system's fixation on money.

These defects in the system are serious, pervasive, and intractable. The Supreme Court is wrong to say that such effects, taken together, do not provide a sufficiently compelling justification for limits on independent expenditures in elections.[33]

The Court has acknowledged the dangers of direct *contributions* to campaigns, saying that such gifts can be limited because they either are or can appear to be akin to bribes. But the Court has refused to extend its reasoning to *expenditures*—that is, money spent to support a campaign or candidate that does not flow through that campaign's or candidate's own treasury. The Court's mistake has both doctrinal and empirical elements. The doctrinal mistake is to see direct expenditures as implicating free speech interests more directly than contributions do. Both are expressions of viewpoints, to be sure. But spending money for a candidate is no closer to the heart of the free speech clause than giving the same money directly to the same candidate. That is a distinction without a First Amendment difference. The empirical mistake is to assume that "independent" expenditures are in fact independent.[34] The concerns about the reality and appearance of the improper influence of moneyed interests on campaigns are identical—or nearly so.[35] The Supreme Court can and should be more nuanced in its campaign finance doctrine, and it can and should be more sophisticated in its understanding of how the world of politics works.

These problems with the dominance of money in politics—and the problems with the Court's rulings—are the same whether we are talking about spending by corporations or natural persons. Money's corrosive effects on politics derive from politicians' unquenchable thirst for it and its skewing effects on policy, not its source. One cannot justify particularly harsh regulation of *corporate* spending on the problem of money's corrosive influence since the corporate identity of the speaker does not lead to more influence. A million dollars from Sheldon Adelson has the same impact in an election as a million dollars from Chevron or the United Auto Workers. A dollar of skewing is a dollar of skewing, regardless of its origin.

The question is whether there are reasons to worry about *corporate* money in politics. As discussed in the previous chapter, in some ways there is reason to worry *less* about corporate money. Because of their purpose and nature, well-managed corporations have to take the long view. They have to be mindful that their customers, employees, shareholders, and suppliers come from varying places in the political spectrum. Heavy involvement in the political sphere will frequently come at a cost; many companies will want to avoid those potential costs. But there are three ways in which corporations pose special considerations because of their nature and purpose.

Difference 1: Corporations Are Collective Enterprises

The first distinction arises from the fact that a corporation is a collective enterprise. Though the Supreme Court's analysis of corporate rights often assumes that the corporation is a mere association of its shareholders, a corporation is more accurately seen as a collective enterprise of a variety of actors.[36] A number of different stakeholders contribute to the work of the firm, and they all deserve to know how their contributions are being used. This need for disclosure extends to the values espoused by the corporation using corporate assets.

One implication for this insight is that a requirement that a corporation disclose its political spending to its stakeholders would not be constitutionally problematic. As with the mandated disclosures of other truths about the corporation, as long as the disclosures are truthful and material, they would be consistent with the purpose of corporations and would not raise free speech problems. The Securities and Exchange Commission has invited comments on a proposal requiring corporations to disclose their political spending, but as of this writing no rule has been promulgated.[37] The Commission should not drag its feet for constitutional reasons. Requirements that corporations disclose their political activities would be constitutionally appropriate, even if such a requirement for natural persons would be problematic.

Also, in considering the collective nature of corporations, we should avoid mistaking corporate law rules for constitutional doctrine. Corporate law in the United States has long assumed that the primary obligations of management run toward a corporation's shareholders first and foremost. Many instances of corporate speech in the political arena are examples of corporations using their political influence on behalf of shareholders or management at the expense of other stakeholders. Corporate opposition to minimum-wage increases or consumer protection laws, for example, operate economically as a transfer of wealth away from employees and consumers and toward shareholders and management. Such efforts are rarely questioned since we simply take for granted that it is proper for corporations to use their resources to fight *for* shareholders and *against* employees and consumers (and others).

But such assumptions are not required as a matter of constitutional doctrine, even if they are assumed as a matter of corporate doctrine. For example, a jurisdiction could—without offending the First Amendment—require that corporations vet their political involvement with a broader range of stakeholders. In effect, a state could say, "Yes, corporations can speak, but we want to ensure such speech advances the interest of the corporation as a whole."

The Supreme Court equated corporations to "associations of citizens" in *Citizens United*.[38] It would not be inconsistent with the First Amendment for a state to define such "associations of citizens" to include all those who contribute meaningful investments to the company and to seek to protect all such citizens within the corporation from having their contributions used against them. Corporate law has long been a matter of state law. If a state wanted to define corporations as being an association of citizens that included employees, customers, and other stakeholders, the First Amendment would not stand in its way.

Difference 2: Corporations Are Dominated by Management

One of the distinctive characteristics of corporations is their dominance by management. A company's various stakeholders entrust their contributions (whether money, effort, infrastructure, or knowledge) to managers who are empowered to use those assets for the betterment of the corporate collective. This managerial empowerment is the key mechanism corporations use to overcome what would otherwise be significant collective-action and coordination problems among the various contributors. This "separation of ownership and control," as it is known in corporate law parlance, poses difficulties that matter when it comes to corporate political involvement.[39]

A risk exists that management will act in its own interests rather than those of the company and its stakeholders. Corporate stakeholders are likely to be passive and detached from matters of corporate governance, and the law makes it difficult for shareholders and other stakeholders to have their preferences heard within the firm. This is by design, and the benefits often outweigh the costs of such an arrangement. The risk of managerial disloyalty is a part of all corporate decisions, but the risk is greater when it comes to political involvement. Directing corporate assets to further a point of view contrary to the views of the company's contributors not only misuses funds, but also forces contributors to subsidize the expression of views contrary to their own. And because management by its very nature overcomes collective-action and coordination problems, corporations can engage in political activity more easily, more often, and on a broader range of issues than membership associations with less managerial power.

These disjunctures between managerial behavior and stakeholder views are not only a problem for corporate law. They have constitutional meaning as well since they are a function of law—corporate law's protection of managerial prerogative—and amount to the kind of harm that the coerced speech doctrine is meant to avoid.[40] This concern is not just for the interests of shareholders. Other stakeholders—whether employees, communities, or creditors—make contributions to the firm that may be highjacked for purposes of influencing political outcomes with which they disagree.

The Court in *Citizens United* assumed that the availability of corporate law remedies mitigated this concern. The Court said there was "little evidence of abuse that cannot be corrected by shareholders through the procedures of corporate democracy."[41] This assumption has been roundly criticized, and rightly so.[42] The likelihood of shareholders influencing management's decisions about political expenditures through mechanisms of corporate "democracy" approaches zero, especially without a comprehensive obligation on the part of corporations to disclose and vet such expenditures. And even if shareholders could influence management, there is no "procedure[] of corporate democracy" in the United States that empowers *other* stakeholders to have a say on such matters. U.S. corporate law does not obligate management to consider the views of non-shareholder stakeholders when making any decision, including decisions about political involvement. Indeed, when corporations speak politically, it is commonplace that they speak out *against* the interests of one stakeholder or the other, such as proposed increases in the minimum wage or greater consumer protections. One can safely say the one constituency never targeted for opposition by corporate political speech is management.

One might argue that the ability to abandon their link to a company—to exit—is a sufficient remedy for shareholders and stakeholders who believe their contributions have been commandeered by management for political purposes with which they disagree. Or one could suggest that by voluntarily making investments in companies, stakeholders have accepted the risk that their contributions will be aggrandized for political purposes by management.[43] If they do not like it, they can get out.

This argument has weaknesses from both corporate and constitutional law perspectives. Among the key stakeholders, shareholders have the most ability to "exit" a company by selling stock or to decline to "enter" by refusing to buy it. But it is not correct to say that shareholders consent to the misuse of their investments by management, nor is it correct to say that exit is cost-free or seamless. Also, the threat of exit fails to impose any real costs or constraints on management unless so many shareholders sell their shares because of a political expenditure that the stock price falls—a very low-probability event.[44] The notion of voluntariness often used in corporate law theory is quite circular in that it bases a justification of the legal rule of deference to managers on the assertion that shareholders have consented to that legal rule.[45] The assumption of knowledgeable consent is especially unpersuasive with regard to corporate political involvement. Shareholders should not be seen to have consented to managerial use of corporate funds for political activity when the involvement is not salient or disclosed and when the rule whether to allow such involvement is itself contested and in flux. And the notion that other stakeholders have consented is almost laughable, given the lack of disclosure and the cost of exit.

As a matter of constitutional law, the question of consent is the flip side of the question of coercion. The Court has not said in any of the coerced speech cases that coercion must be akin to physical entrapment or mandate. There are always choices; the question as a constitutional matter is how costly the alternatives are. Even the schoolchildren who refused to say the pledge in *Barnette* had a choice—they could go to a private school.[46] But the Court thought that was too high a price to pay. If the alternative to the required speech comes at a sufficiently high cost, then the Constitution sees coercion.[47] In the context of corporate political spending, it is quite costly for a potential shareholder to avoid investments in companies that empower managers to spend corporate funds for political purposes since all (or nearly all) companies are so structured. The choice is between being involved in the market or not, and it is virtually impossible to avoid the market or divest completely. And both choices are quite costly. The cost of avoiding a marketplace where the involvement of corporations in politics is both universally allowed and cloaked in secrecy is sufficiently high that an investor's decision to be involved looks more like coercion than choice.

These arguments are even more powerful for employees and some other stakeholders. It is not persuasive to say that employees consent to having management use the corporate surplus created by their labor for political expenditures. Employees and other stakeholders have even less say in management than shareholders, and management under current corporate law is not required to take into account their interests in making political decisions any more than other corporate decisions. What's more, the costs of refusing or exiting employment are significant. In other words, the typical mechanisms of organizational influence—voice, exit, and lawsuit—are not available to employees or other stakeholders to any meaningful extent.[48] All of this is true even when a company's political involvement is disclosed and salient. And the reality is much short of that.

The most that can be said about the consent of shareholders and other stakeholders is really a matter of implied or "constructive" consent. Because the corporate form endows management with power to make decisions on behalf of the collective, those who contribute to the firm implicitly consent to the use of their contributions *for the betterment of the firm as a whole*. If management is advancing the interests of the firm, it is not persuasive for stakeholders to argue their resources are being coercively used to advance causes contrary to their own views. But if management is using corporate resources to advance its own selfish interests or the interests of one stakeholder against another, the argument that such speech is coercive becomes stronger. This is in addition to the argument that such speech does not serve to advance the ability of the firm to fulfill its social and institutional role.

The key implication of this corporate difference—that corporations are run by management agents—is that it would be consistent with free speech guarantees for a government jurisdiction to insist that corporate political involvement be limited to matters germane to the company's business. When corporate speech is germane to a company's business and aimed at advancing the company's fortunes as a whole, it is less likely to be coercive to the company's stakeholders, and its claim to constitutional protection will be stronger. Speech that is further afield will be more regulable, as it is more likely to be coercive.

In this light, consider the statute at issue in *First National Bank of Boston v. Bellotti*. The Massachusetts law prohibited the use of corporate funds to purchase advertising "for the purpose of . . . influencing or affecting the vote on any question submitted to the voters, other than one materially affecting any of the property, business or assets of the corporation."[49] The Court struck down that law as too limiting of corporate speech. Under the reasoning explained here, that statute would have stood on much firmer constitutional ground.

Difference 3: Corporations Are Advantage-Seeking Economic Entities

A third way in which corporations pose particular difficulties for free speech doctrine is their economic nature. Humans are more pluralistic and multifaceted than corporations. Human beings are motivated by self-interest, but it is the rare human who reduces all decisions to the economic. It may be possible for for-profit corporations to care about the non-economic, just as humans can care about the economic. But the nature of corporations is that they are uniquely and particularly focused on, and involved in, the workings of the economic and financial markets. Such is their nature and purpose, and they survive over time only if they are successful in that respect.

The fact that corporations are economic in nature is not itself a constitutional problem, and economic motivations for speech should not necessarily receive a lower level of constitutional respect than non-pecuniary motivations. Outside the public debate theory of free speech, there is no intrinsic reason why economic arguments and values are constitutionally different from the charitable. And even within that theory, democratic debate often depends on economic matters and would benefit from the views and expertise of those involved in the market.

It matters that corporations are economic in nature because their pecuniary motivations turbocharge the benefits of political involvement and pervert the competitive marketplace. The marketplace is a product of legal infrastructure and a function of legal rules. Within that infrastructure and those rules, companies must compete to succeed by improving their products and services to satisfy their customers and investors. But if the legal rules themselves are subject to corporate influence, then companies can succeed not by improving their performance in the marketplace, but by skewing the legal framework in their favor.[50] This can come at the expense of their competitors, customers, employees, and even the public interest.[51]

Economists call this kind of behavior "rent seeking," not because corporations are landlords but because "rent" is an economic term that describes extra-competitive gains flowing to the owner of some resource. Market imperfections such as monopoly power or externalities lead to an increase in "rent," and economists agree that rent seeking imposes a deadweight loss on society.[52] It distorts the marketplace away from efficiency, empowering lower-performing companies to survive and making survival for better companies more difficult. Companies with political influence will find it easier to rent-seek. As Anat R. Admati has written, "In the name of maximizing shareholder value, profit-maximizing corporations gain economic and political power that they often use successfully to benefit at the expense of society."[53] Leo Strine and Nicholas Walter explain that "corporations will only make expenditures in favor of candidates who will help the corporation make money," and those candidates will "favor the corporations' regulatory agenda . . . rules whereby the corporation is more likely to externalize the negative costs of its activities on to society."[54]

Because corporations are economic entities, they will be indifferent between a competitive advantage gained because of political influence or because their products and services are cheaper or better. If it is cheaper to buy success by spending money on politics, then companies will do so. If they can lobby more effectively for regulatory or legislative benefits by promising political spending on behalf of their supporters or against their opponents, corporations will do so.[55] Their economic nature makes them eager to use this strategy, even when it creates net losses for society as a whole. As legal scholar Robert Sitkoff has argued, "In the market for legislation . . . corporations might be particularly pernicious rent seekers."[56] You can think of this rent seeking as a negative externality of corporate political spending. And these externalities are likely to be worse from corporate political activity than the activity of natural persons.

The implications that businesses are economic rent seekers cut the opposite way from the implications of the second consideration that businesses are dominated by management. Under the latter, we should worry most about speech far afield from the company's business. As we have seen, the reasons to protect corporate speech are strongest when the speech is germane to the company's business. However, the propensity to use political expenditures to rent-seek is a more acute problem the closer the contested matters are to the business of the corporation. Corporations do not have an incentive to skew the marketplace if they won't benefit from it, but when they can achieve economic benefits from their political activities, they have every incentive to do so.

Even though the free speech interests of corporations are at their strongest when the speech in question has the tightest connection to their business activities, there are legitimate—and, at times, even compelling—reasons to be skeptical of corporate speech claims that operate to benefit the companies economically. One needs to be careful here—economic benefit does not necessarily mean the companies' speech claims and interests are illegitimate. But cor-

litical spending is misused to benefit either the management itself or a subset of those involved in the corporation at the expense of the others. In areas outside of speech, it would be beyond question that a jurisdiction could establish governance rules to protect against such misappropriation or misallocation of funds. Nothing in free speech doctrine should prevent jurisdictions from protecting against the use of political activities that misallocate or misappropriate corporate resources. The First Amendment does not include within it an allegiance to shareholder or management primacy.

4. *That corporate political activity be limited to matters and questions germane to the company's business.*

In general, corporate speech serving the social and institutional purposes of corporations should be protected; corporate speech further afield can be regulated at a lower level of governmental justification. This is simply a matter of applying the oldest statement about corporate rights in our jurisprudence: Chief Justice Marshall's statement two centuries ago that a corporation "being the mere creature of law, possesses only those properties which the charter of its creation confers upon it either expressly or as incidental to its very existence."[63] Speech necessary for corporations to fulfill their social role within a competitive marketplace is "incidental to" the "very existence" of those companies. Speech not germane to that role should not be seen as incidental and is thus open to regulation.

5. *That corporations should abide by anti-discrimination and public access laws, even when contrary to corporate beliefs, when exceptions to those laws would give those companies an advantage in the marketplace.*

Companies are rent-seeking entities by nature. It would be inconsistent with the role of corporations for some to be able to skew the marketplace by asserting speech and association rights in ways that provide competitive advantages.

For those who carry deep skepticism of corporate power, the analysis of the last two chapters will likely seem too protective of corporate constitutional prerogatives. While this evaluation of both the purpose of the right to free speech and the role of corporations would suggest the need for significant adjustments in current doctrine, corporations will still be participants in the public square. Those who worry about corporate influence in public policy and corporations' dangerous tendency to extract rents in the market for legislation will be disappointed with the lack of easy constitutional remedy. They also will be disappointed that under this analysis, corporations are people too—at least some of the time.

The best hope for constraining corporate power and legitimizing corporations' participation in the public square is not an adjustment in constitutional doctrine but an adjustment to corporate governance within corporate law. And there, the best hope is not to deny corporate personhood but to champion it. That is the focus of this book's final chapters.

SEVEN

More Personhood, Please

Corporations are people, at least some of the time and for some purposes. But are they *citizens?*

Corporations often tout their corporate "citizenship" in their web pages, annual reports, public relations materials, and advertising. They point to their charitable giving, sponsorship of beneficial activities, and kindness toward the communities where they have facilities. They have corporate citizenship departments and issue corporate citizenship reports.[1] Paid consultants and nonprofit institutions help corporations achieve and maintain good corporate citizenship. My home institution of Boston College houses the Center for Corporate Citizenship, which claims hundreds of corporate members and hosts trainings and conferences attended by corporate executives and managers.[2]

No corporation is saying that it is a citizen in the legal sense. Corporations do not have passports; they cannot vote. As scholar Adam Winkler explains, "Citizens are generally thought to be natural people who belong by law to one country. They are members of a political community who owe their allegiance and support to a particular polity."[3] Neither is true for corporations as a descriptive matter.

It is sometimes difficult to figure out what "citizenship" means even for natural humans. Disagreements erupt over who can claim citizenship, what rights it bestows, and what obligations it imposes.[4] Our ideas of citizenship evolve and mutate over time.[5] At its core, however, the concept of citizenship captures a bundle of rights and obligations. Many of these would be impossible to apply or attach to a corporation or any collective body, as they are typically thought of as pertaining only to individuals. A corporation cannot serve on a jury, for example, because such service is intrinsically connected to one's having a physical presence in the courtroom. A corporation cannot be conscripted into the armed services because such service is intrinsically connected to having a body that is pressed into service. A citizen's right to vote cannot be exercised by a corporation any more than by any other collective bodies, whether they be unions, the PTA, or the Boy Scouts.

Yet some aspects of citizenship could be extended to corporations. There is nothing in the nature of the corporation that would protect it from being charged with treason, for example. Corporate bodies are subject to criminal proceedings for malfeasance of many kinds, and there is nothing in the crime of treason that would make it impossible to impose it on a corporate entity. If a corporation chartered in the United States used corporate assets to give aid or comfort to our enemies, then a treason charge might be appropriate. One could imagine a U.S.-based corporation engaging in, say, corporate espionage of a presidential election in service of a hostile foreign power that would subject not only its principals but also the business itself to an indictment for treason.

The only difficult question is whether corporations *ought* to have an obligation of national loyalty sufficiently strong that its violation would merit a charge of treason. The best answer is that a corporation chartered in the United States and receiving legal personhood and the rights going along with it, constitutional and otherwise, should be held to a duty of loyalty to the country. Different countries may make different judgments on this front, but there is nothing inherent in the corporate form that makes it nonsensical to hold businesses to an obligation that they not give aid and comfort to a nation's enemies.

Holding corporations to an obligation of national loyalty sufficient to support a duty not to engage in treason is an outgrowth of the fact of corporate personhood. For those who oppose corporate constitutional rights, one implication of their views would be that corporations would be free from any sense of national loyalty. Relieving corporations from obligation would certainly be an odd outcome of an effort to control corporate power.

It is also possible to hold corporations to the more abstract obligations of citizenship. Some scholars point to a duty of "alignment" and participation.[6] The former describes a sense of national loyalty, a sense of identification with and support for the nation's interests. The latter is a duty to participate in the public life of the nation. Corporations could be held to both as a matter of norm; that is exactly how such obligations are enforced for individuals.

Even scholar Bruce Ackerman's suggestion that "citizenship" requires a consideration of the public good could be projected onto corporate entities, either by norm or by legal rule.[7] It may be "a plain social fact," as scholar Amy Sepinwall has argued, "that corporations are not expected to participate in the central institutions of citizenship."[8] But that is a function of corporate law rules as much as social expectations. Our social expectations of corporations are a function of corporate law rules, which can be changed. It is important to evaluate whether corporate assertions of citizenship rights undermine the citizenship rights of natural persons or the obligations of corporations to pursue their institutional roles as producers of goods and services and creators of wealth. In other words, the discussion about corporate citizenship depends not only on the definition of citizenship, but also on the nature of corporations, how we conceptualize them, and what we require of them.[9]

There is one area of the law in which corporations are already deemed citizens. Under Article III of the Constitution, federal courts can hear only certain kinds of cases. One kind arises under so-called "diversity jurisdiction," defined as lawsuits in which the parties are "citizens of different states."[10] This provision arose from the worry that parties from one state would not get a fair hearing in the courts of another state. Federal courts would stand ready to adjudicate disputes between "citizens of different states." Early in the nation's history, the Court determined that corporations could take advantage of diversity jurisdiction. It did so initially not by looking at the state citizenship of the company but the state citizenship of the shareholders.[11] The Court disregarded the corporate form for diversity purposes. That rule became untenable over time as corporations became more complex, with thousands and then millions of shareholders from a variety of states. Now, for purposes of federal diversity jurisdiction, corporations are deemed "citizens" of the state where they are incorporated and have their principal places of business.[12] While natural persons are citizens of only one state for diversity purposes, corporations are often citizens of two. This means individuals will find it easier to get into federal court than corporations will.

Bestowing "citizenship" under Article III may be problematic for strict textualists. But for most constitutional scholars, the application of diversity jurisdiction to corporations makes sense as a functional matter. The risk of state court bias against out-of-state parties is present when the party is a corporation just as when the party is a natural person. And as we saw in chapter 3, corporations must be able to depend on fair judicial process to fulfill their social and institutional role as creators of economic wealth. This right of citizenship flows from both the purpose of the right and the nature of corporations.

But when corporations and others discuss corporate "citizenship," it is not an assertion of a right to vote, serve on a jury, or even sue in federal court. Instead, it is shorthand for a description of the role of corporations in society, in the public space. The assertion of corporate citizenship is more a recognition of obligations than of rights. Corporations are "good citizens" when they are magnanimous toward the communities where they do business, generous with charitable contributions, mindful of the interests of employees and other stakeholders, conscientious about their environmental impacts, and willingly compliant with law. "Corporate citizenship" indicates the corporation has obligations that extend beyond the financial—that a corporation can and should be measured not only by its bottom line, but also by its behavior toward a broad group of stakeholders and society.

The general parlance of corporate citizenship is more about corporate governance than constitutional law and norms. It represents the notion that corporations have a social contract that goes beyond the creation of value for shareholders and that such a contract should have implications for the ways in which the corporation is managed. As a matter of internal corporate governance, "citizenship" stands in contrast to "shareholder primacy," the notion that shareholder interests are the sum by which corporations should be measured. This is not to say that those who advocate for corporate citizenship believe it should be mandated by law, for that is a separate question. But it certainly implies that managers should be *permitted*—as a matter of law—to take non-shareholder interests into account when making decisions on behalf of the company.

Citizens United and *Hobby Lobby* changed this discussion. Instead of corporate citizenship being about obligations, both cases were about corporations asserting rights. In neither case did the Court say the corporations were "citizens," but it certainly assumed that the corporation's role in the public space was that of an entity—a legal person—that had a right to participate in public debate, with rights vis-à-vis the state. And the Court, in both cases, used assumptions about the role of corporations in society that eased the Court's path to recognizing corporate rights of speech and religious conscience. In *Citizens United*, the Court saw corporations as offering important opinions about matters of public concern beyond the merely commercial. In *Hobby Lobby*, the Court recognized the possibility that corporations care about more than just the bottom line and could have religious commitments worthy of deference.

One might claim that both cases are consistent with the work of progressive corporate law scholars who had argued for decades in favor of corporate "citizenship" as a matter of corporate governance. They argue that corporations have a role in the public space; they urge the limitations of corporate "conscience"; they suggest corporations should accept commitments that go beyond the bottom line. *Citizens United*'s and *Hobby Lobby*'s recognition of corporations' assertions of political and religious rights were, perhaps ironically, consistent with those progressive arguments. If progressive corporate law scholars were a more influential bunch, one might even suggest that *Citizens United* and *Hobby Lobby* were their fault.[13]

But as described above, a belief that corporations have moral and social obligations going beyond shareholder value does not inevitably lead to the results the Court produced in *Citizens United* and *Hobby Lobby*. The ruling in *Hobby Lobby* was an embodiment of shareholder primacy, allowing the religious views of the dominant shareholders to be projected onto the corporate form, notwithstanding the views of the company's other stakeholders. Moreover, allowing corporations to gain religious exemptions from laws that govern other similarly situated businesses upends the level playing field of the market. In *Citizens United*, the problem with the Court's ruling was not its acknowledgment that corporations have something to contribute in the public space. The problem was the Court's unwillingness to see how money distorts democratic decision making and how unique aspects of the corporate form can make these distortions worse.

These finer points have been lost, even among progressives. Many on the ideological left have begun to champion shareholder primacy as a way to fight back against *Citizens United*, in effect abandoning the notion of corporate citizenship in the process. They argue that corporate political activity goes against shareholder value, that corporate political activity should be subject to shareholder veto, and that the money spent for political campaigning belongs to shareholders. These are all ideas that depend on and embody shareholder primacy, motivated by an urge to push corporations back into a narrow, private sphere where they attend to a constricted set of obligations and do not roam about in the public square. Instead of embodying hope for change, corporate "citizenship" is now a source of fear.

Because of this fear, we are seeing calls to have both constitutional and corporate law retreat. In constitutional law, the notion that "corporations are not people" embodies a simplistic response that would undermine genuinely important advances in several areas of constitutional jurisprudence. In taking up the banner of shareholder primacy, the opponents of *Citizens United* are sacrificing the potential for real change in corporate governance that corporate citizenship could offer.

Corporate citizenship is worth saving.

I. The Downside of Corporate Personhood

Perhaps it is not easy to hear that corporations deserve constitutional rights, especially when the implication of that argument is that corporations can assert rights in ways that seem selfish and contrary to public policy. Corporations can contribute to political campaigns? They can spend money to influence outcomes in ballot referenda or votes in Congress? Corporations can speak out on public issues in ways that affect public opinion? For those who are skeptical of any exercise of corporate power or influence in the public space, these assertions of rights are an affront.

But that is more about *corporate* citizenship than *constitutional* citizenship. What the "corporations are not people" crowd is railing against is not at heart that corporations are asserting constitutional rights. Rather, they are objecting to the underlying ends the corporations are seeking through their rights claims. These objections deserve to be acknowledged.

To date, many of the instances in which corporations have raised constitutional claims have been for reasons that—frankly—stink. Corporations do not want to print warnings on cigarette packages or disclose their use of conflict minerals.[14] They want to be able to buy and sell patients' medical information.[15] They want to sell video games that put children in the virtual act of graphically raping, murdering, and dismembering victims.[16] Corporations are now the plaintiffs in roughly half of all First Amendment cases in federal courts,[17] not because they believe it is their moral duty to fight for the right to espouse politically unpopular views in the public square. No; they are asserting constitutional rights to resist regulatory obligations. And they have gained sufficient success that some scholars now see the First Amendment operating as a constitutional get-out-of-regulations-free card, much as the due process clause was used by businesses in the *Lochner* era to resist progressive-era restrictions on corporate power.[18]

Corporations have asserted rights vis-à-vis the public in order to benefit the corporation narrowly, seemingly contrary to the public interest. And when corporations participate in the political sphere, their resources are brought to bear disproportionately to benefit the affluent classes, from which their management and prominent shareholders spring. Corporate treasuries—the products of contributions by all stakeholders—are used to fight on behalf of the managerial and financial elite and against others who contribute to the companies' success. Corporate money is often used to fight against minimum-wage increases, workplace safety regulations, consumer protections, and government initiatives to retard global warming.

Not all assertions of corporate rights would survive under the analysis offered by this book, but many probably would. As a constitutional matter, one cannot devise a defensible theoretical rationale to exclude corporations entirely from the protections of the free speech clause and other constitutional provisions without either undermining the ability of corporations to meet their institutional and social role or offending the purpose and meaning of the constitutional rights at issue.

As a matter of constitutional law, then, we have to be willing to accept corporations as persons. That does *not* mean, however, that we must accept corporate power and prerogative. For this we have a possible remedy. The solution to the problem of corporate personhood in the *constitutional* space is corporate personhood in the *corporate* law space.

II. The Inhumanity of Shareholder Primacy

We need *more* corporate personhood, not less.

Under current corporate governance law and practice in the United States, corporations are managed primarily to serve the interests of shareholders. There is disagreement among corporate law scholars as to whether this servitude is legally required. Some say that the "business judgment rule" of judicial deference to man-agerial decisions is so elastic that it gives sufficient discretion to managers that they in effect do not owe an enforceable duty to shareholders.[19] But even with such discretion, there is little doubt of the hierarchy among those who contribute to, and hold stakes in, American companies: shareholders come first. Executives cannot admit to prioritizing other needs or interests without fear of suit.[20] Only shareholders can vote at annual meetings, elect directors, or sue those directors to enforce fiduciary duties. Shareholders are the only ones who can propose resolutions in proxy materials or pro-pose and approve changes in bylaws. As the chief justice of the Del-aware Supreme Court warned in 2015, executives who take care of an "interest other than stockholder wealth" breach their fiduciary duties.[21] This stands in contrast to the corporate governance laws of a number of other nations, which hold corporations and their executives to a broader range of obligations.

Even though corporations are collective enterprises reliant on the contributions of a range of stakeholders, they are managed by people who operate within a set of norms and laws that direct their atten-tions primarily to shareholders. While the business judgment rule might protect managers who choose to take into account a broader set of interests, they are certainly not required to do so by anything within corporate governance. And when they do, even if the business judgment rule protects management from lawsuit, it does not protect them from punishment in the market. Shareholders—that is, Wall Street investors—usually have sufficient market power to punish a company that does not put them first.

The law and the market act as though the corporation is a sim-ple enterprise that can be managed robotically by always asking one question: What is best for shareholders? There will be disa-greements about the answer, and sometimes being magnanimous toward other stakeholders may be the best strategy for benefiting shareholders. But the ultimate goal is clear, and executives who disregard that goal do so at the risk of lawsuits or termination.

Shareholder primacy means that corporations not only will, but also should take care of the environment, workers, community, or ethics only when doing so serves the shareholders in the end. In the words of the Delaware Supreme Court, a corporate "board may have regard for various constituencies in discharging its responsibilities, *provided there are rationally related benefits accruing to the stockholders.*"[22]

Consider the situation in which a board of directors of a public company faces a choice between two alternatives. Option One benefits its employees but imposes real, long-term costs on shareholders. Option Two benefits shareholders at a cost to employees. Also assume that the board has determined that Option One's benefits to the employees would far outweigh the costs to shareholders, while Option Two's benefits to shareholders would be swamped by the costs to employees. From a social perspective, as well as from the perspective of the company as a whole, Option One is the better choice. But most lawyers would advise directors to choose Option Two. If they choose Option One anyway, the directors might be able to protect themselves from suit through the deference of the business judgment rule—but only if they lie about their motivation and suggest that they are really acting in the long-term interests of the shareholders. While directors might get away with such subterfuge some of the time, it will clearly be a reach in other situations. The shareholder plaintiff law firms and the courts will eventually catch on. Moreover, the market will punish the managers severely. The stock price will fall, making it harder for the company to finance its ventures, perhaps even targeting the company for takeover. Companies whose managers act as though they have duties to stakeholders other than shareholders are squeezed out of the market.

Shareholder primacy not only narrows management's view of its responsibilities, but it also squeezes that view temporally, incentivizing a focus on the short term.[23] Shareholders increasingly expect high returns quarter to quarter, and if they do not get such returns, they punish the companies failing to provide them. Shareholders do not have loyalty to the companies whose stock they hold; the only loyalty is that which is earned by high returns. If they don't get the returns they expect, they can sell quickly and easily. What's more, most shareholders are not actually investors in the companies whose stock they own. Most own stock not because they gave the company money but because they purchased stock from someone who purchased stock from someone who purchased stock from someone (and so on) who did. Sure, some shareholders buy their shares at the time of the initial public offering. But the vast majority of shareholders buy their stock on the secondary market from another shareholder, who at some earlier point (months or minutes before) had also purchased shares in the secondary market. If a stock is not performing in the short term, there will always be a more appealing company. Not surprisingly, the average stock turnover in the United States is over 150 percent a year.[24] Short-termism is made worse by the size and power of institutional shareholders such as mutual funds, pension funds, hedge funds, banks, and insurance companies, which now own more than two-thirds of all public corporate equities and have their own incentives to maximize the value of their portfolios in the short term.[25]

Shareholder primacy restricts management, keeping it focused on the short term and on shareholder interest. Any company that wants to take the long-term view—or thinks it important to take into account the interests of other firm stakeholders—will be punished in the securities markets.[26] Shareholder primacy thus guarantees that talk from management about the company's responsibility toward society will likely be primarily for show; it will mean that legal requirements intended to protect other stakeholders will be seen as costs rather than commands.[27] Any externality that does not translate into a corporate cost will be disregarded. Non-shareholder stakeholders are left to depend on mechanisms outside corporate law to protect their interests. These mechanisms primarily appear in the form of express contracts or government regulation, both seriously imperfect.

This hierarchy within corporate law has the predictable effect of moving resources from employees to holders of shares. A rule of shareholder primacy creates a push toward greater economic inequality since most of the capital in the United States is held by those already well off. Data show that less than half of Americans own any stock at all,[28] and the richest 10 percent of American families own as much as 80–90 percent of the nation's stock wealth.[29] So decisions made within companies will tend to preference the interests of the already-well-off over the interests of the less-well-off working class, exacerbating economic inequality.[30] What's more, the efforts of corporations in the public space will have a similar effect. If corporations use their constitutional personhood to fight for a decrease in the capital gains tax while opposing increases in the minimum wage or overtime pay, inequality is the result. If corporations lobby for regulations making it more difficult for people to get out of credit card debt in bankruptcy or easier for companies to defund pensions, inequality is the result. If corporations spend money helping elect judges who uphold business-friendly arbitration clauses in employment contracts or refuse to certify class actions against companies accused of discrimination, inequality is the result.

Norms of corporate decision making, persistently putting the interests of shareholders above all other stakeholders, stand in such contrast to how human beings responsibly behave that they can be called inhuman. They are inhuman not in that the decisions are mean-spirited or lacking in pity but in that they lack the qualities of humans. Though managers of large, powerful corporations are required to act as though one metric should be the measure of all decisions, humans acting as though only one thing matters are seen as odd and obtuse. Humans cannot act in life as though there is one solitary rule for judgment. They have to balance their obligations over time. Parents cannot prioritize their children over their jobs in every case, or they would not be successful in their careers. They cannot prioritize their jobs over their children in every case either; they would not be good parents. If you know someone who puts everything aside for one goal and one goal only, you do not set him or her up as a paragon of good decision making even if that goal is reached. Sometimes reaching that goal can be beneficial in the short or medium term. But someone who obsesses about a solitary goal over the long term at the expense of all else is not our human-istic model of good decision making.

My point is that our expectations for corporations and their executives are odd. Corporations depend on a multitude of inputs, and their outputs affect a multitude. But by law and norm, we ask companies to ignore most of these contributors and even social welfare. Companies can take these interests into account if, and only if, doing so benefits shareholders.

Corporations, everyone agrees, are collective enterprises with the institutional role of creating economic wealth for society. They are the economic engines of society, in contrast to other social institutions (universities, churches, families, charities, hospitals, governments), the roles for which are primarily non-economic. And under current law, norm, and practice, corporations must satisfy their social role of creating wealth for society by focusing on shareholders *to the exclusion of social good*. Corporations are created for the good of society but must ignore social good in their decision making and corporate structure.

The cure for this fixation on the interests of those who own shares is to ask companies and their managers to take a broader view of their obligations. That is, to ask corporations to be more human.

More personhood, please.

EIGHT

Six Bad Arguments for
Shareholder Primacy

It has long been understood in the United States that corporations are to be managed primarily for the benefit of shareholders. Managers are to look after the interests of other stakeholders and investors only to the extent necessary to maintain the corporation as a going concern and ultimately to benefit those who own shares. This requirement of shareholder primacy imposes myriad costs on society as a whole and on corporations themselves. It also affects the discussion of corporate constitutional rights. When corporations assert those rights to fight regulatory restrictions and obligations, the norm of shareholder supremacy means that such assertions will be in service of a narrow sliver of American citizenry. And because that sliver tends to be financially better off and more politically connected than the rest of us, the norm of shareholder primacy tends to worsen not only economic inequality, but political inequality too.

It need not be that way. We could ask corporations for more. We could expect corporations to abide by a social contract more robust than they now do and more like we observe in many other industrialized democracies. We could expect them to act less robotic; we could ask them to take into account a wider range of interests. We could ask them to act more like people.

Given the costs of shareholder primacy and the availability of alternatives, one might suppose the arguments in favor of such a position are strong. But, in fact, they wither under scrutiny.

Argument 1: The Shareholders Own the Company

Let's say you have a house with a back yard, and you want to decide whether to add a play structure for your kids. You get to decide, not your neighbors. Why? Because you are the owner, and your neighbors are not. Even if your neighbors might care one way or the other, they do not have the legal right to decide for you. It's your yard.

This is the argument most often used for shareholder primacy. Shareholders are the owners, so they are supreme. The corporation is managed for their benefit because they own it. Managers are merely agents acting on behalf of the owners of the company. If managers were to act on behalf of other stakeholders, it would be akin to your babysitter prioritizing the needs of the neighbors' kids over your own.

This ownership argument is the one heard most often in the popular press and is implicit in most discussions of corporate governance. It is perhaps the most intransigent of all assumptions about corporations, how they are regulated, and what rights they have. The shareholder-as-owner assumption forms the basis of many critiques of *Citizens United* (for example, that political spending is inconsistent with shareholder value) and forms the backbone of many policy responses to it (such as calls for corporate political spending to be disclosed to or approved by shareholders).[1]

This way of arguing for shareholder primacy is long-standing but mistaken. The ownership argument is circular. Because shareholders are owners, they should be treated as owners. Other stakeholders, who are not owners, should not be treated as owners.[2] But in a discussion about corporate governance, the question that needs to be answered is the following: Who, in property terms, "owns" the firm? Are shareholders the only owners, or is the corporation best seen as having multiple owners? If the question of whether management owes a duty to employees and other stakeholders turns on who owns the firm, then to posit shareholders as owners is to answer that question. If one posits that shareholders are supposed to control the firm and equates directors with trust fiduciaries who control shareholders' money, that is simply defending current doctrine by restating it as the conclusion.[3]

Another common mistake is to equate the term "investor" with shareholder, implicitly making the ownership argument. Shareholders invest, the argument goes, and therefore should have their interests protected; other stakeholders are parties to contracts with the company and should protect their own interests through contract or by the petitioning government to help them. Shareholders are investors; other stakeholders are costs. The flaw in this argument is that shareholders are not the only investors in the firm. They contribute capital, to be sure, and they ought to have legal protections for that investment. But others invest in various ways too, and they deserve protections.

Once we set aside the circular assumptions, we see that shareholders are not owners in any meaningful sense. They do not enjoy the rights normally associated with ownership. A shareholder cannot freely access the company's place of business, exclude others, or decide what happens on a day-to-day basis. Even if you own a share of Ford Motor Company, you will be tossed out of its headquarters as a trespasser if you try to enter without an appointment. In fact, if you try to exercise dominion over its property, you will be arrested. Even if you own Ford stock, you cannot go to your local Ford dealer and escape with a new Escape unless you pay for it.

Shareholders do, of course, own their shares. But bondholders own their bonds, suppliers own their inventory, and workers own their labor. Each of these "owners" contributes something of essential value to the corporate enterprise, and each expects to make a profitable return. They are all investors, and if any one of these investors backs out from the enterprise, it is doomed. Corporations are simply the mechanism to bring together various investments to produce goods and services for profit.[4]

So what do people mean when they say shareholders "own" the corporation? They are not saying anything about property rights. Rather, they are using the language of property rights as shorthand to describe managerial obligations. Managers are to run corporations with the interests of shareholders first and foremost in their minds.

This is not argument. It is assertion. Shareholders are owners because they own. Shareholders are supreme because they are supreme. But one cannot justify shareholder primacy by pointing out that shareholders are primary.

Argument 2: Shareholder Interests Are the Same as the Company's

A more thoughtful defense of shareholder primacy is that shareholder interests are the same as the company's or that shareholder interests are the best proxy for the interests of the company as a whole. An executive who prioritizes shareholder interests will be better at managing a company over time than an executive who takes into account a broader set of interests. And because there is unity between the interests of the firm and those of shareholders, managers acting with care and loyalty toward shareholders will automatically satisfy the interests of the company.

This argument depends on the notion that the shareholders are the "residual claimants" of the companies in which they hold stock. That means their financial claims against the firm are paid only after all other creditors are paid. Because of this, as one scholar has argued, shareholders "have the greatest incentive to maximize the value of the firm."[5] The financial interests of other stakeholders are "largely fixed and senior to those of the shareholders."[6] While other stakeholders can be satisfied without the firm's making a profit, shareholders benefit only when the firm prospers. They enjoy "the perspective of the aggregate" because if the firm is managed in such a way as to benefit shareholders, then the whole firm, and everyone associated with it, benefits.[7]

There are a number of ways to answer the residual claimant argument, but perhaps the most important is to point out that the rules of liquidation do not require a particular governance structure for a company as a going concern. There is nothing about the right to receive the financial residual that automatically couples it with the power to control a company. Equity ownership and voting power are frequently divided.[8] Some companies issue non-voting stock; other companies place creditor (rather than equity) representatives on governing boards as a result of bond negotiations and the like. The inclusion of employee representatives on company boards is routine in Europe, meaning that those companies have split the residual financial claim from the right to control the company or even from the right of shareholders to be the sole beneficiaries of fiduciary duties. As scholar Jonathan Macey explains, "once we view the shareholders as simply the residual claimants . . . it is far from self-evident that shareholders are necessarily entitled to control the firm, i.e., to have managers' and directors' fiduciary duties flow exclusively to them."[9]

As to the point that looking after the interests of shareholders is the best proxy for looking after the interests of the firm as whole, notice three implicit jumps in logic buried in the claim. First, the purpose of corporations, and corporate law, is to benefit society. Second, the best way to benefit society is to maximize the value of corporations. Third, the best way to maximize the value of corporations is for management to act as though only shareholders matter. The last two jumps are contestable and depend on political as well as financial judgments.

The best way to benefit society may *not* be to maximize the value of corporations. The building of wealth is a crucial goal of society, and corporations are a fundamental—indeed central—part of that effort. But other values matter as well, such as stability, fairness, and sustainability. Moreover, left to their own devices, corporations are indifferent between making profit by building wealth and making profit by extracting economic rents from society by externalizing social costs, utilizing political advantage, or merely shifting financial surplus from others to themselves.

Even when corporations in fact create wealth rather than shift it around, social welfare is not maximized unless that wealth is widely distributed. The importance of distribution is partly economic. Because of the diminishing utility of money, widely shared wealth raises social welfare more than concentrated wealth. Its importance is partly political; democracy thrives better in a society without huge economic disparities. And the importance of distribution is partly social; inequality creates the context for crime, social unrest, and other ills. For social welfare to be maximized, we need to care not only about the *creation* of firm value, but its *allocation* as well. And shareholder primacy is unlikely to lead to a balance of wealth creation and wealth distribution.

The assumption that the best way to maximize corporate value is for management to act as though only shareholder interests matter is contestable for a straightforward reason. The interests of shareholders and the firm do not, in fact, coalesce in all circumstances.

Shareholders, because they hold the financial residual, benefit disproportionately when the firm does well, and because of limited liability, they are disproportionately protected when the firm does poorly. That means that if shareholder interests are all that matters, the firm will be managed to prefer endeavors with high potential payoffs that are also high risk and have high variability. The more leveraged the firm—the greater the amount of debt in relation to equity—the more shareholders will stand to benefit from such risky strategies, and the less likely such strategies will actually maximize firm value.[10] (The global financial crisis is a perfect, and tragic, example of this very thing.)

The description so far is simply a restatement of a financial truism. From a broader perspective, the distinction grows. Shareholders typically invest in a number of different companies and have diversified portfolios. As a result, they do not care a great deal about the risks that any one particular firm is taking. Shareholders will prefer decisions that provide high potential payoffs but risk bankruptcy over those that provide lower potential returns but have less risk of pushing the firm into liquidation. Shareholders are indifferent toward a specific company's liquidation risk as long as their portfolios as a whole maximize their expected returns.

In fact, shareholders with large pools of capital to allocate—think of institutional investors and hedge funds—can use the rules of shareholder primacy to manipulate management decisions in companies across their portfolios to hurt some companies and help others. Depending on their stake, large shareholders can force management in Company A to act in ways that hurt that company but benefit Company B. If an investor owns more of Company B than Company A, then the investor is better off, even if Company A ends up worse off. In such a situation, management's attentiveness to shareholder preferences in Company A depletes its resources, is detrimental to the company, and hampers its long-term success.[11]

By way of comparison, now look at a corporation whose management considers not only the interests of shareholders, but of employees as well. The first thing to notice is that like shareholders, employees have financial interests in their companies that tend to be positively correlated with firm value. Employees' financial interests rise and fall with the fortunes of their employers, and this means they have an interest in company success just like shareholders do. Some employees' wage and salary claims (though not all) may be fixed in the short term, but employees also have both implicit and explicit claims against the enterprise that are more valuable when the company does well and are worth less (or nothing) when the company does poorly. Unfixed, explicit claims against the company might include pension plans, 401(k) accounts, or other retirement benefits. These can constitute a significant percentage of an employee's net worth and are at risk of evaporation if the company fails. Unfixed, implicit claims might include understandings about job security or promotion policies, the development of firm-specific human capital, and the safety of working conditions. When a company's management makes good decisions for the enterprise as a whole, workers' fortunes improve even if their wages or salaries remain the same. When a company's management makes poor decisions for the enterprise, workers' fortunes decline even if their wages or salaries are unchanged in the short term.

Employees often care *more* about the success of their company than shareholders do. While shareholders are largely indifferent as to whether any particular firm fails, employees are vitally interested in the success of their employers and are not indifferent about whether their company goes belly up. When their company goes bankrupt, employees will often lose their jobs, the value of any firm-specific skills, and sometimes retirement or pension benefits. Employees thus prefer that the management of their company not make risky decisions, even when such decisions have a possibility of a high return. Employees instead prefer decisions that value stability and long-term growth.

Will including employee interests into firm governance mean that firms will fail more often? Just the opposite. It will encourage firms to be more dedicated to their own success. Because shareholders want companies to take risks that other stakeholders do not, there is little doubt that shareholder primacy results in more companies going under than if companies were required to take into account the interests of other stakeholders.

Once the difference in risk aversion is considered, the argument for shareholder primacy depends on the claim that employees and other stakeholders care *too much* about the fortunes of their firm. A proponent of the shareholder-centered view of corporate law has to make the ironic argument that it is better for society as a whole for the decision making of each individual firm to be dominated by shareholders, who care little about the fortunes of each firm. On its own terms, this is hardly self-evident, and it is not what shareholder proponents typically say. The argument is usually that shareholders are the only ones who care about the success of the firm. But employees and other stakeholders care too.

Argument 3: Shareholder Interests Are the Same as Those of Other Stakeholders

One argument made in favor of shareholder primacy is related but distinct to the point that shareholders' interests are the same as those of the company as a whole. This third argument is that managers do not need to take into account the interests of other stakeholders because shareholder interests coalesce with those of other stakeholders over time. An executive need not be concerned with the claims of employees, bondholders, customers, or host communities because in the long run, their interests will be served by a dedication to shareholders. Shareholder interests and the interests of other stakeholders are really the same.

One hears this argument in various guises, from both ideologically conservative and progressive commentators. From the traditional conservatives, one hears the argument that shareholder value helps employees and other stakeholders. From the progressives, one hears that taking care of stakeholders will inure to the benefit of shareholders. ("Doing well by doing good," some say.) But regardless of its source or direction, the argument is ultimately unpersuasive.

Stakeholder and shareholder interests are simply not the same. A company that makes money for shareholders does not necessarily create wealth for others or for society. Without a mechanism within the corporation to force it to absorb externalities or to share profits with all stakeholders, there is no sure gain on the part of employees, for example, even when the firm is making a great deal of money. The "trickle down" is not inevitable. Shareholder gain could come, in fact, as a result of a transfer of wealth from labor or from society.[12]

Moreover, as mentioned above, shareholders will prefer that a company make riskier decisions than other stakeholders will prefer. Because of limited liability, shareholders are protected from bearing the full downside costs of risky decisions, whereas on a societal basis, all costs have to be accounted for. The upside for shareholders is higher (since they have the residual financial claims), and their downside is less severe (because of limited liability and because they have diversified portfolios). An executive maximizing value to shareholders will make riskier decisions than employees, bondholders, and communities will prefer. If the company loses the bet implicit in the risky decision, the shareholders' losses will be mitigated by the winning payouts from other companies in their portfolios. Other stakeholders will not be so lucky, either because the nature of their investment does not enable them to share in the upside (bondholders, for example) or because the nature of their investment limits their ability to mitigate their risk through diversification (employees and communities).

Another reason the argument that the long-term interests of stakeholder and shareholder coalesce is unpersuasive is that, in the words of famous economist John Maynard Keynes, "In the long run we are all dead."[13] There is truth in this sarcasm. Even if the shareholder primacists are correct that such coalescence occurs, the time horizon assumed is many years in the future.

This weakens the argument significantly. It is a financial truism that short-term losses or gains swamp long-term gains or losses. All economists assume that gains or losses in the future are less important than similar gains or losses in the present. The difference is a function of what is called the discount rate, the measure of how much a dollar in the future should be discounted to compare with a dollar today. Because future gains and costs are discounted, the current financial implications of decisions trend toward zero as the time horizon moves further out. For example, at a 7 percent discount rate (the rate assumed by the U.S. government for some projects, based on a typical rate of return for private investments),[14] a $100 benefit in one hundred years is worth only twelve cents today. That means that economically rational shareholders would prefer a thirteen-cent gain today over a $100 gain in a hundred years, even if all the future gain inured to them rather than others.[15] Even catastrophic costs, if far in the future, have little financial meaning in present value and can be rationally ignored. For example, if shareholders were convinced that climate change will be a major crisis in the long-term, causing $100 trillion in damage five hundred years from now, the rational amount they would be willing to spend now to avoid such catastrophe would be just twenty cents. Any solution costing twenty-one cents or more would not pay off financially. (And if shareholders assume that some of the costs can be externalized to others, they will be willing to pay even less.) All this is to say that shareholders will not likely push for decisions that benefit the firm as a whole—much less other stakeholders—if the payoff is likely to be far in the future.[16]

For the same reason, long-term benefits to stakeholders need to be discounted. Stakeholders are told to be patient. Managers can focus on shareholders, and benefits will trickle to other stakeholders eventually. But for long-term benefits to count, they need to be sufficient to outweigh the operation of the discount rate. It cannot be that future benefits to shareholders should be discounted to present value but that those accruing to stakeholders should not.

At heart, the argument for shareholder primacy is that attention to shareholder interests will naturally, as by an invisible hand, benefit other stakeholders. A necessary corollary to this claim is that corporate managers should be *prohibited* from taking into account the interests of other stakeholders. But note the audacity of this claim: the best way to benefit other stakeholders is for managers never to consider their interests. Not even Adam Smith, who created the notion of the invisible hand, ever suggested that those in charge of capital should be prohibited from taking into account the implications of its use on others.[17]

The claim about the long-term interests of other stakeholders reduces to the notion that the bare survival of companies is the best way to benefit all stakeholders. It is true that a failing business is not much good to anyone with any kind of investment in the firm. But the general claim that shareholder interests and stakeholder interests are the same can be true only, if at all, in the longest of long terms and only if a host of other conditions is met. One example will suffice to illustrate the tenuous nature of the claim. Imagine a company facing the choice of whether to close a unionized, high-wage factory and move production to a sweatshop in a country that has no health and safety protections for workers. Shareholders will certainly prefer the change, all else being equal. The decrease in labor costs will flow to the corporation's bottom line, available for distribution to shareholders. Revenue flowing to labor shifts from one locale to another and decreases in the aggregate. How is labor, or society as a whole, benefited? Only if the benefit to the shareholders or to the company outweighs the net costs suffered by the employees *and those benefits (eventually) flow from the shareholders to others.* To believe they will, one has to rely on "trickle-down" economics or entrust the redistributional efforts of government. The former is dubious; the latter is contentious and unreliable.

What are the implications of the failure of Argument 3? We cannot blithely assume that pursuing shareholder value is good for other investor-stakeholders. We have to be more sophisticated in our analysis of which policies benefit which groups. Some decisions and governance policies would likely be in the interests of all stakeholders, such as limits on executive compensation. Others would benefit none of them, such as judicial deference to "selfish" charitable spending by management. Some policies benefit one stakeholder at the expense of another. A high minimum wage, for example, most likely benefits employees and costs shareholders. Limited liability for shareholders unquestionably benefits shareholders but comes with increased costs and risks to employees, customers, suppliers, and others interacting with the company.[18]

The nature of the corporation as a collective enterprise means that tough choices and trade-offs are unavoidable. But under existing law and norm, shareholders must win anytime there is a tough choice or trade-off.

The best way to reveal that such choices are inevitable is to propose that we change the rule of shareholder primacy to one of stakeholder inclusion. If tough choices and trade-offs were nonexistent or rare, shareholder advocates would not care much about the legal rule of fiduciary duty. But shareholders do care, and they care a great deal. Just propose toppling shareholders from the summit of the corporate pyramid and listen to them cry foul.

Argument 4: Shareholders Need More Protection Than Other Stakeholders

Another prominent argument for shareholder primacy is that shareholders need more protection from managerial avarice and laziness than other stakeholders. The other stakeholders, the argument goes, can protect themselves by contract and regulation; the shareholders are at the mercy of the management because of the long-term and vague nature of the relationship. In this view, shareholders are the exclusive beneficiaries of the managers' fiduciary duties because "shareholders face more daunting contracting problems than other constituencies."[19] In other words, shareholders need the law to protect them. Employees, communities, and other stakeholders can protect themselves.

The notion that employees, communities, and other stakeholders have more power than the financial sector is ludicrous. Even setting aside questions of power, there are reasons to believe that fiduciary obligations would be at least as important in the relationship between management and other stakeholders as in the shareholder-management relationship. Fiduciary duties usually arise from relationships, and most shareholders of public corporations have little genuine relationship with the companies in which they hold stock. They may not even know what stocks they hold, and their holding periods are shorter than ever—sometimes only milliseconds. Meanwhile the relationships between companies and other stakeholders commonly last for years. Also, shareholders have ways to protect themselves other than fiduciary duties. Their ability to exit a particular company by selling shares comes at a tiny cost. Capital markets are liquid, and moving one's capital from one stock to another is a low-cost proposition. The costs of exit for employees and host communities are much higher. Sometimes exit is a costly strategy even for customers—have you tried to cancel your cable television contract lately?

The nature of the capital markets will protect shareholders even in the absence of fiduciary duty. The fluidity of the capital markets will mean any managerial decision hurting shareholders will be very quickly revealed in a drop in the company's stock price (assuming that both the decision and its effects are publicly known). And any decision that benefits shareholders will be revealed in a bump in the stock price. Managers will lose or gain reputation among shareholders very quickly. Meanwhile, the fluidity and price responsiveness of the labor market is much less than in the capital markets. The nexus between managerial decisions and employee wages—or community tax basis or consumer prices, for that matter—will be much more attenuated. Inevitably, then, management will naturally prioritize the interests of shareholders at the expense of other stakeholders even without a fiduciary "kicker" that adds to shareholder power.

This is not to say that shareholders merit no protection against mismanagement or malfeasance on the part of those who run the company. But it is to say that the claim that they need more protection than other stakeholders is quite weak.

A related argument is that stakeholders do not need the protections of corporate law fiduciary duties because they can adequately protect themselves by way of negotiated contracts or other kinds of regulation. Stakeholders do not need additional protection because they "contract with the firm and can either contract for limits on risk or demand compensation for the risk they assume." If stakeholders are not successful in reaching the bargain they want, "employees can quit their jobs and customers can take their business to other suppliers if they are dissatisfied."[20]

This argument reduces to the notion that the free market should be trusted as the primary mechanism to protect stakeholders. If stakeholders want protection, they should bargain for it. If they cannot win that right, they should go elsewhere.

These arguments are fanciful to anyone keeping up with the state of working America in the early twenty-first century. To suggest, for example, that workers should depend on collective bargaining to protect themselves, in an era in which unions represent less than 7 percent of the private workforce in America, is to whistle past the graveyard.[21] To suggest that the right to quit one's job and find a different one provides anything close to the power of capital to move fluidly from market to market, country to country, is laughable.

Those who urge employees and other stakeholders to depend on the marketplace for their protection do not generally apply this same advice to shareholders. Employees and other stakeholders should depend on self-help; shareholders need not. Such an argument would be persuasive only if the market offered *less* power to shareholders than to other stakeholders. But that is exactly opposite from what one observes in the real world.

Argument 5: Managers Can Have Only One Master

One prominent argument in favor of shareholder primacy is that a broadening of corporate responsibilities would actually make it easier for managers to avoid responsibility altogether. The claim goes like this: if corporate managers have more than one "master," they can avoid real responsibility to any one party by claiming their actions are to further the interests of another party. Economists call this an "agency costs" argument: enlarging the duties of management will increase the agency costs inherent in managing the firm since it will be more difficult to monitor whether the managers are doing their jobs carefully and in good faith.

It is worth noting that this "too many masters" concern is inconsistent with an objection to stakeholder governance discussed above—namely, that corporate law need not worry about stakeholder interests because looking after shareholders will inevitably help other stakeholders as well. Of course, shareholder advocates cannot have it both ways. If the interests of shareholders and other stakeholders are not in conflict, then agency costs will not increase much if the law requires managers to take into account the interests of other stakeholders. And if they do conflict, shareholder advocates cannot claim stakeholders can be ignored since attentiveness to shareholders will also help other stakeholders.

A more accurate view is that there is conflict between the interests of shareholders and other stakeholders in a range of cases, especially in the short term. Such conflict, however, is not a reason to fear that managers are unable to handle increased responsibility or that it would be impossible to know whether managers are doing their jobs well. It is true, in a mundane way, that someone who has two responsibilities may have more difficulty meeting both than meeting only one. But people routinely have more than one responsibility, some of them even conflicting. Humans are quite accustomed to having a range of obligations. Even in business, managers are asked to balance a multitude of obligations, some arising from corporate law, some from other areas of law, and some from the market. For example, corporations regularly issue different classes of stock that afford different rights, but current law still obligates directors to owe fiduciary duties to all shareholders even when the interests of the various classes are in conflict.

The only way in which having more and broader responsibilities would make it easier for managers to avoid responsibility is that it would allow them to use one obligation as a defense against a claim that they failed to satisfy another. This, however, is not a function of the number and scope of responsibilities but how they are enforced. And corporate law duties are simply not enforced in a way that would allow managers to play one duty off the other.

Consider the duty of care. When enforced at all, courts reduce it essentially to a procedural obligation—namely, to investigate various alternatives, to consider various possible outcomes, to take the time necessary to deliberate effectively, and to erect certain monitoring systems to ensure the smooth flow of information from throughout the company to the centralized management. If managers were required to take account of employees' interests, the duty of care could be enforced by looking at process, the same way it is now. No managers would be able to erect a defense to a shareholder claim by saying they were unable to pay attention to the impact of the decision on shareholders because they were thinking at the time about employees. The managers would have to do both. Yes, this may be more difficult. But it is not impossible, and it is certainly not the kind of difficulty that throws up such dust that one cannot discern if the board is doing its job.

Similarly, the duty of loyalty would not be loosened if managers were required to look after a broader set of stakeholders. In corporate law, loyalty requires managers not to engage in self-dealing. Such an obligation would not be undermined by including employees among the beneficiaries of managers' fiduciary duties. Rather, adding to the number of people who benefit from managers' fiduciary duties will make it *less* likely that managers will be able to get away with self-dealing. More corporate stakeholders will have an interest in monitoring managerial conflicts of interest.

Beneath the surface of the agency cost argument, one finds that the real worry of the shareholder primacists is that adding to the responsibilities of management will make it less likely that managers will act like agents of the shareholders. They are likely correct that managers will change their behavior in that way. But whether that change is a problem depends on whether managers should serve only the interests of the shareholders.

For a similar reason, the existence of shareholder agency costs is not a persuasive argument either. Other stakeholders have agency costs since they, too, depend on management to use their contributions to create wealth. A shareholder primacy rule makes it more difficult for these other stakeholders to rely on management, a situation that raises the stakeholders' agency costs. A relaxation of the shareholder primacy model might increase the agency costs of shareholders, but it will *decrease* the agency costs of non-shareholder stakeholders, which are just as important as shareholders' agency costs. To say that only shareholders should have a rule that lowers their agency costs assumes shareholder primacy. But we cannot justify the rule of shareholder primacy by pointing to shareholder agency costs unless the agency costs of other stakeholders are discounted. Those costs can be discounted only if shareholders are supreme.

At base, the "too many masters" argument is founded either on a prior assertion of shareholder primacy or on an empirical assertion that broadening fiduciary duties "just won't work." The first argument is circular. The second argument is disproven by the multitude of institutions—both profit and nonprofit—around the world holding their leadership to a set of robust duties greater than to shareholder value alone.

Argument 6: Protecting Stakeholders Is Counterproductive

Some scholars have argued that even if the rationales behind stakeholder protections are strong, we should nevertheless refuse them because they would be counterproductive. The argument often follows this syllogism: employees and other stakeholders benefit from a vibrant economy; stakeholder protections make the economy less vibrant; therefore, stakeholders are hurt by protections. "Job creation has been much better in economies that make it easier for employers to dismiss employees," one scholar posits. "Thus shareholder control is probably the best arrangement for each firm's employees."[22] By this logic, to help employees and other stakeholders is to hurt them.

There is some truth in this. The protection of *any* investor can go so far as to retard economic vibrancy. If employees are protected from termination even when they perform poorly, the economy suffers. The economy also suffers when environmental protections are set so high that companies cannot build new facilities or when protections for creditors are set so high that businesses cannot borrow money. But the economy also suffers when protections for *shareholders* are set too high, whether by having standards of disclosure that are too stringent, setting the fiduciary obligations of management too high, or providing a guarantee for shareholder investment.

But sometimes protection for investors (of all kinds) can facilitate investment and make the economy more vibrant. Shareholder advocates recognize this truth when it comes to shareholders but are generally blind to it with regard to the others who invest in the firm. That may be because of the distinction they make between shareholders—who are often seen as the sole investors—and the other stakeholders—who are seen as costs. But once we recognize the collective nature of the firm, it is much more difficult to make these distinctions, and, in fact, the arguments in favor of shareholders can also be applied to employees and other stakeholders as well.

Consider the point made by proponents of shareholder rights that legal protections for shareholders lower the cost of capital. Shareholder rights "will reassure investors that America is the safest place to put their money," so more institutions and individuals will want to buy stock in U.S. companies, lowering the cost of capital for those companies.[23] The protections for capital will make holders of capital more likely to invest.

The same argument applies to others who invest in the firm. If legal protections lower the cost of capital, then they should lower the cost of other investments as well. And the lack of legal protections will increase the cost of those inputs. For example, employees will be less likely to invest their labor in a legal regime in which their investment gives them no say in corporate governance and no redress other than exit, leaving them vulnerable to the exploitation or expropriation of firm-specific skills. A legal regime that disregards their interests will not "reassure [workers] that America is the safest place" to work. They will protect themselves to the extent they can in other ways. They may demand a higher wage; they may demand more explicit job security protections; they may moderate their effort; they may solicit their legislators to protect them in other ways.

My point is simply that any argument about the counterproductivity of legal protections for employees can also be made vis-à-vis shareholders. And any argument about the benefit of legal protections toward shareholders can be made vis-à-vis employees. This notion is so often missed because of the lack of parallel structure in how the "counterproductivity argument" is typically made. In considering shareholder protection, the benefits are the focus: legal protections lower the cost of capital, making the economy more vibrant. Ignored are the costs of the legal protection (SEC regulations, the fiduciary obligations of managers, the framework of shareholder voting, the structure of securities markets). When the frame shifts to employee and stakeholder protection, it is the costs that are mentioned. The potential benefits of stakeholder protections are largely ignored, and shareholder primacy theorists have particularly undervalued the potential benefits of increased employee protection. The more enlightened shareholder advocates may recognize that employees deserve more protection than they receive, but they believe these protections should come from outside of corporate law and governance. From the perspective of the company as a whole, however, costs are costs. This is true whether they come in the form of external regulations of the corporation (the mandate of a minimum wage, for example, or protection from hazardous chemicals) or in the form of a mandate that the internal processes of the firm take into account the interests of employees by way of adjusting fiduciary duties or the structure of the board. It is likely that employees can be made better off at a lower cost through the use of corporate governance reforms than through other regulatory mechanisms.

The arguments for prioritizing shareholders are either weak or apply to other stakeholders at least as well. The reality of shareholder primacy, both in law and norm, is instead based on power. The owners of financial capital simply have the economic power to force businesses to pay them heed. And because corporations can assert constitutional rights, the economic power enjoyed by the financial elites can all too easily be transformed into, and cemented by, political power.

We are left with a legal framework for corporations that both devalues the contributions of most Americans to the nation's economic well-being and isolates those Americans from political influence. Corporations that simultaneously exercise muscular constitutional rights while prioritizing the interests of their most affluent investors will not serve the public interest. They are instead dangers to democracy and economic flourishing.

NINE

The Promise of Corporate Personhood

After *Citizens United*, corporate personhood has been a focus of serious opposition because corporations have claimed constitutional rights as if they were "persons" or "citizens" protected by the First and Fourteenth Amendments and other constitutional guarantees. The protests of "corporations are not people" are shorthand for an argument that corporations should not be protected by the Constitution. As we have seen, this kind of corporate "citizenship" and "personhood" can be justified in many cases. But it can also be problematic when brought to bear in ways that serve only a sliver of the American citizenry.

Corporate "citizenship" is also a term used as shorthand for the idea that corporations owe a robust set of duties to society and to stakeholders that go beyond shareholder primacy. A dedication to these norms and requirements of corporate citizenship—in corporate governance terms—will make corporations *more* like people. Companies will be governed more pluralistically, with an eye toward the interests of the real persons who invest in them and work for them. Worries about corporate personhood and citizenship as a *constitutional* matter will be ameliorated by corporate personhood and citizenship as a *corporate governance* matter.

I. Stakeholder Governance with Person-ality

Scholars have disagreed for more than a century over what obligations corporations have and how they should be governed. But there is little disagreement about one thing: corporations are collective bodies—legal mechanisms for bringing together various investments in order to produce goods and services for profit. When this basic truth is brought forward, two fundamental problems of the corporate form are made plain. One is how to induce investment from the various contributors to the firm. The second is how to allocate the financial surplus that is created.

The solution to both problems, according to the view of mainstream corporate law doctrine and scholarship, is that we need to worry only about the investment of and allocation to one of the many investors—namely, the shareholders. This fixation on shareholder value causes businesses to ignore social harms (or potential social benefits, for that matter) of business decisions. It tends to incentivize the transfer of as much wealth from labor to capital as possible. It leads corporations to act with disregard toward non-shareholder stakeholders. It inures to the benefit of the most well-off Americans and hurts the rest.

This way of organizing and regulating corporations is not the only way. We could structure and regulate corporate governance differently, using corporate law as a tool to provide broader benefits to society, without eroding the ability of corporations to build wealth for those who contribute to it.

The way to do this is to make corporations *more* like people, through a set of governance reforms that adjusts corporate decision making in ways that bring it closer to the good decision making of humans. Reform begins with a rejection in law and norm of the robotic use of the one-metric guide of shareholder primacy. Reform would also include changes in the structure of corporate decision-making bodies to include a wider range of viewpoints and perspectives, which humans need to guard against groupthink and confirmation bias. And courts should abandon the conventional judicial deference given to managers' decisions because humans behave more responsibly when they are asked to be accountable for their actions and decisions.

The lodestar for successful management of particular companies and business as a whole should be long-term, sustainable stakeholder governance. Stakeholder governance is the notion that the concerns of *all* the firm's investors should be brought into the governance of the firm, based on a recognition that non-shareholder stakeholders are investors too and have interests that should be taken into account. Stakeholder governance is based on a conviction that as law is used to overcome impediments to shareholder investment, law can also be used to overcome impediments to investment by other stakeholders. Support also springs from the belief that stakeholder governance provides a mechanism to protect the interests of stakeholders that is more efficient as a regulatory matter than other forms of legal protection. Finally, stakeholder governance grows from a confidence that corporations themselves will be better managed over time when management is held to consider the interests of all key investors of the firm, not just a small subset.

Stakeholder reforms would improve not only corporate governance, but also the nature of corporate involvement in the public space. The fact that corporations assert political influence is not itself problematic in most cases. The problem has been that their influence is brought to bear on behalf of the managerial and financial elite rather than all those who contribute to the success of the business. If corporations were required to take into account the interests of all their stakeholders and include their views within a pluralistic, more democratic corporate structure, the voices of corporations themselves would be more pluralistic and democratic.

Instead of responding to cases such as *Citizens United* and *Hobby Lobby* with cries of "Corporations Are Not People," we should be chanting "Let's Make Corporations Human Again" or "If Corporations Are People, They Should Act Like It." More corporate personhood should be our goal, not our fear.

Dismantling shareholder primacy is hardly an extreme idea. A growing number of commentators, both within and outside industry, believe that "companies need a bigger and better purpose than simply maximising shareholder value."[1] "Employees and customers often know more about and have more of a long-term commitment to a company than shareholders do."[2] "It feels as though we are at the dawn of a new movement—one aimed at overturning the hegemony of shareholder value."[3] Shareholder primacy is "the dumbest idea in the world,"[4] and "shareholders are ruining American business."[5] Even the conservative prime minister of the United Kingdom has suggested that British companies should place employee representatives on their boards.[6]

We should be cautious, however, about the traditional alternative to shareholder primacy—*managerial* primacy, taking away shareholder power and giving it to management.[7] The managerial remedy depends completely on the benevolence of managers. Explosions in executive compensation and perquisites, the manipulation of financial reporting and disclosure, self-dealing in various guises, and judicial rubber-stamping of questionable decisions are more common than benevolence.

This conceptual dichotomy between shareholder supremacists on the one hand and managerialists on the other has dominated the thinking for decades. But in neither do the interests of other stakeholders bear much weight. Customers, employees, bondholders, communities, and suppliers are protected haphazardly, inefficiently, and imperfectly through antitrust law, environmental law, labor law, and the like.

There is a third way.[8] Managerial obligation to all stakeholders could be increased. Fiduciaries of companies could be subject to meaningful constraints and duties, enforceable by courts, without a disabling of the ability of corporations to fulfill their institutional role of generating wealth and economic gain. The fiduciary obligations of management would run to the firm as a whole, and management would be responsible for taking into account the interests of all those who make material investments in the firm. It would be a violation of fiduciary duties to prioritize one stakeholder over others consistently or to fail to consider the interests of all stakeholders in significant corporate decisions. Corporate directors and executives would not be able to make decisions in which the only metric that mattered was stock price, measured day to day or even quarter by quarter. It would continue to be improper for management to self-deal, act carelessly, or exercise something less than good faith judgment.

This would not make corporations into altruistic or charitable institutions. The best way for corporations to serve the public interest is to create wealth, primarily by selling worthwhile goods and services for a profit. We should simply define wealth broadly and require corporations to have both a greater awareness of the costs inherent in its creation and the benefits that flow from broadly distributing it.

We must cease thinking of corporations as pieces of property owned by shareholders. We should conceptualize businesses as team-like collective economic enterprises making use of a multitude of inputs from various kinds of investors and stakeholders, all of which contribute to a firm's success. That success depends on maintaining all of these contributions, and the governance of corporations should recognize those contributions.

Broader fiduciary duties would benefit companies over time. Fiduciary obligations build trust in those who contribute since they know management has a duty to look after their interests. If management owes obligations of care and loyalty to all the firm's important stakeholders, they are more likely both to invest in the first place and to leave their investment in place over time. This has long been thought to be true of shareholders, but it is true for other kinds of "investors" as well. Employees, for instance, will be more loyal and willing to invest in developing firm-specific skills benefiting the company. They will take less of an us-versus-them attitude toward management when they do not fear their interests will be shoved aside any time they are in conflict with short-term profitability. (Evidence from Europe bears this out; countries that have strong worker involvement in corporate governance enjoy higher rates of worker productivity and fewer days lost to strikes than in countries without such involvement.)[9]

The best way to operationalize a broader, more robust set of fiduciary duties would be to change the actual structure of company boards to allow for the nomination and election of members who embody or can credibly speak for the interests of stakeholders. Currently, boards of U.S. companies embody the interests of two groups: senior management and those with large financial stakes in the company. Once we recognize that a variety of stakeholders make essential contributions to the firm, it becomes clear that the current structure does not serve most of those stakeholders well. The way to change this is to require boards to reflect a broader cross section of those who contribute to their companies' success.

It would be straightforward to elect employee representatives; either we could use the German model, in which employee representatives are selected by the company workforce, or we could simply issue each employee one share of a special class of stock and have a number of board seats elected by that class. If we wanted other stakeholders represented, there are various ways it could be done. Community leaders in the localities where the company has a major presence could nominate a director; long-term business partners and creditors could be represented as well. We could also seize on the idea of calling on companies to include a "public-interest director" on their boards, whose special obligation would be to vet company decisions from the standpoint of the public.[10]

These mechanisms would need testing and development. But we are not in uncharted waters. There is much experience, at both the company and country levels, that we can take advantage of going forward. Companies are trying various ways to take into account stakeholder interests, and countries are trying numerous ways to strengthen the social contract of businesses. Some of these attempts work, and some fail. That is to be expected. But shareholder primacy is not sustainable over the long term at either the company or national level. We need to work to develop alternative structures and legal frameworks that are.

II. The Upsides of Stakeholder Governance

Why go to so much trouble? The potential benefits of stakeholder governance are significant, and they include the organizational, economic, and political.

Better Decision Making

The fact that the corporation has a sophisticated group decision maker at the top of the structural hierarchy is seen as a distinctive element of the success of the corporation as a business form.[11] When working properly, boards offer significant benefits as compared to solitary, individual decision makers typical in sole proprietorship or to small groups of decision makers typical in partnerships or similar enterprises. In complex organizations such as corporations, group decision making is crucial since "the effective oversight of an organization exceeds the capabilities of any individual" and "collective knowledge and deliberation are better suited to this task."[12] And when working well, groups improve on the decision making of individuals by exposing and mitigating bias and mistake.

But these organizational benefits can vanish—and indeed transform into costs—if the group reinforces bias and submerges mistakes, worsening irrationalities.[13] Groupthink—when like-minded participants reinforce rather than challenge underlying biases and validate rather than expose mistakes—is the most common example of this phenomenon.[14] Dissent is essential to good group decision making, and social bonds often make disagreement less likely when it is most needed.[15] Another group tendency that worsens decision making is the inclination for discussion within groups of individuals with similar worldviews and perspectives to harden those perspectives and views.[16] These tendencies are greater within groups that are homogeneous in perspective and in racial, gender, and class composition since "defective" decision making is "strongly correlated" with structural flaws such as "insulation and homogeneity."[17] As legal scholars Christine Jolls and Cass Sunstein have articulated, "Erroneous judgments often result when deliberations are undertaken by like-minded people."[18]

These defects should be a serious concern for those who care about corporate governance. Homogeneity is a defect in groups, and corporate boards may be the least diverse powerful institutions in the United States.[19] Men hold about 80 percent of board positions of Fortune 500 companies, and people of color hold only about 14 percent of Fortune 500 director seats.[20] And a lack of racial and gender diversity is only one slice of the problem.

Corporate decision making could be improved with greater board pluralism, used to encourage dissent, create genuine discussion, and expose and mitigate bias. In the words of Aaron Dhir, "Establishing a level of 'cognitive diversity' in the boardroom is ... a key strategic asset which serves to assist the firm in averting the perils and docile conduct associated with groupthink."[21] A growing body of evidence bears this out. For example, boards with more women have been shown to be more active and independent in monitoring management, more likely to engage with the company's stakeholders, show more attention to risk oversight and control, and be concerned about social responsibility.[22] There is also evidence that the presence of women on a board improves the quality of board deliberations,[23] in part by empowering "constructive dissent," leading to "board unity," which is "essential to setting a clear strategic direction and to overseeing risk and resources."[24] One notable finding is that male directors attend more board meetings when the board is more gender diverse.[25] Other recent findings indicate that more diverse business teams are able to take advantage of a wider pool of relevant knowledge.[26]

Gender and racial diversity is only one kind of diversity that matters. Other kinds of pluralism are also likely to be effectual in debiasing board decisions and protecting against groupthink. For example, some observers have explained Germany's relative success at avoiding the worst of the global financial crisis in 2008 by pointing to German companies' inclusion of employee board representatives, a structure that "introduce[d] a range of new perspectives" at the board level.[27] Class differences are sometimes better proxies for distinctiveness of perspective than racial and gender differences. Adding employee and other stakeholder views to company boards will likely lead to improved decision making at the level of corporate governance.

This makes sense. No one on a stakeholder board wants the firm to fail. All the decision makers will bring their different perspectives and areas of expertise to bear. Groupthink will be less likely, and managerial self-dealing and carelessness will more likely be found out. As with any pluralistic decision-making group, there will be squabbles, especially when making choices that in effect distribute the corporate economic surplus among the parties represented. Compared to situations in which the board uniformly serves shareholders or management, a more diverse body will have more disagreements and make decisions in a way that may appear less efficient. But the potential for conflict and real or apparent inefficiencies should not dissuade us from stakeholder governance. The potential for genuine gain in the quality of decisions is more than worth the risk. This is especially true if one counts, on the positive side of the ledger, possible gains flowing to all the company stakeholders and the company itself rather than just to shareholders alone.

Decreases in Economic Inequality

Another benefit flowing from stakeholder corporate governance is likely to be gains in economic equality. The causes of inequality are varied and complex, but little doubt exists that inequality springs in part from the behavior of corporations— low wages for the working class, exorbitant compensation for corporate executives, and a disproportionate amount of shareholder gains going to the richest among us.[28] And even though inequality in part springs from the actions of corporations, few have advanced changes in corporate governance as a possible and partial remedy.[29] Without considering corporate governance, the policy tools we have available to address such inequality are incomplete at best. We can advocate for an increase in the minimum wage, but the benefits diminish above the lowest rungs of the economic ladder. We can seek to empower labor unions, but in the United States less than 7 percent of the nation's private workforce is organized.[30] We can redistribute financial wealth from the rich by way of the tax system, but that creates resentment even among those who would benefit and arguably decreases the incentives to produce in the first place.

In comparison, changes in corporate fiduciary duties and the makeup of company boards would mean that the allocation of the financial surplus created by successful corporations is likely to be fairer to all concerned as an initial matter. Because the allocation of corporate surplus is one of the most important decisions for boards and senior management, a change in board duties and composition is bound to make a difference. Moreover, executives presently receive the compensation they do in part because directors and executives are members of what amounts to a private club of financial elites, all of whom look after one another. Adding fiduciary duties to interests outside the group will diminish this tendency, and the inclusion of employee representatives and other stakeholder advocates at the board level will make such "insiderism" transparent and less pervasive.

This improvement in the initial allocation of wealth is bound to be more efficient in lessening inequality than having government redistribute wealth after the fact. Fairness in the initial distribution will cause less resentment than post-hoc redistribution using the tax system. Further, employees receiving a fair wage will reciprocate good will toward their employers, increasing productivity and decreasing the need for strict monitoring.[31] These effects do not exist at all with a regimen of government redistribution. In comparison to increases in the minimum wage, which focuses on assisting those at the bottom rungs of the wage ladder, a stakeholder-oriented corporate governance system would benefit stakeholders up and down the economic hierarchy.

Reducing "Short-Termism"

That "short-termism" is a problem is one of the few notes of agreement between business commentators and academics on both the right and the left of the ideological spectrum. The problem is exemplified by the increasingly short time horizon of shareholders, who now hold their stocks on average for only a few months at a time. The turnover rate for shares of most companies is over 150 percent per year,[32] and the daily volume in the United States of high-frequency trading, in which investors hold stocks for seconds or less, is as much as 70 percent.[33]

This pattern of short-term holding means that shareholders will tend to ignore or disregard any change in the value of their stock occurring at a later time. They will prioritize the short term in their choice of shares to hold and in their influence on management in companies whose shares they hold. Management adhering to the interests of those shareholders will prioritize short-term gains even if the result is long-term difficulties.[34]

One reason why short-termism is a real problem springs from the fact that the discount rate of shareholders is higher than that of society. Much of one's calculus about the present depends on how one values the future, and the amount one values the future is captured in the "discount rate." From a shareholder's perspective, benefits gained in the future will be discounted to a present value. The present value of a long-term gain or loss depends on the rate at which such future amounts are reduced to a current value—the discount rate. As a financial matter, the higher the discount rate, the less future gains and losses will matter in the present.

From a social perspective, the discount rate is quite low—perhaps in the range of 1 percent.[35] That is simply another way of saying that society values future gains and losses quite highly; they are not as important as present gains and losses, but almost. Society has a long time frame; a gain or loss ten years from now (whether financial, environmental, or in terms of human lives) should be valued highly. On the other hand, shareholders—or managers who are required to act as if their interests dominate—will have a higher discount rate. Even if shareholders invest for what they think is the "long term," the long term for shareholders is shorter than the long term for society in general. The future will not be valued as highly as the present, and the discount rate will reflect that. Concretely, if the discount rate is even 7 percent—a figure the United States uses in calculating many capital projects[36]—the assessment of future value will approach zero quite quickly. (To make matters worse, the discount rate used by corporations to evaluate future gains and losses is likely significantly greater than 7 percent and may be increasing.)[37] According to scholar Frank Partnoy, "Discount rates for public corporations can be estimated based on market prices of corporate bonds or loans, and are typically well above government bond yields; discount rates for private corporations can be even higher. For example, venture capitalists typically use discount rates in the range of 30%–70%, and discount rates during the start-up stage of venture capital investments are commonly between 50%–70%."[38] At those high rates, future costs and benefits trend toward zero very quickly. The short term receives a massive thumb on the scale in calculating proper corporate choices.

For these reasons, there is little doubt that society's valuation of future gains and losses is greater than that of private economic actors such as corporations. And the gap between society's net present value and that of corporations is essentially an externality—a social cost. Corporations will underinvest in projects with future benefits and under-deter future costs. One example would be that corporations will underinvest in projects that will save lives in the future and overinvest in projects that will cost human lives in the future.[39] Corporations may act completely rationally as an economic matter, but the fact that they have a private discount rate out of sync with the social discount rate imposes social costs. If a corporation values a future gain less than society does, then a dead weight loss occurs (from a social perspective) when a corporation fails to invest in future gains or fails to avoid future losses at the same rate society would. And because corporations are society's greatest private source of long-term investment and economic growth, such social costs should not be ignored.

Why does this matter for our discussion of shareholder supremacy and stakeholder governance? A governance structure that takes into account the interests of a broad range of stakeholders will act as though long-term costs and benefits matter more than a governance structure that prioritizes the interests of shareholders only. The more the structure generally mimics the makeup of society, the more likely the discount rate assumed in corporate decisions will be that of the broader society. In other words, a corporate structure that includes the views of all of a company's most important stakeholders will be more likely to consider the long term than the current structure we see in American corporations. The social cost created by the differential between the corporate and social discount rates will decrease. It will not decrease to zero since no private actor will likely value the long term as much as society does. But it is reasonable to believe that it will decrease some because employees and other stakeholders will have a longer time frame than shareholders. Future gains will be valued more highly; future losses will be taken into account more seriously.

For these reasons, a board that accounts for the cost-benefit analyses of its stakeholders will tend to act with more social awareness than a board that takes into account only the interests of shareholders. And this change would not come about because the company would be more altruistic, or even more "socially responsible" in the traditional sense. It would come about in part because the costs and benefits to other stakeholders would matter. And it would come about in part because the costs and benefits that occur in the future would be valued more significantly.

This description of discount rates is simply a technical way of making the point that including broader stakeholder concerns at the senior level of corporate decision making will help roll back the pervasive short-termism of corporations. Stakeholders in general, and employees and communities in particular, know their interests are not well served by prioritizing the short term. They hope to have their jobs and their neighborhoods for more than a year; they are unwilling to assume away risk when they are the ones who would bear the costs if those risks play out. One might say that there is less moral hazard with boards that include a diversity of interests. A more straightforward way of describing this is that people don't play with fire when it's their own house that will burn.

I have spent much of my career arguing that the way we regulate and govern corporations in America undermines our democratic ideals, worsens the quality of the decision making by corporate managers and executives, and undervalues the contributions of millions of Americans who contribute to the success of business other than through ownership of stock. These arguments have been seen as marginal or even extreme, even though they have deep historical roots and find embodiments in the reality of how some other nations govern business.

But because of the global financial crisis, many people are more willing than ever to question fundamental principles of U.S. corporate governance and regulation. And the backlash to *Citizens United* also made many of us question even further the nature and risks of corporate power. We may be in a moment of historical opportunity when we can gather the political will to adjust corporate governance to become more pluralistic, incentivizing businesses to become better corporate citizens. Ironically, we may be at a moment when we stand on the verge of making real what the Supreme

Court assumed in *Citizens United:* that corporations are "associations of citizens."

The risk, however, is that those who oppose corporate power will push corporations away from the public sphere out of fear of what they do there. But the negative impact of corporations is a function of the shareholder primacy of their corporate governance. The danger they pose in the public sphere is not that they have power, but for whom they exercise that power. To fall back on assumptions about shareholder primacy as the basis for taking away the constitutional rights of corporations, as so many in the "corporations are not people" crowd have done, is a mistake. The focus on shareholders undervalues the importance of corporate constitutional rights and understates the dangers of shareholder primacy.

We can do better. The best way to start down the better route is to jettison shareholder primacy and shareholder value as the lodestars of corporate governance. Once we do that, we can move forward in both corporate law and constitutional law. We can move forward in a way beneficial to our economy and our citizens—the real, human being citizens who populate our nation.

POSTSCRIPT

Making Corporations Citizens

Corporations are not citizens, though they have some of the rights of citizens to assert beliefs, speak out on important issues, and exert influence in electoral politics. Since the Supreme Court decided *Citizens United* in 2010, the political rights and the electoral influence of corporations have been at the forefront of our national debate. For many, the answer is to push corporations back into a confined constitutional space where they cannot assert any of these rights. "Corporations are not people" embodies the understandable desire to rid our politics of the outsized influence of corporations and the people who control them.

But the notion of taking rights away from corporations is both simplistic and counterproductive. It is simplistic because it is nearly impossible to come up with a workable system of constitutional rights that meaningfully constrains government without including corporate bodies within its protective scope, at least some of the time and in some circumstances. It is counterproductive because while the influence of corporations is often worrisome—when energy companies deny climate change or when financial companies work against banking reforms—it is often helpful or necessary—when employers decry laws allowing discrimination against trans people or when media companies oppose government's efforts to surveil their customers.

The concerns about corporate influence over our politics and economy are well taken, but they are less a matter of constitutional governance than of corporate governance. When corporations are constitutionally empowered, as they must be, the question of who controls them is ever more important. When corporate influence is at its worst, it is because the voices of corporations have been appropriated by the managerial and financial elites who control them. And that appropriation is virtually assured by our system of corporate governance.

Looking at our current constitutional and governance systems together, one would be hard-pressed to imagine a system that more readily justifies a worry about corporate power: robust corporate constitutional rights married to a framework of corporate governance that is insular, exclusive, and elitist. Corporate governance norms and laws delegate corporate power to a tiny fraction of managerial and financial elites, and then constitutional law turbocharges that power. And that power can be used not only to skew politics but to distort the rules of the marketplace itself. Worse: the power can be marshaled to oppose any reform to that power.

A danger exists, however, if the response to this situation focuses on the constitutional side to the exclusion of the governance side. There should be adjustments to constitutional doctrine based on a better understanding of the nature and purpose of corporations. Corporate constitutional rights should be more limited than they are at present, especially in the electoral context. But a broad attack on corporate constitutional rights is neither workable nor advisable. Worse: the recent push to limit the constitutional personhood of corporations has gone hand in hand with arguments that corporations should stay out of the public square and focus their energies on shareholder interests. This is the wrong direction.

The best fix for the problem of the misuse of corporate power in politics and in society is not a constitutional one, nor should it push corporations into a narrow box where they care only about the economic interests of shareholders. The best solution is a corporate governance solution that encourages—even requires—corporations to take seriously their public commitments.

We should not exclude corporations from democracy, but inject democracy into them. Instead of rejecting corporate personhood, we should embrace it. To make corporate citizenship less of a threat and more of a promise, corporations should become more like the real persons who make them up. Corporate governance structures should include representatives of the people who contribute to them, and management should focus not only on the interests of shareholders, but on those of other stakeholders as well.

Corporations should be more like people. Corporations should take into account a multitude of obligations—as people do. They should act as though more than one thing matters—as people do. They should care about the implications of their decisions, even if it does not affect them financially—as people do.

If corporations were more like people, corporate personhood—indeed corporate citizenship—could be a positive force in our society and even in our politics.

Notes

Introduction

1. Franklin D. Roosevelt, Message to Congress on Curbing Monopolies (Apr. 29, 1938), online by Gerhard Peters and John T. Woolley, The American Presidency Project, http://www.presidency.ucsb.edu/ws/?pid=15637.
2. President Dwight D. Eisenhower, Farewell Address (Jan. 17, 1961); Final TV Talk 1/17/61 (1), Box 38, Speech Series, Papers of Dwight D. Eisenhower as President, 1953–61, Eisenhower Library; National Archives and Records Administration.
3. Margaret Ebrahim, *Fat Cat Hotel: How Democratic High-Rollers Are Rewarded with Overnight Stays at the White House*, 2 NEWSLETTER OF THE CENTER FOR PUBLIC INTEGRITY (Aug. 1996), available at https://iw-files.s3.amazonaws .com/documents/pdfs/fat_cat_hotel_1996_08.pdf.
4. Michael Abramowitz & Steven Mufson, *Papers Detail Industry's Role in Cheney's Energy Report*, WASH. POST (July 18, 2007).
5. Bob Ivry, Bradley Keoun, & Phil Kuntz, *Secret Fed Loans Gave Banks $13 Billion Undisclosed to Congress*, BLOOMBERG MARKETS (Nov. 27, 2011), https:// www.bloomberg.com/news/articles/2011-11-28/secret-fed-loans-undis closed-to-congress-gave-banks-13-billion-in-income (reporting over $7 trillion of commitments to save financial system); Brent Snavely, *Final Tally: Taxpayers Auto Bailout Loss $9.3B*, USA TODAY (Dec. 30, 2014), https://www .usatoday.com/story/money/cars/2014/12/30/auto-bailout-tarp-gm-chrys ler/21061251/.

6. *New York Times Co. v. United States,* 403 U.S. 713 (1971).
7. *Virginia State Board of Pharmacy v. Virginia Citizens Consumer Council, Inc.,* 425 U.S. 748 (1976).
8. *Citizens United v. Fed. Election Comm'n.,* 558 U.S. 310 (2010).
9. Dan Eggen, *Poll: Large Majority Opposes Supreme Court's Decision on Campaign Financing,* WASH. POST (Feb. 17, 2010), http://articles.washingtonpost.com /2010-02-16/politics/36773318_1_corporations-unions-new-limits; Gary Langer, *In Supreme Court Ruling on Campaign Finance, the Public Dissents,* ABC NEWS (Feb. 17, 2010), http://blogs.abcnews.com/thenumbers/2010/02/in -supreme-court-ruling-on-campaign-finance-the-public-dissents.html.
10. *See* Public Citizen, DEMOCRACY IS FOR PEOPLE, http://www.citizen.org/doc uments/DIFP-Corporations-are-Not-People-Citizens-United-Fact-Sheet .pdf.
11. *Trs. of Dartmouth Coll. v. Woodward,* 4 Wheat. 518, 636 (1819).

ONE

In Defense of Corporate Persons

1. Attributed to Edward Thurlow, 1st Baron Thurlow, who was Lord Chancellor of Great Britain from 1778 to 1783. *See* John C. Coffee, Jr., *"No Soul to Damn: No Body to Kick": An Unscandalized Inquiry into the Problem of Corporate Punishment,* 79 MICH. L. REV. 386, 386 (1981).
2. *See* Ashley Parker, *Romney Stands by Corporations Remarks,* N.Y. TIMES (Aug. 25, 2011).
3. The first case to allow a constitutional claim by a corporation—the right to sue in federal court—was *Bank of United States v. Deveaux,* 9 U.S. (5 Cranch) 61 (1809). For a comprehensive history of the development of corporate constitutional rights, *see* ADAM WINKLER, WE THE CORPORATIONS (2018).
4. *Citizens United v. Fed. Election Comm'n.,* 558 U.S. 310 (2010).
5. 2 U.S.C. § 441(b) (2000 ed.); *Citizens United,* 558 U.S. at 320.
6. *Buckley v. Valeo,* 424 U.S. 1 (1976).
7. *Austin v. Michigan Chamber of Commerce,* 494 U.S. 652 (1990) (upholding limits on corporate expenditures in candidate elections). The Court had previously struck down limits on corporate spending on referenda—*see First National Bank of Boston v. Bellotti,* 435 U.S. 765 (1978)—but the *Austin* Court believed the risk of corruption was greater in candidate elections than in referenda elections.
8. *Austin,* 494 U.S. at 659 (quoting *FEC v. Massachusetts Citizens for Life, Inc.,* 479 U.S. 238, 257 (1986)).
9. *Austin,* 494 U.S. at 660.
10. For a chart outlining the range of different proposals in Congress, *see Con-*

stitutional Amendments, UNITED 4 THE PEOPLE, http://united4thepeople.org
/amendments/; Other Amendments, MOVE TO AMEND, https://moveto
amend.org/other-amendments; *Our Comparative Analysis of Amendment Bills
in the 113th Congress*, FREE SPEECH FOR PEOPLE, http://freespeechforpeople
.org/node/593.

11. *See* Amy Gardner & Felicia Sonmez, *In Formal Campaign Kick-Off, Obama
Dings Romney's "Corporations Are People" Line*, WASH. POST (May 5, 2012),
https://www.washingtonpost.com/politics/obama-to-showcase-technology
-at-kickoff-rallies-saturday/2012/05/05/gIQAZNA32T_story.html?utm
_term=.ddo11ef074f3; Mark Lander, *Obama Formally Kicks Off Campaign
in Ohio and Virginia*, N.Y. TIMES (May 5, 2012), http://www.nytimes.com
/2012/05/06/us/politics/obama-holds-large-campaign-rallies-in-ohio-and
-virginia.html.

12. *See* David A. Fahrenthold, *Sen. Elizabeth Warren, the Teacher, Reminds Demo-
crats That "Rally" Is a Verb*, WASH. POST (Oct. 28, 2014), http://www.washing
tonpost.com/politics/sen-elizabeth-warren-has-become-a-master-of-the
-stump-speech/2014/10/28/acfee026-5e0e-11e4-8b9e-2ccdac31a031_story
.html.

13. Matea Gold & Anne Gearan, *Hillary Clinton's Litmus Test for Supreme Court
Nominees: A Pledge to Overturn Citizens United*, WASH. POST (May 14, 2015),
https://www.washingtonpost.com/news/post-politics/wp/2015/05/14/hil
lary-clintons-litmus-test-for-supreme-court-nominees-a-pledge-to-overturn
-citizens-united/?utm_term=.d32b15971d0b.

14. *See* Pete Kasperowicz, *Sanders Proposes Amendment to the Constitution That
Would Limit Free Speech*, THE HILL (Dec. 9, 2011).

15. *Resolutions & Ordinances*, MOVE TO AMEND, https://movetoamend.org/reso
lutions-map; *Voters in Four States Reject Citizens United in Landslide Victories
on Election Day*, MOVE TO AMEND (Nov. 15, 2016), https://movetoamend
.org/press-release/voters-four-states-reject-citizens-united-landslide-victo
ries-election-day.

16. *See Achievements by the Movement to Restore Democracy*, DEMOCRACY IS FOR
PEOPLE, http://www.democracyisforpeople.org/infographic.cfm; Byron Tau,
Obama Calls for Constitutional Amendment to Overturn Citizens United, POLI-
TICO (Aug. 29, 2012), http://www.politico.com/blogs/politico44/2012/08/
obama-calls-for-constitutional-amendment-to-overturn-citizens-united
-133724; Caitlin MacNeal, *Citizens United Constitutional Amendments Introduced in the Senate*, HUFFINGTON POST (June 19, 2013), http://www.huffing
tonpost.com/2013/06/19/citizens-united-constitutional-amendment_n_346
5636.html.

17. Paul Blumenthal, *SEC Petition for Corporate Spending Rule Reaches Half-Million
Comments*, HUFFINGTON POST (Apr. 16, 2013), http://www.huffingtonpost
.com/2013/04/16/sec-corporate-political-spending_n_3093121.html.

18. *Money in Politics*, COMMON CAUSE, http://archive.is/xdHHC; Robert Reich, *Amend 2012*, *People over Politics*, https://www.youtube.com/watch?v=eg3-yr Znxeo.

19. *A Constitutional Amendment to Keep Corporate Money out of Elections: Corporations Are Not People*, PUBLIC CITIZEN, http://www.citizen.org/documents /DIFP-Corporations-are-Not-People-Citizens-United-Fact-Sheet.pdf.

20. *The People's Rights Amendment*, FREE SPEECH FOR PEOPLE, http://org2.salsa labs.com/o/7003/p/salsa/web/common/public/content?content_item_KEY =5624.

21. *See, e.g.*, JEFFREY D. CLEMENTS, CORPORATIONS ARE NOT PEOPLE 13 (2012) ("Most Americans understand the fundamental truth that corporations are not people and that large corporations already have far too much power in America"); *Bill Moyers and Stephen Colbert Talk Corporations, Racism*, HUFF-INGTON POST (Jan. 11, 2012), http://www.huffingtonpost.com/2012/01/11 /bill-moyers-stephen-colbert-corporations_n_1199503.html (quoting Moyers as saying, "You cannot have a people's democracy as long as corporations are considered people"); Jamie Raskin, *Corporations Aren't People*, NPR (Sept. 10, 2009), http://www.npr.org/templates/story/story.php?storyId=112714052 ("The sovereign actors of American democracy—we, the people—have also understood that business corporations, which are magnificent agents of capital accumulation and wealth maximization in the economic sphere, pose extreme dangers in the political sphere. Our best leaders have wanted business to prosper but never to govern").

22. *Legal Advisory Committee*, FREE SPEECH FOR PEOPLE, https://freespeechfor people.org/about/legal-advisory-committee/.

23. Patient Protection and Affordable Care Act, Pub. L. No. 111–148, 124 Stat. 119.

24. Religious Freedom Restoration Act of 1993 (RFRA), 42 U.S.C. 2000bb et seq.

25. 42 U.S.C. 2000bb-1(a) and (b).

26. 1 U.S.C. § 1–8 (2012).

27. I was one of the principal authors of the brief. *See* Brief of Corporate and Criminal Law Professors as Amici Curiae in Support of Petitioners, *Burwell v. Hobby Lobby Stores, Inc.* (Nos. 13–354 and 13–356), available at https://www .americanbar.org/content/dam/aba/publications/supreme_court_preview /briefs-v3/13-354-13-356_amcu_cclp.authcheckdam.pdf.

28. Lynn A. Stout, *The Corporation as Time Machine: Intergenerational Equity, Intergenerational Efficiency, and the Corporate Form*, 38 SEATTLE U. L. REV. 685 (2015).

29. I co-authored a similar brief in a case argued in the fall of 2017. In *Masterpiece Cakeshop, Ltd. v. Colorado Civil Rights Comm'n.*, a bakery refused to sell a wedding cake to a same-sex couple. The bakery claimed a First Amendment

right to be exempted from Colorado anti-discrimination law, saying such sale would force the baker to violate sincerely held religious beliefs. The brief I filed on behalf of roughly thirty corporate law professors argued that the baker's religious and political views cannot be projected onto the bakery itself without violating the principle of corporate separateness. *See* Brief of Amici Curiae Corporate Law Professors in Support of Respondents, *Masterpiece Cakeshop, Ltd. v. Colorado Civil Rights Comm'n.*, (No. 16–111), available at http://www.scotusblog.com/wp-content/uploads/2017/11/16-111_bsac_corporate-law-professors.pdf.

30. *On Scene Coordinator Report*, Deepwater Horizon Oil Spill (2011) at 33, http://www.uscg.mil/foia/docs/dwh/fosc_dwh_report.pdf.

31. *New York Times Co. v. United States*, 403 U.S. 713 (1971).

32. *Planned Parenthood of Southeastern Pa. v. Casey*, 505 U.S. 833 (1992).

33. Devlin Barrett & Jay Greene, *Microsoft Wins Appeals Ruling on Data Searches*, Wall St. J. (July 14, 2016), https://www.wsj.com/articles/microsoft-wins-appeals-ruling-on-data-searches-1468511551; Sam Thielman, *Apple v. the FBI: What's the Beef? How Did We Get Here and What's at Stake?*, Guardian (Feb. 20, 2016), https://www.theguardian.com/technology/2016/feb/20/apple-fbi-iphone-explainer-san-bernardino.

34. *The People's Rights Amendment Protects Freedom of the Press*, Free Speech for People, https://freespeechforpeople.org/wp-content/uploads/archive/FSFP%20on%20freedom%20of%20the%20press.pdf.

35. *The People's Rights Amendment*, Free Speech for People, http://org2.salsalabs.com/o/7003/p/salsa/web/common/public/content?content_item_KEY=5624.

36. *The People's Rights Amendment Protects Property Rights*, Free Speech for People, https://freespeechforpeople.org/wp-content/uploads/archive/FSFP%20on%20property%20rights.pdf.

37. *The People's Rights Amendment Protects Property Rights*, *supra*.

38. *See* Kent Greenfield, *Hobby Lobby and the Return of "The Negro Travelers' Green Book*," The Am. Prospect (Mar. 26, 2014), http://prospect.org/article/hobby-lobby-and-return-negro-travelers-green-book.

39. *See Masterpiece Cakeshop, Ltd. v. Colorado Civil Rights Comm'n.* (No. 16–111) (argued Dec. 5, 2017). *See also* n. 29 above.

40. Brandon L. Garrett, *The Constitutional Standing of Corporations*, 163 U. Pa. L. Rev. 95, part I (2014).

41. *Dartmouth Coll.*, 4 Wheat. 518, 636 (1819).

42. *First Nat'l. Bank v. Bellotti*, 435 U.S. 765 (1978).

43. *Id.* at 824 (Rehnquist, J. dissenting).

44. *See* Kent Greenfield, The Failure of Corporate Law: Fundamental Flaws and Progressive Possibilities (2006).

45. *Hale v. Henkel*, 201 U.S. 43 (1906).

46. John Dewey, *The Historical Background of Corporate Legal Personality*, 35 Yale L. J. 655 (1926).
47. Kent Greenfield, *Do Corporations Have Religious Liberty?*, Bos. Globe (Mar. 2, 2014), https://www.bostonglobe.com/opinion/2014/03/02/unfair-advantage-would-spur-abuse-exempt-status/jKhgXAMJyxaiC3vjb7qGxH/story.html.
48. *FCC v. AT&T Inc.*, 562 U.S. 397, 410 (2011).
49. This statement is subject to the straightforward caveat that commercial speech should not receive protection that is so great so as to undermine the economic role of corporations. For example, fraud and misrepresentation—even if protected in other speech contexts; *see United States v. Alvarez*, 567 U.S. 709 (2012)—need not be protected in commercial speech. In other words, intermediate scrutiny—current doctrine—is about right for commercial speech. *See Cent. Hudson Gas & Elec. Corp. v. Pub. Svc. Comm'n.*, 447 U.S. 557 (1980). More on this in chapter 6 below.
50. For purposes of comparison, germaneness is a matter of constitutional importance in construing the rights of unions and union members. Under *Abood v. Detroit Bd. of Educ.*, 431 U.S. 209, 235–36 (1977), public employees have a First Amendment right not to have their union dues or fees used by the union for "the advancement of ideological causes not germane to its duties as collective bargaining representative."
51. *Virginia State Board of Pharmacy v. Virginia Citizens Consumer Council, Inc.*, 425 U.S. 748 (1976).
52. *Citizens United*, 558 U.S. at 365. *See* Winkler, We The Corporations, *supra*, at 290–300.
53. *See* Winkler, We The Corporations, *supra*, at 300.
54. *Buckley*, 424 U.S. 1, 14 (1976).
55. *Citizens United*, 558 U.S. at 350; *Buckley*, 424 U.S. at 48–49.
56. *See, e.g.*, Zephyr Teachout, Corruption in America: from Benjamin Franklin's Snuff Box to Citizens United (2016).
57. *Harper v. Canada* (Attorney General), [2004] 1 S.C.R. 827, 2004 SCC 33, 62 (Can.) ("Wealth is the main obstacle to equal participation [in elections]. . . . These provisions seek to create a level playing field for those who wish to engage in the electoral discourse. This, in turn, enables voters to be better informed; no one voice is overwhelmed by another").
58. *See generally* opensecrets.org. This is the web-based database for the Center for Responsive Politics. The site does not organize the data in a way that makes it simple to search for corporate donors. Nevertheless, within the donor lists of the major Super PACs for the 2016 cycle, very few for-profit, publicly traded companies appear. No corporate donor is listed for the top pro-Clinton Super PAC, Priorities USA Action. The top pro-Trump Super PAC, Get Our Jobs Back, lists only two businesses as donors, and both are

privately held. The top pro-Trump company was NY Post Publishing, which donated just over $300,000. Jeb Bush's Super PAC had ten corporate donors, but nine of them are privately held and appear to have been conduits for individual money. The single public company donor was NextEra Energy, a clean energy company, which gave $1 million. The Senate Leadership Fund (a pro Republican PAC) had only three corporate donors listed for 2016, with Chevron the only publicly traded company appearing on the list. Chevron gave $2 million. The Congressional Leadership Fund (a pro Republican PAC) had two public company donors—Chevron at $1.3 million and Devon Energy at $500,000.

59. Dave Levinthal & Tarini Parti, *5 Money Takeaways from 2012*, POLITICO (Nov. 17, 2012), http://www.politico.com/story/2012/11/five-money-take aways-from-2012-083655?o=0; *Post-Election Money in Politics Analysis*, CITIZENS FOR RESPONSIBILITY AND ETHICS IN WASHINGTON, 7, http://s3.ama zonaws.com/storage.citizensforethics.org/wp-content/uploads/2016/07 /20022643/2012_Election_Analysis.pdf; Ciara Torres-Spelliscy, *Safeguarding Markets from Pernicious Pay to Play: A Model Explaining Why the SEC Regulates Money in Politics*, 12(2) CONN. PUB. INTEREST L. J. 361, 402 (2012–2013).

60. *See* Associated Press, *Super Bowl Ads Cost Average of $3.5M*, ESPN.COM (Feb. 6, 2012), http://www.espn.com/nfl/playoffs/2011/story/_/id/7544243/super -bowl-2012-commercials-cost-average-35m.

61. *2012 Top Donors to Outside Spending Groups*, THE CENTER FOR RESPONSIVE POLITICS, https://www.opensecrets.org/outsidespending/summ.php?cycle =2012&disp=D (select "2012," "Individuals," and "All Outside Spending Groups"); *Political Nonprofits: Top Election Spenders*, CENTER FOR RESPONSIVE POLITICS, https://www.opensecrets.org/outsidespending/nonprof_elec .php?cycle=2012 (select "2012"); Andrew Prokop, *40 Charts That Explain Money in Politics*, Vox (July 30, 2014), http://www.vox.com/2014/7/30/5949581 /money-in-politics-charts-explain; *The Koch Network: A Cartological Guide*, CENTER FOR RESPONSIVE POLITICS (Jan. 7, 2014), https://www.opensecrets .org/news/2014/01/koch-network-a-cartological-guide/.

62. *See* opensecrets.org.

63. According to the *New York Times*, as of February 2016, in the heat of the primary season, eighty-seven donors had given at least a million dollars to a candidate or a candidate's Super PACs. Of those eighty-seven, only nine donors were for-profit corporations. Of those nine, only one was publicly traded. Of the eight private companies, most appear to be dominated by a single owner. *See* Wilson Andrews et al., *Million-Dollar Donors in the 2016 Presidential Race*, N.Y. TIMES (Feb. 9, 2016), http://www.nytimes.com/inter active/2016/us/elections/top-presidential-donors-campaign-money.html; Theo Francis, *Despite Citizens United, Corporate Super PAC Contributions Trail Individuals, Study Finds*, WALL ST. J. (Nov. 2, 2016), http://www.wsj.com

/articles/despite-citizens-united-corporate-super-pac-contributions-trail
-individuals-study-finds-1478059201; LANDSCAPE OF CAMPAIGN CONTRIBU-
TIONS (Committee for Econ. Dev. of the Conf. Board, Nov. 2016), available
at https://www.ced.org/pdf/Election_Spending_Report_-_Nov_2016.pdf.

64. These figures are derived from a spreadsheet of all corporate expenditures in
2016, provided to the author by the Center for Responsive Politics.

65. *See* https://www.opensecrets.org/overview/topindivs.php?cycle=2016.

66. *Right to Rise USA,* Contributors, 2016 Cycle, CENTER FOR RESPONSIVE
POLITICS, available at https://www.opensecrets.org/pacs/pacgave2.php?cy
cle=2016&cmte=C00571372. *See also 2016 Top Donors to Outside Spending
Groups,* CENTER FOR RESPONSIVE POLITICS, available at https://www.open
secrets.org/outsidespending/summ.php?cycle=2016&disp=D&type=O&su
peronly=N.

67. *See* GREENFIELD, THE FAILURE OF CORPORATE LAW, *supra;* LYNN A. STOUT,
THE SHAREHOLDER VALUE MYTH: HOW PUTTING SHAREHOLDERS FIRST
HARMS INVESTORS, CORPORATIONS, AND THE PUBLIC (2012).

68. Kent Greenfield, *Defending Stakeholder Governance,* 58 CASE W. RES. L. REV.
1043 (2008); Kent Greenfield, *Sticking the Landing: Making the Most of the
"Stakeholder Moment,"* 2015 EUR. BUS. L. REV. 147 (2015).

69. ALINE CONCHON, BOARD-LEVEL EMPLOYEE REPRESENTATION RIGHTS IN
EUROPE: FACTS AND TRENDS, 7–8 (2011), http://www.etui.org/Publica
tions2/Reports/Board-level-employee-representation-rights-in-Europe; *see also
MAP: Board-Level Representation in the European Economic Area,* WORKER-
PARTICIPATION.EU, http://www.worker-participation.eu/National-Industrial
-Relations/Across-Europe/Board-level-Representation2/MAP-Board-level
-representation-in-the-European-Economic-Area2.

70. CONCHON, BOARD-LEVEL EMPLOYEE REPRESENTATION RIGHTS IN EUROPE,
supra.

71. *See* Kent Greenfield & John Nilsson, *Gradgrind's Education: Using Dickens and
Aristotle to Understand (and Replace?) the Business Judgment Rule,* 63 BROOK. L.
REV. 799 (1998).

TWO
Corporations and the "Damn Public"

1. There are three competing versions of the interview, but the most likely is
the one mentioned in the text. *See* JOHN STEELE GORDON, THE BUSINESS OF
AMERICA 96–99 (2001). This quote is often misattributed to William Henry's
father, "Commodore" Cornelius Vanderbilt. *See, e.g.,* THE DICTIONARY OF
CULTURAL LITERACY 436 (E. D. Hirsch, Jr., et al., eds., 1988) (attributing
quote to Cornelius Vanderbilt).

2. GORDON, THE BUSINESS OF AMERICA, *supra*, at 96.
3. Cartoon viewable at Kent Greenfield, *Corporate Law's Original Sin*, WASH. MONTHLY, http://www.washingtonmonthly.com/magazine/januaryfebruary _2015/features/sidebar_corporate_laws_origina053536.php?page=all. For a comprehensive treatment of the comment and the stories surrounding it, *see* GORDON, THE BUSINESS OF AMERICA, *supra*, at 96–99.
4. *See* ADAM WINKLER, WE THE CORPORATIONS (2018), at 104 ("Many of the railroads that followed would similarly use cash or stock to sway elected officials to approve railroad measures. Graft was treated as a cost of doing business. Over the second half of the nineteenth century, bribery of public officials would become as commonplace as the leaden smoke billowing from the engines of the B&O's imitators"); *id.* at 197 ("To win favorable legislation in this changing environment, corporations turned to lobbying, special favors, and, when that failed, flat out bribery").
5. *The Homestead Strike*, PBS: AMERICAN EXPERIENCE, http://www.pbs.org /wgbh/amex/carnegie/peopleevents/pande04.html.
6. *See* Adam Winkler, *The Corporation in Election Law*, 32 LOY. L.A. L. REV. 1243, 1246 (1999) (quoting ROBERT E. MUTCH, CAMPAIGNS, CONGRESS, AND COURTS: THE MAKING OF FEDERAL CAMPAIGN FINANCE LAW 7 (1988), quoting Republican reformer William E. Chandler).
7. *Id.* at 1246 n. 10 (quoting RICHARD HOFSTADTER, THE AGE OF REFORM: FROM BRYANT TO F.D.R. 225 (1955)).
8. This appeared in PUCK, Vol. 12, 98 (Google digitized 2015) (1882) (available as free Google ebook at https://books.google.com/books?id=hWBHAQA AMAAJ&printsec=frontcover&source=gbs_ge_summary_r&cad=o#v=one page&q&f=false).
9. *Lochner v. New York*, 198 U.S. 45 (1905).
10. *Id.* at 63.
11. *Muller v. Oregon*, 208 U.S., 412 (1908).
12. *See, e.g.*, the Keating-Owen Child Labor Act of 1916, c. 432, 39 Stat. 675.
13. *See Hammer v. Dagenhart*, 247 U.S. 251, 276–77 (1918).
14. UPTON SINCLAIR, JR., THE JUNGLE (1906).
15. *See, e.g.*, M. Todd Henderson, *Everything Old Is New Again: Lessons from Dodge v. Ford Motor Company*, *in* CORPORATE LAW STORIES (J. Mark Ramseyer, ed., 2009).
16. These figures can be extrapolated from the opinion itself in *Dodge v. Ford Motor Company*, 204 Mich. 459 (1919). During the years leading up to the suit, the Ford company paid out regular quarterly dividends equal to 5 percent monthly of the capital stock of $2 million. That would mean that the Dodge brothers, who had made an initial investment in the company of $10,000, were receiving regular dividends of $10,000 per month. In addition to regular dividends, the company also paid out special dividends of $1 mil-

lion in 1911, $4 million in 1912, $10 million in 1913, $11 million in 1914, and $10 million in 1915. The Dodge brothers thus received over $4 million in special dividends from their $10,000 initial investment, a return of over 40,000 percent in special dividends alone.

17. *See, e.g.*, Vincent Curcio, Henry Ford (2013); Max Wallace, The American Axis: Henry Ford, Charles Lindbergh, and the Rise of the Third Reich (2003); Victoria Saker Woeste, Henry Ford's War on Jews and the Legal Battle against Hate Speech (2012); Michael Dobbs, *Ford and GM Scrutinized for Alleged Nazi Collaboration*, Wash. Post (Nov. 30, 1998), https://www.washingtonpost.com/wp-srv/national/daily/nov98/nazicars30 .htm.

18. *See* Thomas Edison, *Henry Ford Explains Why He Gives Away $10,000,000*, N.Y. Times (Jan. 11, 1914), at A01.

19. Henderson, *Everything Old Is New Again*, *supra*, at 18.

20. *Henry Ford's Rouge*, The Henry Ford, https://www.thehenryford.org/visit /ford-rouge-factory-tour/history-and-timeline/fords-rouge/#millennium; Alisa Priddle, *Be Dazzled at New Ford Rouge Factory Tour*, Detroit Free Press (Feb. 1, 2015), http://www.freep.com/story/money/cars/ford/2015/02/01/ford -rouge-factory-tour-renovated/22698457/.

21. *See* Henderson, *Everything Old Is New Again*, *supra*, at 21–22 n. 14 (quoting Alexander R. Crabb, Birth of a Giant: The Men and Incidents that Gave America the Motorcar 359 (1969)).

22. Henderson, *Everything Old Is New Again*, *supra*, at 21–22 n. 14 (quoting Henry Ford, My Life and Work 162 (1922)).

23. Allan Nevins & Frank E. Hill, Ford: Expansion and Challenge, 1915–1933 (1957).

24. Henderson, *Everything Old Is New Again*, *supra*, at 21–22 n. 14.

25. *Dodge*, 204 Mich. 459, 505 (1919).

26. Henderson, *Everything Old Is New Again*, *supra*, at 23–24.

27. *Id.* at 24.

28. *Dodge*, 204 Mich. at 491.

29. Jamie L. Carson & Benjamin A. Kleinerman, *A Switch in Time Saves Nine: Institutions, Strategic Actors, and FDR's Court-Packing Plan*, 113 Pub. Choice 301 (2002).

30. *See* Cass Sunstein, After the Rights Revolution 20 (1993) ("For the New Deal reformers . . . the common law was hardly neutral or prepolitical, but instead reflected a set of explicit regulatory decisions"). The intellectual leaders of the legal realist movement are owed credit for this insight. *See, e.g.*, Felix Cohen, *Transcendental Nonsense and the Functional Approach*, 35 Colum. L. Rev. 809 (1935); Robert L. Hale, *Coercion and Distribution in a Supposedly Non-Coercive State*, 38 Pol. Sci. Q. 470 (1923).

31. *West Coast Hotel Co. v. Parrish*, 300 U.S. 379, 399 (1937).

32. *Id.*
33. *See Wickard v. Filburn,* 317 U.S. 111 (1942) (upholding regulation of farm prices and production); *United States v. Darby,* 312 U.S. 100 (1941) (upholding federal minimum wage and maximum hour laws established in the Fair Labor Standards Act); *NLRB v. Jones & Laughlin Steel Corp.,* 301 U.S. 1 (1937) (upholding the National Labor Relations Act of 1935).
34. *Jones & Laughlin,* 301 U.S. at 57.
35. *West Coast Hotel,* 300 U.S. at 399.
36. Securities Act of 1933 §§ 1–26, 15 U.S.C. §§ 77a–77bbbb (2006); Securities Exchange Act of 1934 §§ 1–37, 15 U.S.C. §§ 78a–78nn (2006).
37. 49 STAT. 449 (1935), 29 U.S.C. § 151 (Supp. 1937).
38. Fair Labor Standards Act of 1938, 29 U.S.C. §§ 201–19 (1982).
39. ADOLF A. BERLE & GARDINER C. MEANS, THE MODERN CORPORATION AND PUBLIC PROPERTY (1932).
40. Dalia Tsuk, *Corporations without Labor: The Politics of Progressive Corporate Law,* 151 U. PA. L. REV. 1861, 1885 (2003).
41. *See* BERLE & MEANS, THE MODERN CORPORATION AND PUBLIC PROPERTY, *supra,* at 345 (discussing how Adam Smith's concepts "tend to mislead in describing modern enterprise as carried on by the great corporations" and that they are "inapplicable to a dominant area in American economic organization").
42. Tsuk, *Corporations without Labor, supra,* at 1885.
43. BERLE & MEANS, THE MODERN CORPORATION AND PUBLIC PROPERTY, *supra,* at 357. *See also* Tsuk, *Corporations without Labor, supra,* for an excellent treatment of the Berle & Means argument in this regard.
44. BERLE & MEANS, THE MODERN CORPORATION AND PUBLIC PROPERTY, *supra,* at 353.
45. *Id.* at 355.
46. *Id.* at 356.
47. *Id.*
48. *Id.*
49. Tsuk, *Corporations without Labor, supra,* at 1861.
50. *See, e.g., A. P. Smith Mfg. Co. v. Barlow,* 13 N.J. 145, 98 A.2d 581 (1953).
51. *See, e.g., Shlensky v. Wrigley,* 95 Ill. App. 2d 173, 237 N.E.2d 776 (App. Ct. 1968).
52. *See* RACHEL CARSON, SILENT SPRING (1962), and RALPH NADER, JOEL SELIGMAN, & MARK GREEN, TAMING THE GIANT CORPORATION (1976); RALPH NADER, UNSAFE AT ANY SPEED (1965).
53. *See* SUNSTEIN, AFTER THE RIGHTS REVOLUTION, *supra.*
54. *See* Lawrence E. Mitchell, *A Theoretical and Practical Framework for Enforcing Corporate Constituency Statutes,* 70 TEX. L. REV. 579, 592–94 (1992); Eric W. Orts, *Beyond Shareholders: Interpreting Corporate Constituency Statutes,* 61 GEO. WASH. L. REV. 14, 24 (1992).

55. *See, e.g.*, William L. Cary, *Federalism and Corporate Law: Reflections upon Delaware*, 83 YALE L. J. 663, 666 (1974).

56. *See Corporate Rights and Responsibilities: Hearing before S. Comm. on Commerce*, 94th Cong. (1976); *Role of the Shareholder in the Corporate World, Part 1: Hearing before the Subcomm. on Citizens and Shareholders Rights and Remedies of the S. Comm. on the Judiciary*, 95th Cong. (1977).

57. JOHN W. SLOAN, THE REAGAN EFFECT: ECONOMICS AND PRESIDENTIAL LEADERSHIP (1999).

58. Franklin D. Roosevelt, Second Inaugural Address (Jan. 20, 1937), available at http://historymatters.gmu.edu/d/5105/.

59. Ronald Reagan, The President's News Conference (June 28, 1983), AMERICAN PRESIDENCY PROJECT, available at http://www.presidency.ucsb.edu/ws/?pid=41535.

60. Milton Friedman, *The Social Responsibility of Business Is to Increase Its Profits*, N.Y. TIMES (Sept. 13, 1970) at 32, available at http://query.nytimes.com/mem/archive-free/pdf?res=9E05E0DA153CE531A15750C1A96F9C946190D6CF. *See* Pascal-Emmanuel Gobry, *What Reagan's Greatest Economic Adviser Thought about Austerity*, Forbes.com (June 5, 2013), https://www.forbes.com/sites/pascalemmanuelgobry/2013/06/05/milton-friedman-on-austerity/#30183fa35628.

61. *See* WALL STREET (American Entertainment Partners 1987); http://www.imdb.com/title/tt0094291/quotes.

62. For a review, *see* RICHARD POSNER, ECONOMIC ANALYSIS OF LAW (3d ed., 1986).

63. *See* Kent Greenfield, *The End of Contractarianism? Behavioral Economics and the Law of Corporations*, in THE OXFORD HANDBOOK ON BEHAVIORAL ECONOMICS AND THE LAW (Eyal Zamir & Doron Teichman, eds., 2014). The foundational texts of this contractarian view are FRANK EASTERBROOK & DANIEL FISCHEL, THE ECONOMIC STRUCTURE OF CORPORATE LAW (1991), and Michael C. Jensen & William H. Meckling, *Theory of the Firm: Managerial Behavior, Agency Costs and Ownership Structure*, 3 J. FIN. ECON. 305 (1976).

64. KENT GREENFIELD, THE FAILURE OF CORPORATE LAW: FUNDAMENTAL FLAWS AND PROGRESSIVE POSSIBILITIES 29–39 (2006).

65. *See generally* Jonathan Macey, *An Economic Analysis of the Various Rationales for Making Shareholders the Exclusive Beneficiaries of Corporate Fiduciary Duties*, 21 STETSON L. REV. 23 (1991).

66. *Executive Profile of Robert L. Nardelli*, BLOOMBERG BUS., https://www.bloomberg.com/profiles/people/14003404-robert-l-nardelli.

67. James Fanto, *Quasi-Rationality in Action: A Study of Psychological Factors in Merger Decision-Making*, 62 OHIO ST. L. J. 1333, 1368 (2001); Kath Hall, *Looking beneath the Surface: The Impact of Psychology on Corporate Decision Making*, 49 MANAGERIAL LAW 93, 99 (2007); Richard Roll, *The Hubris Hypothesis of Corporate Takeovers*, 59 J. BUS. 197 (1986).

68. *See In re Walt Disney Co. Derivative Litig.*, 906 A.2d 27 (2006).

69. *See Kahn v. Sullivan*, 594 A.2d 48, 54–55 (Del. 1991).

70. *Stocks Traded, Turnover Ratio,* THE WORLD BANK, http://data.worldbank.org/indicator/CM.MKT.TRNR?order=wbapi_data_value_2008+wbapi_data_value+wbapi_data_value-first&sort=desc.

71. PETER A. BROOK, A VISION FOR VENTURE CAPITAL: REALIZING THE PROMISE OF GLOBAL VENTURE CAPITAL AND PRIVATE EQUITY, 150 (2009) ("Amid the buyout boom of the early 2000s, private equity investors such as Stephen Schwarzman and David Donderman became the new celebrities of the financial word").

72. *See* FRANK PARTNOY, F.I.A.S.C.O.: BLOOD IN THE WATER ON WALL STREET (2009).

73. Kent Greenfield, *The Puzzle of Short-Termism,* 46 WAKE FOREST L. REV. 627 (2011). *See* Rachelle C. Sampson and Yuan Shi, *Are US Firms and Markets Becoming More Short-Term Oriented? Evidence of Shifting Firm and Investor Time Horizons, 1980–2013* (draft of Jan. 31, 2018), available at https://dx.doi.org/10.2139/ssrn.2837524 (providing evidence of increasing short-termism in U.S. equity capital markets).

74. The best source for U.S. statistics to substantiate these claims is the ECONOMIC POLICY INSTITUTE, www.epi.org, particularly its annual book-length reports entitled *The State of Working America.*

75. *See* THOMAS O. MCGARITY, FREEDOM TO HARM: THE LASTING LEGACY OF THE LAISSEZ FAIRE REVIVAL (2013).

76. Kent Greenfield, *Corporate Law and the Rhetoric of Choice, in* LAW AND ECONOMICS: TOWARD SOCIAL JUSTICE, Vol. 24 OF RESEARCH IN LAW AND ECONOMICS (Dana Gold, ed., 2009).

77. ROY GIRASA, CORPORATE GOVERNANCE AND FINANCE LAW 115–117 (2013).

78. 2006 UK Companies Act, c. 46, § 172 (requiring directors in fulfilling their duties "to promote the success of the company," to "have regard [to] the likely consequences of any decision in the long term," "the interests of the company's employees," and "the impact of the company's operations on the community and the environment," among other things).

79. For a good review, *see* David K. Millon, *New Directions in Corporate Law: Communitarians, Contractarians, and the Crisis in Corporate Law,* 50 WASH. & LEE L. REV. 1373 (1993).

80. *See New York v. United States,* 505 U.S. 144 (1992).

81. *See United States v. Morrison,* 529 U.S. 598 (2000); *United States v. Lopez,* 514 U.S. 549 (1995).

82. *Am. Trucking Assns., Inc. v. EPA,* 175 F.3d 1027 (DC Cir. 1999), overturned by *Whitman v. Am. Trucking Assns.,* 531 U.S. 457 (2001).

83. *United States v. Morrison,* 529 U.S. 598 (2000); *Nat'l. Fed'n. of Indep. Bus. v. Sebelius,* 567 U.S. 519 (2012).

84. *Whitman v. Am. Trucking Assns.*, 531 U.S. 457 (2001).
85. More recently, the First Amendment's guarantee of free exercise of religion is also being used to oppose regulation. *See* Elizabeth Sepper, *Free Exercise Lochnerism*, 115 COLUM. L. REV. 1453 (2015).
86. *Nike, Inc. v. Kasky*, 539 U.S. 645 (2003).
87. *Sorrell v. IMS Health, Inc.*, 564 U.S. 552 (2011).
88. *R. J. Reynolds Tobacco Co. v. FDA*, 696 F.3d 1205 (2012).
89. *Omnicare, Inc. v. Laborers Dist. Council Constr. Indus. Pension Fund*, 575 U.S. ___, 135 S. Ct. 1318 (2015); *Nat'l. Ass'n. of Mfrs. v. SEC*, 956 F. Supp. 2d 43 (D.D.C. 2013).
90. John C. Coates, IV, *Corporate Speech and the First Amendment: History, Data, and Implications*, 30 CONST. COMMENT. 223 (2015). *See also* Joe Pinsker, *How Corporations Took Over the First Amendment*, ATLANTIC (Apr. 1, 2015), https://www.theatlantic.com/business/archive/2015/04/how-corporations-took-over-the-first-amendment/389249/.
91. *See* MARK TUSHNET, A COURT DIVIDED: THE REHNQUIST COURT AND THE FUTURE OF CONSTITUTIONAL LAW (2005); Tamara Piety, *Citizens United and the Threat to the Regulatory State*, 109 MICH. L. REV. FIRST IMPRESSIONS 16 (2010).
92. *See* Russell Korobkin, *What Comes after Victory for Behavioral Law and Economics?*, 2011 U. ILL. L. REV. 1653, 1655 (2011) ("The battle to separate the economic analysis of legal rules and institutions from the straightjacket of strict rational choice assumptions has been won").
93. Edmund L. Andrews, *Greenspan Concedes Error on Regulation*, N.Y. TIMES (Oct. 23, 2008), http://www.nytimes.com/2008/10/24/business/economy/24panel.html.
94. *See Am. Tradition P'ship, Inc. v. Bullock*, 567 U.S. 516 (2012) (striking down long-standing Montana state campaign finance laws).
95. BLAIR BOWIE & ADAM LIOZ, BILLION DOLLAR DEMOCRACY: THE UNPRECEDENTED ROLE OF MONEY IN THE 2012 ELECTIONS 4 (2013).
96. *See* opensecrets.org, Total Outside Spending by Election Cycle, Excluding Party Committees, https://www.opensecrets.org/outsidespending/cycle_tots.php.
97. Justin Fox & Jay W. Lorsch, *What Good Are Shareholders?*, HARV. BUS. REV. (July–Aug. 2012), available at http://www.shareholderforum.com/access/Library/20120700_HarvardBusinessReview.htm.
98. Stefan Stern, *Transcend "Shareholder Value" for All Our Sakes*, FIN. TIMES (Oct. 22, 2014), https://www.ft.com/content/0a288288-583e-11e4-a31b-00144feab7de.
99. Steve Denning, *The Dumbest Idea in the World: Maximizing Shareholder Value*, FORBES (Nov. 28, 2011), http://www.forbes.com/sites/stevedenning/2011/11/28/maximizing-shareholder-value-the-dumbest-idea-in-the-world/#4c2853612224.

100. Joe Nocera, *Down with Shareholder Value*, N.Y. Times (Aug. 10, 2010), http:// www.nytimes.com/2012/08/11/opinion/nocera-down-with-shareholder -value.html. *See also* Lynn A. Stout, The Shareholder Value Myth: How Putting Shareholders First Harms Investors, Corporations, and the Public (2012); Denning, *The Dumbest Idea in the World*, supra; Justin Fox, *How Shareholders Are Ruining American Business*, Atlantic (June 19, 2013), http://www.theatlantic.com/magazine/archive/2013/07/stop-spoiling -the-shareholders/309381/.

101. Steven Pearlstein, *How the Cult of Shareholder Value Wrecked American Business*, Wash. Post: Wonkblog (Sept. 9, 2013), http://www.washingtonpost .com/blogs/wonkblog/wp/2013/09/09/how-the-cult-of-shareholder-value -wrecked-american-business/.

102. Kent Greenfield, *The Stakeholder Strategy*, 26 Democracy: A Journal of Ideas 47 (2012); Dylan Matthews, *In Germany, Workers Help Run Their Companies. And It's Going Great!*, Wash. Post: wonkblog (Oct. 7, 2012), http:// www.washingtonpost.com/blogs/wonkblog/wp/2012/10/07/in-germany -workers-help-run-their-companies-and-its-going-great/.

103. *Statement on Company Law*, Modern Corporation Blog, https://themod erncorporation.wordpress.com/company-law-memo/.

104. Christopher Halburd, *Is Corporate Governance on the Brink of a Revolution?*, LinkedIn (July 9, 2015), https://www.linkedin.com/pulse/corporate-gov ernance-brink-revolution-christopher-halburd.

105. *Citizens United v. Fed. Election Comm'n.*, 558 U.S. 310, 356 (2010).

106. Leo E. Strine & Nicholas Walter, *Conservative Collision Course: The Tension between Conservative Corporate Law Theory and Citizens United*, 100 Cornell L. Rev. 335 (2015); David G. Yosifon, *The Citizens United Gambit in Corporate Theory: A Reply to Bainbridge on Strine and Walter* (Santa Clara Univ. Legal Studies Research Paper No. 4-14, Oct. 2014), available at http://ssrn.com/ abstract=2510967; David G. Yosifon, *It's Law but It Shouldn't Be*, N.Y. Times (Apr. 16, 2015), http://www.nytimes.com/roomfordebate/2015/04/16/what -are-corporations-obligations-to-shareholders/its-law-but-it-shouldnt-be.

107. *See* Stephen M. Bainbridge, *Director Primacy: The Means and Ends of Corporate Governance*, 97 Nw. U. L. Rev. 547 (2003); Lucian Ayre Bebchuk, *The Case for Increasing Shareholder Power*, 118 Harv. L. Rev. 833 (2005); Kent Green-field, *The Third Way: Beyond Shareholder or Board Primacy*, 37 Seattle U. L. Rev. 749 (2014).

108. Friedman, *The Social Responsibility of Business Is to Increase Its Profits*, supra.

109. *Citizens United*, 558 U.S. at 475–76 (Stevens, J., dissenting).

110. *Id.* at 469–70 (Stevens, J., dissenting) (internal citations omitted).

111. *Id.* at 470 (Stevens, J., dissenting) (quoting the American Law Institute, Principles of Corporate Governance: Analysis and Recommenda-tions § 2.01(a), p. 55 (1992)). *See also* Melvin Aron Eisenberg, *An Overview*

of the Principles of Corporate Governance, 48 Bus. Law. 1271 (1993), available at http://scholarship.law.berkeley.edu/facpubs/2024.

112. Robert Barnes, *Justice Stevens' Liberal Legacy Goes beyond Ideology*, Seattle Times (Apr. 10, 2010), https://www.seattletimes.com/nation-world/justice-stevens-liberal-legacy-goes-beyond-ideology/; David G. Savage, *John Paul Stevens' Unexpectedly Liberal Legacy*, L.A. Times (Apr. 9, 2010), http://articles.latimes.com/2010/apr/09/nation/la-na-stevens-legacy10–2010apr10; Jeffrey Toobin, *After Stevens*, New Yorker (Mar. 22, 2010), https://www.newyorker.com/magazine/2010/03/22/after-stevens.

113. *Money in Politics*, Common Cause, http://www.commoncause.org/issues/money-in-politics/.

114. Elizabeth Kennedy, *Protecting Shareholders after Citizens United*, Brennan Ctr. for Just. (July 13, 2011), http://www.brennancenter.org/blog/protecting-shareholders-after-citizens-united.

115. Jamie B. Raskin, *A Shareholder Solution to "Citizens United,"* Wash. Post (Oct. 3, 2014), http://www.washingtonpost.com/opinions/a-shareholder-solution-to-citizens-united/2014/10/03/5e07c3ee-48be-11e4-b72e-d60a9229cc10_story.html.

116. *Burwell v. Hobby Lobby Stores, Inc.*, 573 U.S. ___, 134 S. Ct. 2751 (2014).

117. The Religious Freedom Restoration Act of 1993 (RFRA), 42 U.S.C. 2000bb et seq.

118. *Hobby Lobby*, 134 S. Ct. at 2771.

119. *Id.*

120. Though not unanimously. *See* Kent Greenfield, *A Skeptic's View of Benefit Corporations*, 1 Emory Corp. Gov. & Acct. Rev. 17 (2014).

121. *Conestoga Wood Specialties v. Sec'y. of the U.S. Dep't. of Health & Human Serv.*, 724 F.3d 377, 403 n.18 (3d Cir. 2013) (Jordan, J., dissenting).

THREE

Should Corporations Have Rights?

1. Ashley Parker, *"Corporations Are People," Romney Tells Iowa Hecklers Angry over His Tax Policy*, N.Y. Times (Aug. 25, 2011), http://www.nytimes.com/2011/08/12/us/politics/12romney.html. *See* Adam Winkler, We the Corporations 377–78 (2018).

2. Isolde Raftery, *California Man Says He Can Drive in Carpool Lane with Corporation Papers*, NBC (Jan. 5, 2013), https://usnews.newsvine.com/_news/2013/01/05/16372432-california-man-says-he-can-drive-in-carpool-lane-with-corporation-papers?lite; Aaron Sankin, *Jonathan Frieman, California Political Activist, Asks, 'If Corporations Are People, Can They Ride in the Car-*

pool Lane?,' HUFFINGTON POST (Jan. 7, 2013), http://www.huffingtonpost
.com/2013/01/07/jonathan-frieman_n_2427971.html.

3. *Citizens United v. Fed. Election Comm'n.*, 558 U.S. 310, 356 (2010).

4. *See id.* at 372 ("The First Amendment underwrites the freedom to experiment and to create in the realm of thought and speech. Citizens must be
free to use new forms, and new forums, for the expression of ideas. The civic
discourse belongs to the people, and the Government may not prescribe the
means used to conduct it").

5. *Trs. of Dartmouth Coll. v. Woodward,* 17 U.S. 518, 636 (1819).

6. *The People's Rights Amendment,* FREE SPEECH FOR PEOPLE, http://org2.sal
salabs.com/o/7003/p/salsa/web/common/public/content?content_item_KEY
=5624.

7. *See Church of the Lukumi Babalu Aye, Inc. v. City of Hialeah,* 508 U.S. 520
(1993).

8. *See Rumsfeld v. Forum for Acad. & Inst. Rights, Inc.,* 547 U.S. 47 (2006). The
claims of the Forum for Academic and Institutional Rights (FAIR) won in
the Third Circuit Court of Appeals—*see* 390 F. 3d 219 (2004)—and lost in
the Supreme Court but not on the grounds that the group's corporate status
barred the claim.

9. *Dartmouth Coll., supra.*

10. *See* AVI SOIFER, LAW AND THE COMPANY WE KEEP (1995).

11. *Boy Scouts of Am. v. Dale,* 530 U.S. 640 (2000).

12. *See, e.g., Whole Woman's Health v. Hellerstedt,* 579 U.S. ___, 136 S. Ct. 2292
(2016).

13. *See* LETTER FROM THE FEDERAL FARMER XVI (Herbert J. Story, ed., 1981)
(Jan. 20, 1788).

14. *McCulloch v. Maryland,* 17 U.S. (4 Wheat) 316, 407 (1819).

15. It is quite common for corporations to be considered persons in a wide variety of legal contexts. *See* ERIC W. ORTS, BUSINESS PERSONS (2013).

16. For a recent takings clause case with clear benefits for corporate claimants, *see
Horne v. Dept. of Agric.,* 135 S. Ct. 2419 (2015). *See also* Kent Greenfield & Adam
Winkler, *The U.S. Supreme Court's Cultivation of Corporate Personhood,* ATLAN
TIC (June 24, 2015), https://www.theatlantic.com/politics/archive/2015/06
/raisins-hotels-corporate-personhood-supreme-court/396773/.

17. *McNabb v. United States,* 318 U.S. 332, 347 (1943).

18. *Joint Anti-Fascist Refugee Comm. v. McGrath,* 341 U.S. 123, 179 (1951) (Douglas, J., concurring).

19. Tom R. Tyler, *Procedural Justice, Legitimacy, and the Effective Rule of Law, in*
CRIME AND JUSTICE: A REVIEW OF RESEARCH, 431–505 (Vol. 30, 2003).

20. *See First National Bank of Boston v. Bellotti,* 435 U.S. 765 (1978) (Rehnquist,
J., dissenting) ("There can be little doubt that, when a State creates a corpo-

ration with the power to acquire and utilize property, it necessarily and im-plicitly guarantees that the corporation will not be deprived of that property absent due process of law"). *See Smyth v. Ames*, 169 U. S. 466, 169 U. S. 22 (1898) (extending due process protections to corporations).

21. *See Youngstown Sheet & Tube Co. v. Sawyer*, 343 U.S. 579 (1952).
22. *Nat'l. Fed'n. of Indep. Bus. v. Sebelius*, 567 U.S. 519 (2012).
23. *See, e.g., H. P. Hood & Sons, Inc. v. Du Mond*, 336 U.S. 525 (1949).
24. *Kassel v. Consol. Freightways Corp.*, 450 U.S. 662 (1981); *Dean Milk Co. v. City of Madison, Wis.*, 340 U.S. 349 (1951); *Reading R.R. v. Pennsylvania*, 82 U.S. (15 Wall) 232 (1873).
25. *Silverthorne Lumber Co. v. U.S.*, 251 U.S. 385, 392 (1920) ("The rights of a corporation against unlawful search and seizure are to be protected.").
26. *Hale v. Henkel*, 201 U.S. 43, 75 (1906).
27. *Katz v. United States*, 389 U.S. 347, 360–61 (1967) (Harlan, J., concurring).
28. *Cf.* Orin S. Kerr, *Four Models of Fourth Amendment Protection*, 60 STAN. L. REV. 503 (2007); Brian J. Serr, *Great Expectations of Privacy: A New Model for Fourth Amendment Protection*, 73 MINN. L. REV. 583 (1989); Daniel J. Solove, *Fourth Amendment Pragmatism*, 51 B.C. L. REV. 1511 (2010); Nadia B. Soree, *Whose Fourth Amendment and Does It Matter? A Due Process Approach to Fourth Amendment Standing*, 46 IND. L. REV. 753, 757 (2013); Scott E. Sundby, *"Everyman"'s Fourth Amendment: Privacy or Mutual Trust between Government and Citizen?*, 94 COLUM. L. REV. 1751 (1994).
29. *Vernonia Sch. Dist. v. Acton*, 515 U.S. 646 (1995); *see also Bd. of Educ. v. Earls*, 536 U.S. 822 (2002).
30. *United States v. Drayton*, 536 U.S. 194 (2002).
31. *See* WAYNE R. LaFAVE, SEARCH & SEIZURE: A TREATISE ON THE FOURTH AMENDMENT § 7 (5th ed., 2012–17).
32. *See Marshall v. Barlow's, Inc.*, 436 U.S. 307 (1978); *Fourth Amendment—Administrative Searches and Seizures*, 69 J. CRIM. L. & CRIMINOLOGY 552 (1978).
33. Eve Brensike Primus, *Disentangling Administrative Searches*, 111 COLUM. L. REV. 254, 266 (2011).
34. *See* Primus, *Disentangling Administrative Searches, supra*, at 256–57 ("Instead, courts evaluating administrative searches need only balance the govern-ment's interest in conducting the search against the degree of intrusion on the affected individual's privacy to determine whether the search is reasona-ble. This reasonableness balancing—which scholars often describe as a form of rational basis review—is very deferential to the government, and the re-sulting searches are almost always deemed reasonable").
35. *Barlow's, Inc., supra*, at 311.
36. *City of Los Angeles v. Patel*, 576 U.S. ___, 135 S. Ct. 2443 (2015).

37. The exception is when the very act of producing the document is itself testimonial and incriminating. *See United States v. Hubbell*, 530 U.S. 27 (2000).
38. *Hale*, 201 U.S. at 75.

FOUR

Corporations and Fundamental Rights, Equality, and Religion

1. *Meyer v. Nebraska*, 262 U.S. 390, 399 (1923).
2. *Planned Parenthood of Southeastern Pa. v. Casey*, 505 U.S. 833, 851 (1992) (plurality).
3. *Washington v. Glucksberg*, 521 U.S. 702, 721 (1997) (citing *Palko v. Connecticut*, 302 U.S. 319, 325 (1937)).
4. *Stanley v. Illinois*, 405 U.S. 645 (1972).
5. *Obergefell v. Hodges*, 576 U.S. ___, 135 S. Ct. 2584 (2015); *Loving v. Virginia*, 388 U.S. 1 (1967).
6. *Lawrence v. Texas*, 539 U.S. 558 (2003).
7. *Roe v. Wade*, 410 U.S. 113 (1973) (abortion); *Griswold v. Connecticut*, 381 U.S. 479 (1965) (contraceptives).
8. *Cruzan v. Dir., Mo. Dep't. of Health*, 497 U.S. 261 (1990).
9. *See* Autumn L. Bernhardt, *The Profound and Intimate Power of the Obergefell Decision: Equal Dignity as a Suspect Class*, 25 TUL. J. L. & SEXUALITY 1, 17 (2016); Nancy K. Kubasek et al., *The Analogous Constitutional Protection of Race and Sexual Preference: Recognizing the Shared Vulnerability*, 6 DePAUL J. FOR SOC. JUST. 61 (2012); Courtney A. Powers, *Finding LGBTs a Suspect Class: Assessing the Political Power of LGBTs as a Basis for the Court's Application of Heightened Scrutiny*, 17 DUKE J. GENDER L. & POL'Y. 385 (2010); Stacey L. Sobel, *When Windsor Isn't Enough: Why the Court Must Clarify Equal Protection Analysis for Sexual Orientation Classifications*, 24 CORNELL J.L. & PUB. POLICY 493 (2015).
10. *Sch. Dist. of Abington v. Schempp*, 374 U.S. 203 (1963); *Engel v. Vitale*, 370 U.S. 421, 430 (1962).
11. *Lemon v. Kurtzman*, 403 U.S. 602 (1971).
12. *Zelman v. Simmons-Harris*, 536 U.S. 639 (2002).
13. *Stone v. Graham*, 449 U.S. 39 (1980).
14. *Van Orden v. Perry*, 545 U.S. 677 (2005).
15. *Church of the Lukumi Babalu Aye, Inc. v. City of Hialeah*, 508 U.S. 520 (1993).
16. *Emp't. Div. v. Smith*, 494 U.S. 872 (1990).
17. *Roe v. Wade*, 410 U.S. 113 (1973).
18. *Planned Parenthood of Southeastern Pa. v. Casey*, 505 U.S. 833 (1992).
19. *See, e.g.*, David S. Law & Mila Versteeg, *The Declining Influence of the United*

States Constitution, 87 N.Y.U. L. REV. 762 (2012); Sharmila Murthy, *The Human Right(s) to Water and Sanitation: History, Meaning and the Controversy over Privatization*, 31 BERKELEY J. OF INT. LAW 89 (2013); Adam Liptak, *"We the People" Loses Appeal with People around the World*, N.Y. TIMES (Feb. 6, 2012), http://www.nytimes.com/2012/02/07/us/we-the-people-loses-appeal-with-people-around-the-world.html.

20. For an overview, *see* Brandon L. Garrett, *The Constitutional Standing of Corporations*, 163 U. PA. L. REV. 95 (2014).

21. *See Santa Clara Cty. v. S. Pac. R.R. Co.*, 118 U.S. 394, 404 (1886); Morton J. Horwitz, *Santa Clara Revisited: The Development of Corporate Theory*, 88 W. VA. L. REV. 173 (1985).

22. *Santa Clara Cty. v. S. Pac. R.R. Co.*, 118 U.S. 394, 397 (1886) (headnote).

23. THOM HARTMANN, UNEQUAL PROTECTION: THE RISE OF CORPORATE DOMINANCE AND THE THEFT OF HUMAN RIGHTS 107–8 (2002).

24. *Williamson v. Lee Optical of Okla., Inc.*, 348 U.S. 483, 487–88 (1955).

25. *See Adarand Constructors, Inc. v. Peña*, 515 U.S. 200 (1995).

26. Transcript of Oral Argument at 53, *Burwell v. Hobby Lobby Stores, Inc.*, 573 U.S. ___, 134 S. Ct. 2751, 2771 (2014).

27. *Washington v. Davis*, 426 U.S. 229 (1976).

28. *Emp't. Div. v. Smith*, 494 U.S. 872 (1990).

29. Religious Freedom Restoration Act, 42 U.S.C. § 2000bb-1 (2017).

30. *City of Boerne v. Flores*, 521 U.S. 507 (1997).

31. Richard Jerome, *Holding the Line*, PEOPLE (Feb. 5, 1996), http://people.com/archive/holding-the-line-vol-45-no-5/; Rebecca Leung, *The Mensch of Malden Mills*, CBS NEWS (July 3, 2003), http://www.cbsnews.com/news/the-mensch-of-malden-mills/; Louis Uchitelle, *The Risks of Keeping a Promise*, N.Y. TIMES (July 4, 1996), http://www.nytimes.com/1996/07/04/business/the-risks-of-keeping-a-promise-in-becoming-an-icon-a-mill-owner-bets-his-company.html.

32. Steve Annear, *Woman Allowed to Wear Spaghetti Strainer in Mass. License Photo*, BOS. GLOBE (Nov. 13, 2015), https://www.bostonglobe.com/metro/2015/11/13/woman-allowed-wear-spaghetti-strainer-her-head-mass-license-photo/m8ADuh20S2zk2jrc8503FM/story.html.

33. Verified Complaint, at ¶ 55, *Hobby Lobby Stores, Inc. v. Sebelius*, 870 F. Supp. 2d 1278 (W.D. Okla. 2012) (5:12-cv-01000-HE), *rev'd and remanded*, 723 F.3d 1114 (10th Cir. 2013), *aff'd sub nom. Burwell v. Hobby Lobby Stores, Inc.*, 573 U.S. ___, 134 S. Ct. 2751 (2014); Katie Sanders, *Did Hobby Lobby Once Provide the Birth Control Coverage It Sued the Obama Administration Over?*, POLITIFACT (July 1, 2014), http://www.politifact.com/punditfact/statements/2014/jul/01/sally-kohn/did-hobby-lobby-once-provide-birth-control-coverag/.

FIVE
Corporations and Speech Theory

1. Noel T. Brewer et al., *Effect of Pictorial Cigarette Pack Warnings on Changes in Smoking Behavior*, 176 JAMA INTERNAL MED. 908 (2016); Stanton Glantz, *Compelling Evidence That Graphic Warning Labels on Cigarettes Will Improve Health in the U.S.*, CENTER FOR TOBACCO CONTROL RESEARCH AND EDUCATION (June 6, 2016), https://tobacco.ucsf.edu/compelling-evidence-graphic -warning-labels-cigarettes-will-improve-health-us.

2. *27 Cigarette Warning Labels Nixed by the FDA*, CBS NEWS, http://www .cbsnews.com/pictures/27-cigarette-warning-labels-nixed-by-the-fda/.

3. *W. Va. State Bd. of Educ. v. Barnette*, 319 U.S. 624, 642 (1943).

4. *R. J. Reynolds Tobacco Co. v. FDA*, 696 F.3d 1205 (D.C. Cir. 2012).

5. JEFF CLEMENTS, CORPORATIONS ARE NOT PEOPLE 3 (2012).

6. Tamara Piety, *Why Personhood Matters*, 30 CONST. COMMENT. 361, 365 (2015).

7. William O. Douglas, *Stare Decisis*, 49 COLUM. L. REV. 735, 737 (1949).

8. David Ciepley, *Neither Persons nor Associations: Against Constitutional Rights for Corporations*, J. L. & CTS. 221, 223–24 (2013).

9. *See* FLOYD ABRAMS, THE SOUL OF THE FIRST AMENDMENT (2017); Alex Gray, *Freedom of Speech: Which Country Has the Most?*, WORLD ECON. F. (Nov. 8, 2016), https://www.weforum.org/agenda/2016/11/freedom-of-speech-country -comparison/; Thane Rosenbaum, *Should Neo-Nazis Be Allowed Free Speech?*, DAILY BEAST (Jan. 30, 2014), http://www.thedailybeast.com/articles/2014 /01/30/should-neo-nazis-be-allowed-free-speech.html; Ilya Shapiro & Frank Garrison, *An Important but Limited Victory for Free Speech*, CATO INST. (Apr. 1, 2017), https://www.cato.org/blog/important-limited-victory-free-speech.

10. *Debs v. United States*, 249 U.S. 211 (1919).

11. *Schenck v. United States*, 249 U.S. 47 (1919).

12. *Abrams v. United States*, 250 U.S. 616 (1919).

13. *Id.* at 628 (Holmes, J., dissenting).

14. *Id.* at 630 (Holmes, J., dissenting).

15. *Gertz v. Robert Welch, Inc.*, 418 U.S. 323, 339 (1974).

16. *Whitney v. California*, 274 U.S. 357, 377 (1927) (Brandeis, J., concurring).

17. *Citizens United v. Fed. Election Comm'n*, 558 U.S. 310, 314 (2010).

18. *New York Times Co. v. Sullivan*, 376 U.S. 254, 270 (1964).

19. This story has been questioned, but it remains a good example of the concept. Jimmy Stamp, *Fact or Fiction? The Legend of the QWERTY Keyboard*, SMITHSONIAN.COM (May 3, 2013).

20. *See* KENT GREENFIELD, THE MYTH OF CHOICE: PERSONAL RESPONSIBILITY IN A WORLD OF LIMITS (2011).

21. JEREMY WALDRON, THE HARM IN HATE SPEECH (2014).

22. *Buckley v. Valeo*, 424 U.S. 1, 14 (1976) (quoting *New York Times Co. v. Sullivan*, 376 U.S. 254, 269 (1964)).
23. *Id.* at 48–49.
24. *Austin v. Michigan Chamber of Commerce*, 494 U.S. 652 (1990).
25. *Id.* at 660.
26. *See* Docket Summary (June 29, 2009), Supreme Court of the United States, http://www.supremecourt.gov/Search.aspx?FileName=/docketfiles /08–205.htm.
27. Supplemental Reply Brief for the Respondent-Appellee, *Citizens United v. Fed. Election Comm'n.*, 558 U.S. 310 (2010) (No. 08–205); Transcript of Oral Argument at 48–49.
28. *Citizens United*, 558 U.S. at 361–62 (quoting *First National Bank of Boston v. Bellotti*, 435 U.S. 765, 794 (1978)). *See also id.* at 370 (Roberts, C.J., concurring) (modern technology makes shareholder objections more effective because rapid disclosures "provide shareholders and citizens with the information needed to hold corporations and elected officials accountable for their positions and supporters").
29. *See, e.g.,* Lucian A. Bebchuk & Robert J. Jackson, *Corporate Political Speech: Who Decides*, 124 Harv. L. Rev. 83 (2010); Leo E. Strine, Jr., & Nicholas Walter, *Conservative Collision Course: The Tension between Conservative Corporate Law Theory and Citizens United*, 100 Cornell L. Rev. 335 (2015); Ciara Torres-Spelliscy, *Corporate Democracy from Say on Pay to Say on Politics*, 30 Const. Comment. 431 (2015); David G. Yosifon, *The Public Choice Problem in Corporate Law: Corporate Social Responsibility after Citizens United*, 89 N.C. L. Rev. 1197 (2011).
30. *See McDonnell v. United States*, 579 U.S. ___, 136 S. Ct. 2355 (2016); Zephyr Teachout, Corruption in America: from Benjamin Franklin's Snuff Box to Citizens United (2016).
31. *Whitney*, 274 U.S. at 375 (Brandeis, J., concurring).
32. David A. Richards, *Free Speech and Obscenity Law: Toward a Moral Theory of the First Amendment*, 123 U. Pa. L. Rev. 45, 62 (1974).
33. *See, e.g., Brown v. Entm't. Merchs. Ass'n.*, 564 U.S. 786 (2011).
34. I have tried to sketch what a more robust, less deferential, self-fulfillment free speech clause would require. *See* Kent Greenfield, *Our Conflicting Judgments about Pornography*, 43 Am. U. L. Rev. 1197 (1994).
35. *See* Kent Greenfield, *The Limits of Free Speech*, TheAtlantic.com (Mar. 13, 2015).
36. *See* Avi Soifer, Law and the Company We Keep (1998).
37. *United States v. Alvarez*, 567 U.S. 709 (2012).
38. *See* Dodd-Frank Wall Street Reform and Consumer Protection Act § 1502, 124 Stat. at 2213 (codified at 15 U.S.C. § 78m[p] [Supp. V 2011]). The Securities Exchange Commission implemented the provision by rule at Conflict

Minerals Final Rule, 77 Fed. Reg. 56,274, 56,283 (Sept. 12, 2012) (to be codified at 17 C.F.R. pts. 240, 249b). *See* Karen E. Woody, *Conflict Minerals Legislation: The SEC's New Role as Diplomatic and Humanitarian Watchdog*, 81 FORDHAM L. REV. 1315 (2012).

39. *Nat'l. Ass'n. of Mfrs. v. SEC.*, 800 F.3d 518, 527 (D.C. Cir. 2015) ("whether [the rule] will work is not proven to the degree required under the First Amendment to compel speech"). *See Recent Case: National Ass'n. of Manufacturers v. SEC*, 129 HARV. L. REV. 819 (2016).

40. *Nat'l. Ass'n. of Mfrs.*, 800 F.3d at 530.

41. *Whitney*, 274 U.S. at 375 (Brandeis, J., concurring).

42. Cass R. Sunstein, *Free Speech Now*, 59 U. CHI. L. REV. 255, 301 (1992).

43. Robert H. Bork, *Neutral Principles and Some First Amendment Problems*, 47 INDIANA L. J. 1 (1971); Victor Brudney, *The First Amendment and Commercial Speech*, 53 B.C. L. REV. 1153 (2012); Owen M. Fiss, *Free Speech and Social Structure*, 71 IOWA L. REV. 1405 (1986); Sunstein, *Free Speech Now, supra.*

44. ALEXANDER MEIKLEJOHN, FREE SPEECH AND ITS RELATION TO SELF-GOVERNMENT 24 (1948).

45. *Id.* at 25.

46. For example, under a self-governance theory, *Arizona Free Enterprise Club's Freedom Club PAC v. Bennett*, 564 U.S. 721 (2011), striking down an Arizona law offering public financing to candidates to "level up" to the spending of a competitor, should have come out the other way.

47. *See, e.g., Brown v. Entm't. Merchs. Ass'n.*, 564 U.S. at 790 ("The Free Speech Clause exists principally to protect discourse on public matters."); *Burson v. Freeman*, 504 U.S. 191, 196 (1992) ("Whatever differences may exist about interpretations of the First Amendment, there is practically universal agreement that a major purpose of that Amendment was to protect the free discussion of governmental affairs") (quoting *Mills v. Alabama*, 384 U.S. 214, 218 (1966)); *Eu v. S.F. Cty. Democratic Cent. Comm.*, 489 U.S. 214, 223 (1989) ("The First Amendment 'has its fullest and most urgent application' to speech uttered during a campaign for political office") (quoting *Monitor Patriot Co. v. Roy*, 401 U.S. 265, 272 (1971)).

48. *Books and plays banned in Boston*, http://archive.boston.com/bostonglobe/magazine/galleries/2010/8_8_10_banned_in_boston/.

49. *Brown v. Entm't. Merchs. Ass'n.*, 564 U.S. at 790.

50. *Virginia State Board of Pharmacy v. Virginia Citizens Consumer Council, Inc.*, 425 U.S. 748 (1976).

51. Alexander Meiklejohn, *The First Amendment Is an Absolute*, 1961 SUP. CT. REV. 245, 256 (1961).

52. *See* CLEMENTS, CORPORATIONS ARE NOT PEOPLE, *supra.*

53. *See* Laurence H. Tribe & Scott Greylak, *Get Foreign Political Money out of U.S. Elections*, BOS. GLOBE (June 23, 2016).

54. Alex Kotch, *Outside Money Wins Big in West Virginia Supreme Court Election*, FACING SOUTH (May 13, 2106), https://www.facingsouth.org/2016/05/out side-money-wins-big-in-west-virginia-supreme-co.

55. Tarun Banerjee & Joshua Murray, *What Shapes Corporate Involvement in Voter Referendums? The Case of Opposition to GM Food Labeling*, SOCIOLOGICAL PERSPECTIVES 2015, Vol. 58(3) 464–89.

56. Ciara Torres-Spelliscy, *Safeguarding Markets from Pernicious Pay to Play: A Model Explaining Why the SEC Regulates Money in Politics*, 12(2) CONN. PUB. INTEREST L. J. 361, 402 (2012–2013); Nicholas Confessore, Nicholas Fandos, & Rachel Shorey, *Trump Inaugural Drew Big Dollars from Donors with Vested Interests*, N.Y. TIMES (Apr. 19, 2017) (parent company of R. J. Reynolds gave at least $1 million; telecommunications giants gave over $2 million; energy companies and their executives gave over $10 million).

57. *See* John C. Coates, IV, *Corporate Speech and the First Amendment: History, Data, and Implications*, 30 CONST. COMMENT. 223 (2015).

58. *Citizens United*, 558 U.S. at 356.

59. *See generally* DAN ARIELY, PREDICTABLY IRRATIONAL: THE HIDDEN FORCES THAT SHAPE OUR DECISIONS (2010); DANIEL GILBERT, STUMBLING ON HAPPINESS (2006); DANIEL KAHNEMAN, THINKING FAST AND SLOW (2011); FRANK PARTNOY, WAIT: THE ART AND SCIENCE OF DELAY (2012).

60. Abby Jackson, *Fortune 100 Companies Tell the Supreme Court Why America Still Needs Affirmative Action*, BUS. INSIDER (Nov. 6, 2015), http://www.busi nessinsider.com/fortune-100-companies-issue-amacus-brief-in-support-of -affirmative-action-at-university-of-texas-2015-11. Brief can be found here: Brief of Fortune-100 and Other Leading American Businesses as *Amici Curiae* in Support of Respondents, *Fisher v. Univ. of Tex.*, 136 S.Ct. 2198 (2016) (No. 14–981), http://graphics8.nytimes.com/packages/pdf/opinion/green house/FisherFortune100.pdf.

61. Andrés Martinez, *Give Corporations More Political Power—Seriously*, TIME MAG. (July 10, 2015).

62. *See Updated List: Who Has Spoken for, Against NC's New LGBT Law*, CHARLOTTE OBSERVER, http://www.charlotteobserver.com/news/business/article 69251877.html.

63. Christine Hauser, *Patagonia, REI and Other Outdoor Retailers Protest Trump's Decision to Shrink Utah Monuments*, N.Y. TIMES (Dec. 5, 2017).

64. Martinez, *Give Corporations More Political Power, supra*.

65. *See* Adam Bonica, *Avenues of Influence: On the Expenditures of Corporations and Their Directors and Executives*, 18 BUS. & POL. 367 (2016) (After *Citizens United*, "The anticipated flood of corporate political cash has amounted to no more than a trickle. In the 2012 election cycle, a handful of predominantly privately owned corporations spent roughly $75 million from their

treasuries on federal elections, or roughly one percent of the estimated $6 billion spent in total for the election cycle").

66. *See* Bonica, *Avenues of Influence, supra*. Bonica includes in his figure of $75 million approximately $20 million from shell companies privately held by wealthy individuals and families. That would make the amount from for-profit, publicly traded corporations less than 1 percent of the total.

67. *See* chapter 1 above.

68. Sherlock Holmes, The Adventure of Silver Blaze (1892).

69. As discussed in chapter 1 above, the largest corporate donor to any Super PAC supporting a presidential candidate appears to have been NextEra Energy, a clean energy company that gave a little over $1 million to Right to Rise, a pro-Bush Super PAC. *See* https://www.opensecrets.org/outsidespend ing/contrib.php?cmte=C00571372&cycle=2016. Right to Rise was the sec ond-largest Super PAC in terms of total raised and total spent. *See* https:// www.opensecrets.org/outsidespending/summ.php?chrt=V&type=S. *See also* Bonica, *Avenues of Influence, supra*, at 373.

70. Clare O'Connor, *Target Makes Gay Marriage Support Official after GOP Donation Gaffe*, Forbes (Aug. 7, 2014), https://www.forbes.com/sites/clareocon nor/2014/08/07/target-makes-gay-marriage-support-official-after-gop-do nation-gaffe/#6e07961b5af6.

71. *See Corporations Spent Nearly $140 Million in Eight State Ballot Initiative Races, Crushing the Opposition by as Much as 24-to-1*, Public Citizen (Sept. 28, 2016), https://www.citizen.org/media/press-releases/corporations-spent-nearly -140-million-eight-state-ballot-initiative-races.

72. *See Corporation-Backed Ballot Initiative Campaigns Spent More than $335 Million, Won 62% of Races Where One Side Was Mostly Funded by Corporate Interests*, Public Citizen (Nov. 9, 2016), https://www.citizen.org/media /press-releases/corporation-backed-ballot-initiative-campaigns-spent-more -335-million-won-62.

SIX
Speech and Corporate Purpose

1. *Virginia State Board of Pharmacy v. Virginia Citizens Consumer Council, Inc.*, 425 U.S. 748 (1976).

2. *Cent. Hudson Gas & Elec. Corp. v. Pub. Svc. Comm'n.*, 447 U.S. 557, 564 (1980). *See also Zauderer v. Office of Disciplinary Counsel of the Supreme Court of Ohio*, 471 U.S. 626, 651 (1985) ("An advertiser's [First Amendment] rights are adequately protected as long as disclosure requirements are reasonably related to the State's interest in preventing deception of consumers").

3. *Williamson v. Lee Optical of Okla., Inc.*, 348 U.S. 483 (1955).
4. *United States v. Playboy Entm't. Grp.*, 529 U.S. 803, 813 (2000) ("If a statute regulates speech based on its content, it must be narrowly tailored to promote a compelling Government interest").
5. Chris Bury, *Clint Eastwood's Super Bowl Chrysler Ad Stirs Political Waters*, ABC News (Feb. 6, 2012) http://abcnews.go.com/blogs/business/2012/02/clint-eastwoods-chrysler-ad-stirs-political-waters/.
6. *See Bolger v. Youngs Drug Prods. Corp.*, 463 U.S. 60 (1983). *See generally* Victor Brudney, *The First Amendment and Commercial Speech*, 53 B.C. L. Rev. 1153 (2012).
7. *See* Tamara Piety, Brandishing the First Amendment: Commercial Expression in America (2012).
8. A recent study by the Global Strategy Group found that "Americans continue to believe that corporations should take action to address important issues facing society (81%) and have a responsibility to do so (77%)." Global Strategy Group, *A Call to Action in the Age of Trump; Business and Politics: Do They Mix? 5th Annual Study* (2018), available at http://www.globalstrategygroup.com/thought-leadership/business-and-politics/.
9. *Gertz v. Robert Welch, Inc.*, 418 U.S. 323, 339 (1974). *See United States v. Alvarez*, 567 U.S. 709 (2012) (plurality) (striking down Stolen Valor Act, making it a crime to falsely claim receipt of military decorations or medals).
10. *See* Kent Greenfield, *The Unjustified Absence of Federal Fraud Protection in the Labor Market*, 107 Yale L. J. 715 (1997). Federal law does not make lying to employees a matter of federal concern, though as a matter of economics fraud in the labor market is inefficient as well. Laws punishing fraud on employees would raise no difficult free speech concerns.
11. *Nike, Inc. v. Kasky*, 539 U.S. 654 (2003).
12. Linda Greenhouse, *Free Speech for Companies on Justices' Agenda*, N.Y. Times (Apr. 20, 2003).
13. *Id.*
14. *Id.*
15. *Nike*, 539 U.S. at 657.
16. *Alvarez*, 567 U.S. at 722.
17. *Basic v. Levinson*, 485 U.S. 224 (1988).
18. *See* Greenfield, *Unjustified Absence of Federal Fraud Protection*, *supra*.
19. *See* Conflict Minerals Final Rule, 77 Fed. Reg. 56,274, 56,283 (Sept. 12, 2012) (to be codified at 17 C.F.R. pts. 240, 249b); Bri Holmes, *FSFP Joins Global Witness in Brief Addressing "Conflict Minerals" and First Amendment Claims by Corporations*, Free Speech For People (Dec. 11, 2014), http://freespeechforpeople.org/fsfp-joins-global-witness-brief-addressing-conflict-minerals-first-amendment-claims-corporations/.

20. *Nat'l. Ass'n. of Mfrs. v. SEC*, 800 F.3d 518, 532 (D.C. Cir. 2015) (Srinivassan, J., dissenting) (quoting Appellant Brief).
21. *Id.* at 530.
22. *Id.* at 521.
23. *Id.*
24. *Hurley v. Irish-Am. Gay, Lesbian & Bisexual Grp.*, 515 U.S. 557, 573–74 (1995).
25. *W. Va. State Bd. of Educ. v. Barnette*, 319 U.S. 624, 642 (1943).
26. See *Beef Checkout Compliance*, Cattlemen's Beef Board, http://www.beef board.org/compliance/compliance.asp.
27. *United States v. United Foods*, 533 U.S. 405, 411 (2001).
28. *Johanns v. Livestock Mktg. Assn.*, 544 U.S. 550, 562 (2005).
29. *Id.* at 577 (Souter, J., dissenting).
30. *Wooley v. Maynard*, 430 U.S. 705 (1977).
31. Michael Felberbaum, *Health Groups Weigh in on Lawsuit over Graphic Cigarette Labels*, Huffington Post (Sept. 20, 2011). See *R. J. Reynolds Tobacco Co. v. FDA*, 696 F.3d 1205 (D.C. Cir. 2012) (striking down proposed labels).
32. See Lawrence Lessig, Republic, Lost: How Money Corrupts Congress—And a Plan to Stop It (2011); Zephyr Teachout, Corruption in America: from Benjamin Franklin's Snuff Box to Citizens United (2016).
33. See *Buckley v. Valeo*, 424 U.S. 1, 48–49 ("But the concept that government may restrict the speech of some elements of our society in order to enhance the relative voice of others is wholly foreign to the First Amendment").
34. *Citizens United v. Fed. Election Comm'n.*, 558 U.S. 310, 357 (2010) ("Independent expenditures, including those made by corporations, do not give rise to corruption or the appearance of corruption"); see also *SpeechNow.org v. FEC*, 599 F.3d 686, 694–95 (D.C. Cir. 2010) ("In light of the Court's holding as a matter of law that independent expenditures do not corrupt or create the appearance of quid pro quo corruption, contributions to groups that make only independent expenditures also cannot corrupt or create the appearance of corruption. The Court has effectively held that there is no corrupting 'quid' for which a candidate might in exchange offer a corrupt 'quo'").
35. See, e.g., Nicholas Almendares & Catherine Hafer, *Beyond Citizens United*, 84 Fordham L. Rev. 2755 (2016); Burt Neuborne, Campaign Finance Report and The Constitution: A Critical Look at Buckley v. Valeo 16 (1998) (stating that the possibility that independent expenditures may corrupt just as contributions do "is where the Buckley Court suffers most from having been without a factual record. Enormous independent expenditures were not part of the fictional record the Court considered, mostly because they were not yet part of America's political process. Several scholars . . . have called for a factually based study of independent expenditures' potential for corruption").

36. *See* Margaret M. Blair & Elizabeth Pollman, *The Derivative Nature of Corporate Constitutional Rights*, 56 WM. & MARY L. REV. 1673 (2015).
37. *See* Business and Financial Disclosure Required by Regulation S-K, SEC Release No. 33–10064 (Apr. 13, 2016); Nicholas Confessore, *S.E.C. Is Asked to Require Disclosure of Donations*, N.Y. TIMES (Apr. 23, 2013), http://www.ny times.com/2013/04/24/us/politics/sec-is-asked-to-make-companies-dis close-donations.html.
38. *Citizens United*, 558 U.S. at 356.
39. The originators of this concept were Berle and Means, as discussed in chapter 2 above. *See* ADOLF A. BERLE & GARDINER C. MEANS, THE MODERN CORPORATION AND PUBLIC PROPERTY (1932).
40. Jay Kesten labels the cost of forced subsidy of points of views with which stakeholders disagree a "moral agency cost," to be contrasted with the run-of-the-mill agency costs inherent in the separation of ownership and control. *See* Jay Kesten, *Shareholder Political Primacy*, 10 VA. L. & BUS. REV. 161 (2016).
41. *Citizens United*, 558 U.S. at 361–62 (quoting *First National Bank of Boston v. Bellotti*) ("Ultimately shareholders may decide, through the procedures of corporate democracy, whether their corporation should engage in debate on public issues").
42. *See, e.g.*, Elizabeth Pollman, *Citizens Not United: The Lack of Stockholder Voluntariness in Corporate Political Speech*, 119 YALE J. ONLINE 53, 56–57 (2009); Anne Tucker, *Flawed Assumptions: A Corporate Law Analysis of Free Speech and Corporate Personhood in Citizens United*, 61 CASE W. RES. L. REV. 497, 499 (2011) (arguing that the Supreme Court "ignored . . . five realities of corporate political speech" by failing to examine the question "through a corporate law lens"). Similar criticisms were voiced about *Bellotti*. *See, e.g.*, Thomas W. Joo, *The Modern Corporation and Campaign Finance: Incorporating Corporate Governance Analysis into First Amendment Jurisprudence*, 79 WASH. U. L. Q. 1, 80 (2001) (arguing that the Supreme Court's corporate political activity jurisprudence, as exemplified by *Bellotti*, is not "based on the realities of contemporary corporate governance").
43. *See* Larry E. Ribstein, *The First Amendment and Corporate Governance*, 27 GA. ST. U. L. REV. 1019, 1033 (2011) ("Regulation of corporate decisions to engage in speech collides with the fact that markets operate fairly well to constrain managers' use of shareholders' money, including on corporate speech"). *See also* Robert Sitkoff, *Corporate Political Speech, Political Extortion, and the Competition for Corporate Charters*, 69 U. CHI. L. REV. 1103, 1113 (2002) ("There is nothing special about managerial control over corporate political speech that warrants abandoning ordinary modes of corporate governance in favor of a mandatory rule and criminalization").
44. *See* Kesten, *Shareholder Political Primacy, supra*, at 187–88 (explaining that stock prices will not normally respond to such sales because "demand curves

for most public stocks are horizontal because there are so many substitutes for any given firm's shares").

45. See *Joy v. North* 692 F.2d. 880 (1982); Kent Greenfield, *The End of Contractarianism? Behavioral Economics and Law of Corporations*, in The Oxford Handbook on Behavioral Economics and the Law 518, 520 (Eyal Zamir & Doron Teichman, eds., 2014) (criticizing *Joy v. North*).

46. See *Barnette*, 319 U.S. at 656 (Frankfurter, J., dissenting) ("But West Virginia does not compel the attendance at its public schools of the children here concerned").

47. See generally Kent Greenfield, The Myth of Choice: Personal Responsibility in a World of Limits (2011); Kent Greenfield, *Free Will Paradigms*, 7 Duke J. of Const. L. & Pub. Pol. 1 (2011).

48. See Kesten, *Shareholder Political Primacy*, *supra*, at 177 (discussing the work of Albert Hirschman, who described the strategies of exit and voice for organizational members, and adding litigation as a "third option." See Albert O. Hirschman, Exit, Voice, and Loyalty: Responses to the Decline in Forms, Organizations, and States (1970)).

49. Massachusetts General Laws ch. 55 § 8, cited in *Bellotti*, 435 U.S. at 768.

50. For powerful evidence of this, see Jeffrey R. Brown & Jiekun Huang, *All the President's Friends: Political Access and Firm Value*, National Bureau of Economic Research, Working Paper 23356, available at http://www.nber.org/papers/w23356. Brown and Huang performed a massive empirical study of company executives who met with White House policymakers from 2009 to 2015. They found that such meetings were associated with above-market returns for the executives' companies. They conclude that "for multibillion dollar corporations ... a single White House visit by a corporate executive can add hundreds of millions of dollars to shareholder value." Jeffrey R. Brown & Jiekun Huang, *When CEOs Visit the White House, Their Companies Profit*, Politico (May 9, 2017), http://www.politico.com/magazine/story/2017/05/08/why-trump-white-house-visitors-logs-should-public-215116). Brown and Huang find evidence that the reasons for these positive abnormal returns are that such firms "receive more government contracts" and "secure more regulatory relief" and that "the investment of treatment firms becomes less negatively affected by political uncertainty after the meetings." Brown & Huang, *All the President's Friends*, *supra*, at 5.

51. See Sitkoff, *Corporate Political Speech*, *supra*, at 1105–6 (discussing "fear of managerial lobbying for redistributive legislation—that is, corporate rent seeking" and saying that "redistributive corporate rent seeking is socially undesirable and yet rational investors might favor it").

52. Fred S. McChesney, Money for Nothing: Politicians, Rent Extraction, and Political Extortion 12 (1997). See also Fred S. McChesney, *Rent Extraction and Rent Creation in the Economic Theory of Regulation*, 16 J. Legal Stud. 101 (1987).

53. Anat R. Admati, *Financialization and the Political Economy of Corporations* 2 (Jan. 13, 2017), Rock Center for Corporate Governance at Stanford University, Working Paper No. 225; Stanford University Graduate School of Business Research Paper No. 17–11, available at https://law.yale.edu/system /files/area/workshop/leo/leo17_admati.pdf.

54. Leo E. Strine, Jr., & Nicholas Walter, *Conservative Collision Course: The Tension between Conservative Corporate Law Theory and Citizens United*, 100 Cornell L. Rev. 335, 384 (2015).

55. Kesten, *Shareholder Political Primacy, supra,* at 193 n. 153 ("*Citizens United* amplified corporations' lobbying power by allowing corporations to threaten credibly that they will spend against a candidate's re-election in the period leading up to that vote"). *See also* Richard Briffault, *Lobbying and Campaign Finance: Separate and Together,* 19 Stan. L. & Pol'y. Rev. 105 (2008); Brown & Huang, *All the President's Friends, supra,* at 3 ("Firms that contributed more to Obama's presidential election campaigns [were] more likely to have access to the White House" during his administration).

56. Sitkoff, *Corporate Political Speech, supra,* 69 U. Chi. L. Rev. at 1106.

57. Kesten, *Shareholder Political Primacy, supra,* at 211–15.

58. *Burwell v. Hobby Lobby Stores, Inc.,* 573 U.S. ___, 134 S. Ct. 2751 (2014).

59. *Masterpiece Cakeshop, Ltd. v. Colorado Civil Rights Comm'n.* (No. 16–111) (argued Dec. 5, 2017); *Elane Photography v. Willcock,* 309 P.3d 53, 59 (N.M. 2013), *cert. denied,* 134 S. Ct. 1787 (2014); *Colorado Cake Maker Appeals Order to Serve Gays,* Associated Press (Jan. 6, 2014), http://bigstory.ap.org/arti cle/colo-cake-makerappeals-order-serve-gays; Dominic Holden, *Bigotry in Bloom: A Flower Shop Is Refusing to Do Business with a Gay Couple Getting Married —Is That Blatantly Illegal?,* The Stranger (Mar. 13, 2013), http://www .thestranger.com/seattle/bigotry-in-bloom/Content?oid=16232163; Jordan Lorence, *Supreme Court Turns Down Elane Photography Case,* National Review (Apr. 7, 2014), http://www.nationalreview.com/benchmemos/375210 /supreme-court-turns-down-elane-photography-case-jordan-lorence; Todd Stames, *Do Gay Rights Trump Religious Rights? Supreme Court Won't Hear Wedding Photographers' Case,* Fox News (Apr. 7, 2014). *See also* Andrew Koppelman, *A Zombie in the Supreme Court: The Elane Photography Cert Denial,* 7 Ala. C.R. & C.L. L. Rev. 77 (2015).

60. Tim Murphy, *In Indiana, Employers Can Still Fire Workers for Being Gay or Trans—and They Do, All the Time,* Nation (July 21, 2015), https://www.the nation.com/article/in-indiana-employers-can-fire-workers-for-being-gay -or-trans-and-they-do-all-the-time/; Todd Starnes, *Oregon Ruling Really Takes the Cake—Christian Bakery Guilty of Violating Civil Rights of Lesbian Couple,* Fox News (Jan. 21, 2014), http://www.foxnews.com/opinion/2014/01/2 1/christian-bakery-guilty-violating-civilrights-lesbian-couple/; Nina Terrero, *N.J. Bridal Shop Refused to Sell Wedding Dress to Lesbian Bride. Owner Says:*

"*That's Illegal*," ABC News (Aug. 19, 2011), http://abcnews.go.com/US/nj
-bridal-shop-refused-sell-wedding-dresslesbian/story?id= 14342333.

61. *See Boy Scouts of Am. v. Dale*, 530 U.S. 640; *Hurley v. Irish-Am. Gay, Lesbian & Bisexual Grp.*, 515 U.S. 557, 573–74 (1995).

62. Amanda Holpuch, "*Chick-fil-A Appreciation Day Brings Huge Crowds to Fast-Food Chain*," Guardian (Aug. 1, 2012).

63. Trs. of *Dartmouth Coll. v. Woodward*, 4 Wheat. at 636.

SEVEN

More Personhood, Please

1. *See* Boeing, http://www.boeing.com/boeing/companyoffices/aboutus/community/index.page; Microsoft, http://www.microsoft.com/about/corporate citizenship/en-us/; The Walt Disney Company, http://thewaltdisneycompany.com/citizenship.

2. *See Center for Corporate Citizenship*, Boston College, http://ccc.bc.edu.

3. Adam Winkler, We the Corporations 44 (2018).

4. *See Opinion, The 21st Century Citizen* (special series), L.A. Times, Oct. 5, 2014, http://www.latimes.com/nation/la-ed-citizenship-sg-storygallery.html.

5. Peter J. Spiro, Beyond Citizenship: American Identity after Globalization (2008).

6. Amy J. Sepinwall, *Citizens United and the Ineluctable Question of Corporate Citizenship*, 44 Conn. L. Rev. 575, 595, 599 (2012).

7. *See* Bruce Ackerman, We the People: Foundations 298–99 (1991).

8. Sepinwall, *Citizens United and the Ineluctable Question of Corporate Citizenship*, *supra*, at 605.

9. In this respect I differ from Sepinwall, who argues that corporations are not citizens because they do not "bear an expectation of participation [in the] joint project of the United States." There is something to the notion that citizenship springs from obligation, but her argument mostly begs the question as to whether corporations could voluntarily accept those obligations or have them forced on them. *See* Sepinwall, *Citizens United and the Ineluctable Question of Corporate Citizenship, supra*, at 585.

10. U.S. Const. Art III, § 2.

11. *See* Winkler, We the Corporations, *supra*.

12. *Hertz Corp. v. Friend*, 559 U.S. 77 (2010).

13. *See* Sepinwall, *Citizens United and the Ineluctable Question of Corporate Citizenship, supra*, at 582–83 ("While those who employ this rhetoric [of good corporate citizenship] have laudable goals in mind, they may have unwittingly made respectable a conception of the corporation as a legitimate bearer of constitutional rights").

14. *R. J. Reynolds Tobacco Co. v. FDA*, 696 F.3d 1205 (D.C. Cir. 2012); *Nat'l. Ass'n. of Mfrs. v. SEC*, 800 F.3d 518 (D.C. Cir. 2015).
15. *See Sorrell v. IMS Health, Inc.*, 564 U.S. 552 (2011).
16. *See, e.g., Brown v. Entm't. Merchs. Ass'n.*, 564 U.S. 786 (2011).
17. John C. Coates, IV, *Corporate Speech and the First Amendment: History, Data, and Implications*, 30 CONST. COMMENT. 223 (2015).
18. *See* MARK TUSHNET, A COURT DIVIDED: THE REHNQUIST COURT AND THE FUTURE OF CONSTITUTIONAL LAW (2005); Tamara Piety, *Citizens United and the Threat to the Regulatory State*, 109 MICH. L. REV. FIRST IMPRESSIONS 16 (2010). I have discussed this in greater detail in chapter 2 above.
19. *See* Margaret M. Blair & Lynn A. Stout, *A Team Production Theory of Corporate Law*, 85 VA. L. REV. 247 (1999).
20. *See, e.g., Ebay Domestic Holdings, Inc. v. Newmark*, 16 A.3d 1, 11 (Del. Ch. 2010).
21. Leo E. Strine, *The Dangers of Denial: The Need for a Clear-Eyed Understanding of the Power and Accountability Structure Established by the Delaware General Corporation Law*, 50 WAKE FOREST L. REV. 761, 776–77 (2015); *see also* David G. Yosifon, *The Law of Corporate Purpose*, 10 BERKELEY BUS. L.J. 181 (2013).
22. *Revlon, Inc. v. MacAndrews & Forbes Holdings, Inc.*, 506 A.2d 173, 182 (Del. 1986) (emphasis added).
23. *See* Rachelle C. Sampson & Yuan Shi, *Are US Firms and Markets Becoming More Short-Term Oriented? Evidence of Shifting Firm and Investor Time Horizons, 1980–2013* (draft of Jan. 31, 2018), available at https://dx.doi .org/10.2139/ssrn.2837524 (providing evidence of increasing short-termism in U.S. equity capital markets). *See also* Jillian A. Popadak, *A Corporate Culture Channel: How Increased Shareholder Governance Reduces Firm Value* (Oct. 25, 2013), available at https://ssrn.com/abstract=2345384 or http://dx.doi .org/10.2139/ssrn.2345384 (correlating increased shareholder voice in governance with greater attention to short-term tangible results and decreases in attention to intangible sources of long-term value).
24. *See Stocks Traded, Turnover Ratio of Domestic Shares (%) of United States*, WORLD BANK, available at http://data.worldbank.org/indicator/CM.MKT .TRNR?end=2016&locations=US&start=2000. Turnover in the United States peaked at over 400 percent in 2008, during the global financial crisis. *See also* Sampson & Shi, *Are US Firms and Markets Becoming More Short-Term Oriented?, supra* (showing correlation between stock turnover and short-termism).
25. Marshall E. Blume & Donald B. Keim, *Institutional Investors and Stock Market Liquidity: Trends and Relationships*, Working Paper, Wharton School, University of Pennsylvania (Aug. 21, 2012), available at http://finance.wharton .upenn.edu/~keim/research/ChangingInstitutionPreferences_21Aug2012.pdf, at p. 4. *See also* THE CONFERENCE BOARD, 2010 INSTITUTIONAL INVESTMENT REPORT: TRENDS IN ASSET ALLOCATION AND PORTFOLIO COMPOSITION (Nov. 2010).

26. *See* Sampson & Shi, *Are US Firms and Markets Becoming More Short-Term Oriented?, supra.*

27. *See, e.g.,* James D. Cox, *Compensation, Deterrence, and the Market as Boundaries for Derivative Suit Procedures,* 52 GEO. WASH. L. REV. 745, 765 (1984) (stating that corporate fiduciary duties may not have a place in enforcing general law compliance if the illegality is profitable to the corporation because the derivative suit is incapable of being a mechanism of enforcing general law compliance); Frank H. Easterbrook & Daniel R. Fischel, *Antitrust Suits by Targets of Tender Offers,* 80 MICH. L. REV. 1155, 1177 n. 57 (1982) ("Managers not only may but also should violate the rules when it is profitable to do so").

28. Edward N. Wolff, *Household Wealth Trends in the United States, 1962–2013: What Happened over the Great Recession?,* NATIONAL BUREAU OF ECONOMIC RESEARCH, Working Paper 20733 (2014), available at http://www.nber.org/papers/w20733.

29. *See* Edward N. Wolff, *Recent Trends in Household Wealth in the United States: Rising Debt and the Middle-Class Squeeze—An Update to 2007,* LEVY ECONOMICS INSTITUTE OF BARD COLLEGE, Working Paper No. 589 (2010), available at http://www.levyinstitute.org ("Stock ownership was also highly skewed by wealth and income class. The top 1 percent of households classified by wealth owned 38 percent of all stocks in 2007, the top 10 percent owned 81 percent, and the top quintile held 91 percent. Moreover, 84 percent of all stocks were owned by households earning $75,000 or more and 92 percent by households with incomes of $50,000 or more"). *See also* Wolff, *Household Wealth Trends, supra* ("The top 10 percent of families as a group accounted for about 85 to 90 percent of stock shares, bonds, trusts, and business equity" in 2013).

30. *See* Ezra Wasserman Mitchell, *Corporate Governance and Income Inequality: The Role of the Monitoring Board* (draft of Mar. 2017; on file with author) ("I conclude that the principal institution of corporate governance driving income inequality is the modern monitoring board, which began to take shape in the 1970s and was fully formed during the 1980s, the decade of fastest growing economic disparity. The principal normative force motivating the monitoring board to dramatically increase top incomes is the shareholder value norm, which did not find its fullest practical expression until sometime in the later 1990s but which grew out of changes in business and financial practices tracing back to the 1950s and can be seen in practical operation by the mid-1980s").

EIGHT

Six Bad Arguments for Shareholder Primacy

1. *See* John C. Coates, IV, *Corporate Speech and the First Amendment: History, Data, and Implications,* 30 CONST. COMMENT. 223 (2015); Victor Brudney,

> Business Corporations and Stockholders' Rights under the First Amendment, 91
> YALE L. J. 235 (1981); Lucian Arye Bebchuk, *The Case for Increasing Share-*
> *holder Power,* 118 HARV. L. REV. 833 (2005); Paul Blumenthal, *SEC Peti-*
> *tion for Corporate Spending Rule Reaches Half-Million Comments,* HUFFING-
> TON POST (Apr. 16, 2013), http://www.huffingtonpost.com/2013/04/16
> /sec-corporate-political-spending_n_3093121.html.

2. *See* George W. Dent, Jr., *Stakeholder Governance: A Bad Idea Getting Worse,* 58
    CASE W. RES. L. REV. 1107 (2008) (using ownership argument).

3. Joseph William Singer, *The Reliance Interest in Property,* 40 STAN. L. REV. 611,
    637–38 (1988) ("To assume that we can know who property owners are, and
    to assume that once we have identified them their rights follow as a matter
    of course, is to assume what needs to be decided").

4. Jonathan R. Macey, *Externalities, Firm-Specific Capital Investments, and*
    the Legal Treatment of Fundamental Corporate Changes, 1989 DUKE L. J.
    173, 175 (1989) ("Contrary to popular belief, it is not particularly use-
    ful to think of corporations in terms of property rights"); *see also* JESSE H.
    CHOPER ET AL., CASES AND MATERIALS ON CORPORATIONS 28–29 (3d
    ed., 1989) (contractarians "deny that any one class of participants [i.e., the
    shareholders] have a natural right to view themselves as the owners of
    the firm"); Stephen M. Bainbridge, *Community and Statism: A Conserva-*
    tive Contractarian Critique of Progressive Corporate Law Scholarship, 82 COR-
    NELL L. REV. 856, 863 n. 22 (1997) (ownership not a meaningful concept
    in contractarian analysis of corporations); Eugene Fama, *Agency Problems*
    and the Theory of the Firm, 88 J. POL. ECON. 288, 289 (1980) (abandoning
    "the typical presumption that a corporation has owners in any meaningful
    sense").

5. Dent, *Stakeholder Governance, supra,* at 1113 (quoting Jonathan R. Macey,
    Fiduciary Duties as Residual Claims: Obligations to Nonshareholder Constituencies
    from a Theory of the Firm Perspective, 84 CORNELL L. REV. 1266, 1267–68
    (1999)).

6. *Id.*

7. *Id.*

8. Shaun P. Martin & Frank Partnoy, *Encumbered Shares,* 2005 U. ILL. L. REV.
    775 (2005).

9. *See* Jonathan R. Macey, *An Economic Analysis of the Various Rationales for Mak-*
    ing Shareholders the Exclusive Beneficiaries of Corporate Fiduciary Duties, 21
    STETSON L. REV. 23, 27 (1991) (internal quotation omitted).

10. Bebchuk, *The Case for Increasing Shareholder Power, supra,* at 904–5 ("To begin
    with, high leverage produces its own inefficiency distortions. For example,
    high leverage induces management whose wealth is tied to equity value to
    take excessive risks. The greater the leverage, the larger the costs of distor-
    tions arising from it" [citing Michael C. Jensen & William H. Meckling,

Theory of the Firm: Managerial Behavior, Agency Costs and Ownership Structure, 3 J. Fɪɴ. Eᴄᴏɴ. 305, 333–37 (1976)).

11. *See, e.g., Remillard Brick Co. v. Remillard-Dandini Co.,* 109 Cal. App.2d 405, 241 P.2d 66 (Cal. App. 1 Dist. 1952).

12. *See* Anat R. Admati, *Financialization and the Political Economy of Corporations* (Jan. 13, 2017), Rock Center for Corporate Governance at Stanford University, Working Paper No. 225; Stanford University Graduate School of Business Research Paper No. 17–11 n. 405, available at https://law.yale.edu /system/files/area/workshop/leo/leo17_admati.pdf ("If corporations that maximize shareholder value can do so at the expense of, or while harming the public, and if they are able to affect the rules so the harm is tolerated by governments, then models of corporations where the rules are assumed to be exogenous and socially efficient become invalid").

13. Jᴏʜɴ Mᴀʏɴᴀʀᴅ Kᴇʏɴᴇs, A Tʀᴀᴄᴛ ᴏɴ Mᴏɴᴇᴛᴀʀʏ Rᴇfᴏʀᴍ (1924) 80 ("But this long run is a misleading guide to current affairs. In the long run we are all dead").

14. *See* Oꜰꜰɪᴄᴇ ᴏꜰ Mɢᴍᴛ. ᴀɴᴅ Bᴜᴅɢᴇᴛ, Exᴇᴄ. Oꜰꜰɪᴄᴇ ᴏꜰ ᴛʜᴇ Pʀᴇsɪᴅᴇɴᴛ, OMB Cɪʀᴄᴜʟᴀʀ Nᴏ. A-94 Aᴘᴘᴇɴᴅɪx C, Dɪsᴄᴏᴜɴᴛ Rᴀᴛᴇs ꜰᴏʀ Cᴏsᴛ-Eꜰꜰᴇᴄᴛɪᴠᴇɴᴇss, Lᴇᴀsᴇ Pᴜʀᴄʜᴀsᴇ, Aɴᴅ Rᴇʟᴀᴛᴇᴅ Aɴᴀʟʏsᴇs (2015), https:// www.whitehouse.gov/omb/circulars_a094/a94_appx-c [https://perma.cc/LM 5V-9JLC].

15. For an excellent and accessible explanation of this point, *see* Fʀᴀɴᴋ Pᴀʀᴛɴᴏʏ, Wᴀɪᴛ: Tʜᴇ Aʀᴛ ᴀɴᴅ Sᴄɪᴇɴᴄᴇ ᴏꜰ Dᴇʟᴀʏ 236–40 (2012).

16. Some research has shown that the discount rates used by corporate managers to assess future projects are increasing, a trend that will make matters worse from a social perspective. Rachelle C. Sampson & Yuan Shi, *Are US Firms and Markets Becoming More Short-Term Oriented? Evidence of Shifting Firm and Investor Time Horizons, 1980–2013* (draft of Jan. 31, 2018), available at https://dx.doi.org/10.2139/ssrn.2837524 (finding increasing discount rates and increasing short-termism during the previous thirty years).

17. Aᴅᴀᴍ Sᴍɪᴛʜ, Tʜᴇ Wᴇᴀʟᴛʜ ᴏꜰ Nᴀᴛɪᴏɴs (1776).

18. For a graphic representation of some of these tradeoffs, *see* Kent Greenfield, *Sticking the Landing: Making the Most of the "Stakeholder Moment,"* 2015 Eᴜʀ. Bᴜs. L. Rᴇᴠ. 147 (2015).

19. Macey, *An Economic Analysis of the Various Rationales for Making Shareholders the Exclusive Beneficiaries of Corporate Fiduciary Duties, supra,* at 36.

20. Dent, *Stakeholder Governance, supra,* at 1135.

21. Bureau of Labor Statistics, Economic News Release, Jan. 26, 2017, available at https://www.bls.gov/news.release/union2.nr0.htm (private union membership at 6.4 percent in United States).

22. Dent, *Stakeholder Governance, supra,* at 1121.

23. *Id.*

NINE

The Promise of Corporate Personhood

1. Stefan Stern, *Transcend "Shareholder Value" for All Our Sakes*, Fin. Times (Oct. 22, 2014), https://www.ft.com/content/0a288288-583e-11e4-a31b-00144fe ab7de.
2. Justin Fox & Jay W. Lorsch, *What Good Are Shareholders?*, Harv. Bus. Rev. (July–Aug. 2012), available at http://www.shareholderforum.com/access/Library/20120700_HarvardBusinessReview.htm.
3. Joe Nocera, *Down with Shareholder Value*, N.Y. Times (Aug. 10, 2010), http://www.nytimes.com/2012/08/11/opinion/nocera-down-with-shareholder -value.html. *See also* Lynn A. Stout, The Shareholder Value Myth: How Putting Shareholders First Harms Investors, Corporations, and the Public (2012); Steve Denning, *The Dumbest Idea in the World: Maximizing Shareholder Value*, Forbes (Nov. 28, 2011).
4. Denning, *The Dumbest Idea in the World*, *supra*.
5. Justin Fox, *How Shareholders Are Ruining American Business*, Atlantic (June 19, 2013), http://www.theatlantic.com/magazine/archive/2013/07/stop-spoiling -the-shareholders/309381/.
6. Nils Pratley, *Theresa May's Plan to Put Workers in Boardrooms Is Extraordinary*, Guardian, July 11, 2016, available at https://www.theguardian.com/poli tics/nils-pratley-on-finance/2016/jul/11/theresa-may-plan-workers-board room-reform-extraordinary-tories.
7. *See* Stephen M. Bainbridge, *Director Primacy: The Means and Ends of Corporate Governance*, 97 Nw. U. L. Rev. 547 (2003).
8. *See* Kent Greenfield, *The Third Way: Beyond Shareholder or Board Primacy*, 37 Seattle U. L. Rev. 749 (2014).
9. Sigurt Vitols, *Prospects for Trade Unions in the Evolving European System of Corporate Governance*, http://library.fes.de/pdf-files/gurn/00299.pdf, Table 5 (2005). More recent studies show correlation between greater worker participation and lower rates of poverty, higher rates of employment, and greater investment in research and development. *See* Anne-Marie Kortas & Sigurt Vitols, *Worker Participation and the Sustainable Company*, *in* Sustainable Company and Fair Relationships: European Experience for Implementation in Israel 12, 21 tbl.1 (Roby Nathanson & Itamar Gazala, eds., 2015).
10. *See, e.g.*, Norton E. Long, *The Corporation, Its Satellites, and the Local Community*, in The Corporation in Modern Society 202, 202–17 (Edward S. Mason ed., 1960) (advocating public-interest directors from communities in which a corporation operates); Phillip I. Blumberg, *Reflections on Proposals for Corporate Reform through Change in the Composition of the Board of Directors: Special Interest or Public Directors*, 53 B.U. L. Rev. 547 (1973); Thomas M.

Jones & Leonard D. Goldberg, *Governing the Large Corporation: More Arguments for Public Directors*, 7 ACAD. MGMT. REV. 603 (1982); Alfred F. Conrad, *Reflections on Public Interest Directors*, 75 MICH. L. REV. 941 (1976–1977).

11. ALFRED CHANDLER, THE VISIBLE HAND: THE MANAGERIAL REVOLUTION IN AMERICAN BUSINESS (1977).

12. Daniel Forbes & Frances Milliken, *Cognition and Corporate Governance: Understanding Boards of Directors as Strategic Decision-Making Groups*, 24 ACAD. MGMT. REV. 489, 490 (1999).

13. Avishalom Tor, *The Market, the Firm, and Behavioral Antitrust, in* THE OXFORD HANDBOOK OF BEHAVIORAL ECONOMICS AND THE LAW 63 (2013) ("The evidence shows small-groups outperform individual rationality in some cases but at other times exhibit similar or even more extreme judgmental biases and decision errors").

14. Kath Hall, *Looking beneath the Surface: The Impact of Psychology on Corporate Decision Making*, 49 MANAGERIAL LAW 3, 93 (2007); IRVING LESTER JANIS, GROUPTHINK: PSYCHOLOGICAL STUDIES OF POLITICAL DECISIONS AND FIASCOES (1983); Marleen O'Connor, *The Enron Board: The Perils of Groupthink*, 71 U. CIN. L. REV. 1233 (2003).

15. CASS R. SUNSTEIN, WHY SOCIETIES NEED DISSENT (2003) ("The highest performing companies tend to have extremely contentious boards that regard dissent as a duty and that 'have a good fight now and then'"; quoting Jeffrey A. Sonnenfeld, *What Makes Great Boards Great*, 80 HARV. BUS. REV. 106, 111 (2002)).

16. Daniel Isenberg, *Group Polarization: A Critical Review and Meta-Analysis*, 50 J. PERSONALITY AND SOC. PSYCHOL. 1141 (1986); Cass R. Sunstein, *Group Judgments: Deliberation, Statistical Means, and Information Markets*, 80 N.Y.U. L. REV. 962 (2005); Tor, *The Market, the Firm, and Behavioral Antitrust, supra*, at 63 n. 36.

17. SUNSTEIN, WHY SOCIETIES NEED DISSENT, *supra*, at 143.

18. Christine Jolls & Cass R. Sunstein, *Debiasing through Law*, 35 J. LEGAL STUD. 199, 218 (2006).

19. The data on the homogeneity of boards, and the commentary on the implications of that, are voluminous. *See, e.g.*, Lissa L. Broome & Kimberly D. Krawiec, *Signaling through Board Diversity: Is Anyone Listening?*, 77 U. CIN. L. REV. 341 (2008); Devon W. Carbado & G. Mitu Gulati, *Race to the Top of the Corporate Ladder: What Minorities Do When They Get There*, 61 WASH. & LEE L. REV. 1643 (2004); Lisa M. Fairfax, *Board Diversity Revisited: New Rationale, Same Old Story?*, 89 N.C. L. REV. 855 (2011); DOUGLAS M. BRANSON, THE LAST MALE BASTION: GENDER AND THE CEO SUITE AT PUBLIC COMPANIES (2010); DOUGLAS M. BRANSON, NO SEAT AT THE TABLE: HOW CORPORATE GOVERNANCE AND LAW KEEP WOMEN OUT OF THE BOARDROOM (2007); AARON A. DHIR, CHALLENGING BOARDROOM HOMOGENEITY: COR-

PORATE LAW, GOVERNANCE, AND DIVERSITY (2015). As recently as 1996, no woman had ever been the CEO of a Fortune 500 company in the United States. Even more recently, women held less than 3 percent of the CEO positions in the Fortune 1000 in 2010. *See* Branson, THE LAST MALE BASTION, *supra*. As of 2012, only six Fortune 500 chief executives were African American, seven were Asian, and six were Latino. *See* Black Entrepreneur Profiles (2012), https://www.blackentrepreneurprofile.com; DiversityInc (2013), http://www.diversityinc.com.

20. DELOITTE & ALLIANCE FOR BOARD DIVERSITY, MISSING PIECES REPORT: THE 2016 BOARD DIVERSITY CENSUS OF WOMEN AND MINORITIES ON FORTUNE 500 BOARDS (2017). See also Elizabeth Olson, *Study Finds Only Modest Gains by Women and Minorities on Fortune 500 Boards*, N.Y. TIMES (Feb. 5, 2017).

21. Aaron A. Dhir, *Towards a Race and Gender-Conscious Conception of the Firm: Canadian Corporate Governance, Law and Diversity* 35 QUEEN'S L. J. 569, 595 (2010); *see also* DHIR, CHALLENGING BOARDROOM HOMOGENEITY, *supra*, at 151.

22. DAVID A. H. BROWN, DEBRA L. BROWN, & VANESSA ANASTOSOPOULOS, WOMEN ON BOARDS: NOT JUST THE RIGHT THING . . . BUT THE "BRIGHT" THING (Conference Board of Canada, 2002).

23. Ronald J. Burke & Susan Vinnicombe, *Women on Corporate Boards of Directors: International Research and Practice, in* WOMEN ON CORPORATE BOARDS OF DIRECTORS: INTERNATIONAL ISSUES AND OPPORTUNITIES (Susan Vinnicombe et al., eds., 2008); Quinetta M. Robertson & Hyeon Jeong Park, *Examining the Link between Diversity and Firm Performance: The Effects of Diversity Reputation and Leader Racial Diversity*, 32 GROUP & ORG. MGMT. 548 (2007); Morton Huse & Anne Grethe Solberg, *Gender-Related Boardroom Dynamics: How Scandinavian Women Make and Can Make Contributions on Corporate Boards*, 21(2) WOMEN IN MGMT. REV. 113 (2006); Nicholas Van der Walt & Coral Ingley, *Board Dynamics and the Influence of Professional Background, Gender, and Ethnic Diversity of Directors*, 15 CORP. GOVERNANCE 291 (2003).

24. BROWN, BROWN, & ANASTOSOPOULOS, WOMEN ON BOARDS, *supra*, at 5.

25. Renee B. Adams & Daniel Ferreira, *Women in the Boardroom and Their Impact on Governance and Performance*, 94 J. FIN. ECON. 291 (2009).

26. Sander Hoogendoorn & Mirjam van Praag, *Ethnic Performance and Team Performance: A Field Experiment*, Discussion Paper 6731 (Inst. for the Study of Labor, 2012).

27. *See* FINANCIAL TIMES DEUTSCHLAND, Jan. 27, 2011; cited in ALINE CONCHON, BOARD-LEVEL EMPLOYEE REPRESENTATION RIGHTS IN EUROPE: FACTS AND TRENDS, 8 (2011), http://www.etui.org/Publications2/Reports/Board-level-employee-representation-rights-in-Europe.

28. *See* Ezra Wasserman Mitchell, *Corporate Governance and Income Inequality:*

The Role of the Monitoring Board (draft of Mar. 2017; on file with author). For an overview of economic inequality trends, *see* Thomas Piketty & Emmanuel Saez, *The Evolution of Top Incomes: A Historical and International Perspective*, 96 AM. ECON. REV. 200 (2006); Thomas Piketty & Emmanuel Saez, *Income Inequality in the United States, 1913–1998*, 118 Q. J. ECON. 1 (2003).

29. Ezra Mitchell is a notable exception. *See* Mitchell, *Corporate Governance and Income Inequality, supra.* Other than Mitchell, the few corporate governance scholars who have looked at the issue include Paddy Ireland, *Shareholder Primacy and the Distribution of Wealth*, 68 MODERN L. REV. 49–81 (2005); William Lazonick & Mary O'Sullivan, *Maximizing Shareholder Value: A New Ideology for Corporate Governance*, 29 ECON. AND SOCIETY 13, 14 (2000); and Ola Sjoberg, *Corporate Governance and Earnings Inequality in the OECD Countries, 1979–2000*, 25 EUR. SOC. REV. 519 (2009).

30. Bureau of Labor Statistics, Economic News Release, Jan. 26, 2017, available at https://www.bls.gov/news.release/union2.nro.htm.

31. *See* Kent Greenfield, *Using Behavioral Economics to Show the Power and Efficiency of Corporate Law as Regulatory Tool*, 35 U.C. DAVIS L. REV. 581 (2002).

32. *See* World Bank, *Stocks Traded, Turnover Ratio of Domestic Shares (%) of United States;* chart available at http://data.worldbank.org/indicator/CM.MKT .TRNR?end=2016&locations=US&start=2000.

33. LAWRENCE E. MITCHELL, THE SPECULATION ECONOMY: HOW FINANCE TRIUMPHED OVER INDUSTRY 277–78 (2007); Matthew O'Brien, *Everything You Need to Know about High-Frequency Trading*, ATLANTIC, Apr. 11, 2014, available at https://www.theatlantic.com/business/archive/2014/04/everything -you-need-to-know-about-high-frequency-trading/360411/ (about half of trades are high frequency); Shobhit Seth, *The World Of High Frequency Algorithmic Trading*, Investopedia, Sept. 16, 2015, available at http://www.in vestopedia.com/articles/investing/091615/world-high-frequency-algorith mic-trading.asp (60–70 percent during 2009–10, though decreased since).

34. *See* MITCHELL, THE SPECULATION ECONOMY, *supra*, at 1. *See also* Lee Drutman, *The Long Term Value Moment*, AM. PROSPECT, July 9, 2007, http:// prospect.org/cs/articles?article=the_longterm_value_moment (cataloging various studies pointing out the pathologies of short-termism as a business strategy). There are complexities to this description of the problem of short-termism that I do not address here. For a start, *see* Kent Greenfield, *The Puzzle of Short-Termism*, 46 WAKE FOREST L. REV. 627 (2011).

35. *See* FRANK PARTNOY, WAIT: THE ART AND SCIENCE OF DELAY 236–40 (2012) (discussing social discount rates).

36. *See* PARTNOY, WAIT, *supra*, at 236–40.

37. Rachelle C. Sampson & Yuan Shi, *Are US Firms and Markets Becoming More Short-Term Oriented? Evidence of Shifting Firm and Investor Time Horizons*,

1980–2013 (draft of Jan. 31, 2018), available at https://dx.doi.org/10.2139/ssrn.2837524.

38. *See* Frank Partnoy, *Corporations and Human Life*, 40 SEATTLE U. L. REV. 399, 409 (2017); Sanjai Bhagat, *Why Do Venture Capitalists Use Such High Discount Rates?*, 15 J. RISK FIN. 94, 94 (2014).

39. Partnoy, *Corporations and Human Life, supra.*

Acknowledgments

This book is the product of hundreds of conversations I have been fortunate to be a part of over the last several years. Many of its ideas were cultivated while I was co-teaching a seminar on corporate speech with Professor Victor Brudney in the years after *Citizens United* and before his death in 2016. Victor had noticed the problem of corporate speech rights three decades before, and only after *Citizens United* did most of the rest of us take notice. He was a gentle and brilliant man, and I benefited immensely from his friendship. I thank both him and the wonderful students at Boston College Law School who populated that seminar.

I am also indebted to insights offered and engendered by Richard Albert, John Bonifaz, Jeff Clements, John Coates, George Dent, Jean Du Plessis, Garrett Epps, Ron Fein, Tim Glynn, Andrew Gold, Daniel Greenwood, Lyman Johnson, Renee Jones, Daniel Kanstroom, Sheila Krumholz, Tim Kuhner, Gregory Margarian, William Marshall, Eugene Mazo, Ezra Wasserman Mitchell, Charles O'Kelley, Frank Partnoy, Tamara Piety, Elizabeth Pollman, Sashank Prasad, Brian Quinn, Jamie Raskin, Sergio Alberto Gramitto Ricci, Daniel Rubens, Luke Scheuer, Joseph Singer, Katherine Smith, David Souter, Geoffrey Stone, Lynn Stout, Ciara Torres-Spelliscy,

Acknowledgments

Anne Tucker, Adam Winkler, David Wishart, David Yosifon, and Warren Zola. Thanks also to Dean Vincent Rougeau for his support of this project and to Michael and Helen Lee for their financial support of Boston College Law School's research agenda, which inured directly to my benefit. The terrific librarians at Boston College Law School, particularly Mary Ann Neary, have been tireless in their efforts to prevent me from looking stupid by saying something based on poor research.

Some portions of this book appeared in various guises in a number of legal journals, which are cited in the notes. I thank the editors of those journals for their efforts helping me improve my arguments and my exposition of them. I also tested these ideas in scores of lectures at various institutions over the past few years. For their attention and thoughtful responses, I thank students and faculty at the Australian National University, Brown University, Bucerius Law School, Case Western Reserve University, University of Chicago, Chinese University of Hong Kong, Cornell University, Dalhousie University, East China University of Political Science and Law, Harvard University, University of Hong Kong, University of Idaho, University of Iowa, University of Kansas, University of New South Wales, University of Notre Dame, Shanghai University of Finance and Economics, Seton Hall University, Stetson University, University of St. Thomas, University of Sydney, Temple University, Texas A&M University, Tulane University, University of Utah, and Widener University. The American Constitution Society for Law and Policy facilitated a number of these lectures, and I deeply appreciate that organization's dedication to expanding the reach of my ideas.

My excellent research assistants at Boston College Law School will be pleased that I am finally finished with this project. I thank Hannah Marie Farhan, Nima Jama, Loredana Pamfile, Marlin David Rollins-Boyd, Anna Sanders, and Julian Viksman for their help and for forgiving the late-night and weekend e-mails containing seemingly random research questions.

Susan Schulman, my superb agent, offered encouragement and guidance from idea to finished book. At Yale University Press, editors William Frucht and Karen Olson have been patient and incisive, improving the book immensely.

Acknowledgments

My family has been unflagging in its support. My wife Dana McSherry, brilliant and kind, deserves as much credit for this book as anyone. My parents, Harold and Barbra Greenfield, have loved me without question for as long as I remember. I dedicate this book to my children, Liam, Ruby, and Henry. They are the best people I know.

Index

Index

Index

Index

Mitchell, Ezra Wasserman, 259n30,
  265n29
Mitchum, Robert, 150
Modern Corporation and Public Property,
  The (Berle and Means), 40–42
monopoly, 50, 109, 110, 111, 113, 163
moral hazard, 222
mortgage-backed securities, 147
Moyers, Bill, 230n21
mutual funds, 182

Nader, Ralph, xi, 8, 44
Nardelli, Robert, 46
National Association of Manufacturers,
  146–47
National Beef Promotion and
  Research Act (1985), 150
National Federation of Independent
  Business, 73
National Labor Relations Act (1935),
  40
national monuments, 130
National Rifle Association, 60, 120
Neuborne, Burt, 253n35
New Deal, 39, 42–43, 45
New York Times, 64, 65
New York Times Corporation, 3,
  12–13
New York Times v. United States (1971),
  xi
NextEra, 25
Nike, Inc., 50–51, 141–42, 168
Nike, Inc. v. Kasky (2003), 141–42
non-delegation doctrine, 49
nonprofit corporations, 4, 5, 8, 17, 98,
  112
non-voting stock, 190
North Carolina, 130

Obama, Barack, xi, xii, 7, 131, 138–39
Obamacare, 9–10, 73, 96, 97, 100, 166
Occidental Petroleum, 47
O'Connor, Sandra Day, 48, 86
Ovitz, Michael, 46

PACs (political action committees),
  24–25, 52–53, 127
partnerships, 214
Partnoy, Frank, 220
Patagonia, 121, 130
path dependence, 109
peer pressure, 109, 110
pension funds, 182, 193
Pentagon Papers, xi, 13, 22, 65
People's Rights Amendment (PRA), 8,
  13–15, 17, 62–63
perjury, 105
Pfizer, 130, 147
pharmaceuticals, 51; pricing of, xi;
  warning labels for, 152
Piety, Tamara, 103
Planned Parenthood, 13, 60, 64, 65,
  85–86, 119, 120
Planned Parenthood v. Casey (1992),
  85–86
Pledge of Allegiance, 101–2, 146, 149,
  160
political action committees (PACs),
  24–25, 52–53, 127
political candidates, 102
pollution, 70
pornography, 126
portfolio diversification, 165, 193,
  195–96
Powell, Lewis, 106–7
present value, 196–97, 219–20
Primus, Eva Brensike, 244n34

Index

Index

shell companies, 131
Shell Oil, 130
short-termism, 218–22
Siemens, 27
Sinclair, Upton, 33
Singer, Joseph William, 260n3
Sitkoff, Robert, 164, 254n43, 255n51
Sixth Amendment, 67
Smith, Adam, 108, 197
Snowden, Edward, xi
social Darwinism, 33
sole proprietors, 214
Souter, David H., 48, 86
speculation, 47
stakeholder governance, 210–11, 214–23
stakeholder statutes, 44
Stamp Acts, 78
standing, 12, 89; derivative, 15, 17–18, 86; property, 15–17
start-ups, 220
Stevens, John Paul, 55–57
"stickiness," of markets, 109
Stout, Lynn, 10
strict scrutiny, 93, 118, 134, 137
strikes, 213
Strine, Leo, 163
subpoenas, 80
substantive due process, 83, 85, 86–88
Sunstein, Cass, 124, 215, 236n30, 263n15
Super PACs, 24–25, 52–53, 127
supply chains, 102, 141, 148
suspect classifications, 84, 85, 89, 90, 93

takings, 17, 63, 71, 72, 74; constitutional limits on, 13, 15, 67, 70; regulations likened to, 16
Target Corporation, 131–32

taxation, 183
Tea Party, x
telecommunications industry, 127
Ten Commandments displays, 84
Tester, Jon, 8
textualism, 67–68, 174
Thomas, Clarence, 48
threats, 105, 110
tobacco industry, 25, 51, 127
Tor, Avishalom, 263n13
trade secrets, 75, 146
treason, 172–73
trickle-down theory, 195, 197, 198
Truman, Harry, 73
Trump, Donald, 15, 78, 127, 130, 131
Tsuk, Dalia, 41

Uber, 127
unions, 24, 40, 47, 172, 201, 217
United Auto Workers, 155
United Kingdom, 48
universities, 64, 70, 120, 184
unreasonable search and seizure, 13, 67, 74–75, 77–78
Utah, 130

Vanderbilt, William Henry, 29–30, 31, 35
venture capital, 220
Viagra, 147
video games, 102, 117, 125, 178
Virginia State Board of Pharmacy v. Virginia Citizens Consumer Council (1976), xi, 125
voting rights, 20, 82, 172

wage and hour laws, 31, 32
Waite, Morrison, 89–90